Labour Market Regulation and Deregulation in Asia

PUBLISHED BY
ACADEMIC FOUNDATION, NEW DELHI
IN ASSOCIATION WITH

LEE KUAN YEW SCHOOL OF PUBLIC POLICY,
NATIONAL UNIVERSITY OF SINGAPORE

The Editors:

Caroline Brassard has been teaching Development Economics and Statistics at the Lee Kuan Yew School of Public Policy, at the National University of Singapore since 2002. She obtained a B.A. in Mathematics-Economics at the University of Montreal, an M.A. in Economics at the University of Toronto, and a Ph.D. in Economics from the School of Oriental and African Studies at the University of London. She began her career as an economist for the Government of Ontario and quickly moved into the field of international development. Over the next 10 years, she undertook research and long-term consultancy work on poverty reduction strategies for several international non-governmental organisations, including UNICEF in Madagascar, CARE in Bangladesh and Save the Children in Vietnam. Caroline taught empirical analysis techniques for business and economics at the University of London, and obtained a professional accreditation for teaching in higher education. Her current research focuses on the impact of the transitional process towards a market economy in Vietnam, on income distribution, poverty and inequality and more recently, on the development strategy being implemented in Bhutan.

Sarthi Acharya is currently Director, Institute of Development Studies, Jaipur (India). He has earlier been on the faculty of the Tata Institute of Social Sciences, Bombay. He has been a visiting scholar at Boston University in the US, the Institute of Social Studies in the Netherlands, and the Agricultural University at Bogor (Indonesia). He has also been Research Director at the Cambodia Development Resource Institute, and Employment Specialist with the International Labour Organization. He has been a consultant with the World Bank, Asian Development Bank, UN-ESCAP, UNDP and the Mauritius Research Council as well as to various agencies of the Government of India. He has published extensively in academic and professional forums. His main areas of interest are labour and development studies.

Labour Market Regulation and Deregulation in Asia

EXPERIENCES IN RECENT DECADES

Edited by

Caroline Brassard
Sarthi Acharya

Academic Foundation

NEW DELHI

First published in 2006
by :

ACADEMIC FOUNDATION
4772-73 / 23 Bharat Ram Road, (23 Ansari Road),
Darya Ganj, New Delhi - 110 002 (India).
Phones : 23245001 / 02 / 03 / 04.
Fax : +91-11-23245005.
E-mail : academic@vsnl.com
www : academicfoundation.com

in association with :

Lee Kuan Yew School of Public Policy,
National University of Singapore.

Labour Market Regulation and Deregulation in Asia:
Experiences in Recent Decades
edited by:
Caroline Brassard and Sarthi Acharya

ISBN 81-7188-539-X

Typeset by Italics India, New Delhi.
Printed and bound in India.

CONTENTS

List of Figures, Tables and Annexures 9

Acronyms and Abbreviations 11

Contributors to the Volume 13

Preface 17

Part I

Introduction and General Context

1. Introduction and Overview

Sarthi Acharya • Caroline Brassard 21

    1.1. Deregulation: The Rationale

    1.2. Deregulation and Labour—Case For and Against

    1.3. Findings from Country Studies

2. Labour Market Regulation in Comparative Perspective

Sean Cooney 33

    2.1. Introduction

    2.2. What Regulates the Labour Market?

    2.3. Whom does Labour Market Regulation Apply to?

    2.4. Why Formal Labour Market
        Regulation be Ineffective?

    2.5. Can Labour Regulation be made more Effective?

    2.6. Conclusion

...Contd. ...

Part II

Labour Regulation Impacts on Employment, Wages and Economic Growth

3. **Economic Development, Deregulation and Employment Conditions: The Indian Experience**
   SARTHI ACHARYA 57

   3.1. *Introduction*
   3.2. *Growth, Regulations and Deregulation*
   3.3. *Patterns of Recent Development*
   3.4. *Regulation and Deregulation: Wither Labour Welfare?*
   3.5. *Conclusions*

4. **Impact of Wage and Labour Regulation in Vietnam**
   CAROLINE BRASSARD 81

   4.1. *Introduction*
   4.2. *Population and Employment since 1990*
   4.3. *Wage and Labour Regulation in Vietnam*
   4.4. *The Vietnamese Labour Market in Context*
   4.5. *Analysis of Commune Level Data*
   4.6. *Policy Implications and Conclusion*

5. **Potential Winners and Losers from Labour Regulation in the Formal Sector: The Case of Indonesia**
   CHRIS MANNING 111

   5.1. *Introduction*
   5.2. *Labour Standards and Employment:*
        General Consideration
   5.3. *The Economic and Labour Market Context*
   5.4. *Labour Reforms Stage I: Affirmation of*
        Basic Labour Rights
   5.5. *Labour Reform Stage II:*
        Extending Survival and Security Rights
   5.6. *Conclusions*

Part III
Social Impact of Labour Regulation

6. An Analysis of Severance Pay Policies in India and Sri Lanka
Mukul G. Asher • Pundarik Mukhopadhaya 141

6.1. *Introduction*
6.2. *Economic, Demographic, and Labour Market Characteristics*
6.3. *Severance Pay Arrangements*
6.4. *Concluding Observations*

7. An International Comparison of Health and Safety Regulation and Public Policy From a Gender Perspective: The Case of Australia and Southeast Asia
Suzanne Jamieson 165

7.1. *Introduction*
7.2. *Globalisation and Regulation*
7.3. *Feminist Legal Theory*
7.4. *A Role for Trade Unions*
7.5. *Comparative Law: Theory, Methods and Issues*
7.6. *Experiences from Australia*
7.7. *Experiences in Taiwan and Vietnam*
7.8. *Conclusions and Further Questions*

8. Promotion and Regulationof the Informal Economy in Southeast Asia
Lucita Lazo 183

8.1. *Introduction*
8.2. *Understanding the Informal Sector*
8.3. *Policy Implications of the Informal Sector: Experience in Southeast Asia*
8.4. *The Policy Experience in Southeast Asia*
8.5. *Reducing Invisibility: Counting the Informal Workers and their Contribution to the Economy*

...CONTD. ...

    8.6. Voice and Political Representation:
        Organising the Informal Workers
    8.7. Facilitating Access to Productive Resources
    8.8. Regulatory Measures for the Informal Sector
    8.9. Conclusions

9. Pension Regulation in Japan: Issues and Reforms
HARUKA URATA • NORIYUKI TAKAYAMA 197

    9.1. Structure of Japanese Retirement System
    9.2. Environment Surrounding Japanese Retirement System
    9.3. Company-sponsored Plans
    9.4. Retirement Allowance Plans (RAP)
    9.5. Employee Pension Funds (EPF)
    9.6. Qualified Pension Plans (QPP)
    9.7. New DB Plans
    9.8. Deregulations of DB Plan Investment
    9.9. Defined Contribution Plans
    9.10. Scheduled Private Pension Scheme Reform
    9.11. Conclusion

Index *219*

List of Figures, Tables and Annexures

FIGURES

3.1 Organised Sector Employment Industry Division 65

3.2 Number of Person Days Lost due to Strikes and Lock-outs 70

5.1 Real Minimum Wages in Major Industrial Centres
and All Indonesia, 1992-2002
(Rp., '000 per month, 1996 Prices) 128

5.2 Legally Payable Severance, Number of Months Pay
by Years of Service: Indonesia, 1986-2003 130

TABLES

3.1 Total Organised Sector Workers in
Non-agricultural Sectors and Aggregate 60

3.2 Per Cent Distribution of Workers in
Non-agricultural Sectors, 1999-2000 67

3.3 Share of National Income from
the Unorganised Segments, 1996-97 71

4.1 Daily Salary of Males and Females for
Different Types of Agricultural Work for the
Main Staple Food Crop (in Thousands of Dong) 94

4.2 Daily Salary of Northern and Southern
Communes for Different Types of
Agricultural Work for the Main Staple Food Crop
(in Thousands of Dong) 95

4.3 Daily Salary of Males and Females for
Different Types of Agricultural Work for the
Main Industrial or Fruit Crop (in Thousands of Dong) 96

4.4 Daily Salary of Northern and Southern Communes
for Different Types of Agricultural Work for the
Main Industrial or Fruit Crop (in Thousands of Dong) 97

...CONTD. ...

4.5   Monthly Salary of Males and Females in
      Different Industries (in Thousands of Dong) 99

4.6   Monthly Salary of Males and Females in Different
      Industries between the Northern and Southern
      Communes (in Thousands of Dong) 100

4.7   Daily Salary of Adult Males and Females and
      Children in the Textile Industry (in Thousands of Dong) 101

5.1   A Classification of Labour Standards as Rights 113

5.2   The Structure of Indonesian GDP and
      Employment and Output per Workers, 1986-2002 119

5.3   Employment, Wages and Value Added in Large and
      Medium and Small Firms in Indonesian
      Manufacturing, 1995-2002 120

5.4   Growth of Employment, Value Added and Wages in
      TCF and All Industries, 1986-2001 (Per Cent Per Annum) 122

5.5   Months of Severance and Long Service Pay,
      According the Cause of Separation, Indonesia: 2003 131

6.1   India and Sri Lanka: Selected Economics
      and Demographic Indicators, 2003 144

6.2   Selected Labour Force Indicators of India and Sri Lanka 146

ANNEXURES

A-4.1.1   Demographic Indicators of Vietnam (1990-2002) 107

A-4.1.2   Employment Share by Sector (1990-2001) 108

A-4.1.3   Employment by Sector and Unemployment Rate
          in Rural and Urban Areas (1990-2001) 108

A-4.1.4   Unemployment Rate in Urban Area
          by Region (1996-2002) 109

A-4.1.5   Rate of Working Time Used by Employment
          in Rural Areas (1996-2002) 109

Acronyms and Abbreviations

BMA	Bangkok Metropolitan Authority
BPO	Business Process Outsourcing
CEPA	Comprehensive Economic Partnership Agreement
CPI	Consumer Price Index
CPRGS	Comprehensive Poverty Reduction and Growth Strategy
DB	Defined Benefit
DC	Defined Contribution
EPF	Employee Pension Fund
EPI	Employee's Pension Insurance
FDI	Foreign Direct Investments
FTA	Free Trade Agreement
GATT	General Agreements on Trade and Tariffs
GDP	Gross Domestic Product
GIC	Guaranteed Investment Contract
GNP	Gross National Product
GOBU	Government-Owned Business Undertakings
GoI	Government of India
GSO	General Statistics Office
HCMC	Ho Chi Minh City
HEPR	Hunger Eradication and Poverty Reduction
HOMENET	Networks of Homeworkers
HR	Human Resources
IDA	Industrial Disputes Act
ILO	International Labour Organization
IMF	International Monetary Fund
KHM	Kehidupan Hidup Minimum

MAP	Mutual Aid Pension
MOLISA	Ministry of Labour Invalids and Social Affairs
MPI	Ministry of Planning and Investment
MW	Minimum Wage
NGO	Non-Governmental Organisation
NP	National Pension
OECD	Organisation for Economic Cooperation and Development
OHS	Occupational Health and Safety
PBO	Projected Benefit Obligations
PFA	Pension Fund Association
PPA	Participatory Poverty Assessment
PRSP	Poverty Reduction Strategy Paper
PTF	Poverty Task Force
QPP	Qualified Pension Plan
RAP	Retirement Allowance Plans
SME	Small and Medium-sized Enterprise
SMERU	Social Monitoring and Early Response Unit
SNCL	Second National Commission on Labour
SOE	State Owned Enterprise
SRV	Socialist Republic of Vietnam
TCF	Textile, Clothing and Footwear industries
TEWA	Termination of Employment of Workmen Act
TFR	Total Fertility Rate
UNESCAP	United Nations Economic and Social Commission for Asia and the Pacific
UNIFEM	United Nations Development Fund for Women
USD	United States Dollar
VLSS	Vietnam Living Standard Survey
VRS	Voluntary Retirement Scheme
WIEGO	Women in Informal Employment: Globalising and Organising
WTO	World Trade Organization

Contributors

Sarthi Acharya is currently Director of the Institute of Development Studies, Jaipur (India). He has earlier been on the faculty of the Tata Institute of Social Sciences, Bombay. He has been a visiting scholar at Boston University in the US, the Institute of Social Studies in the Netherlands, and the Agricultural University at Bogor (Indonesia). He has also been Research Director at the Cambodia Development Resource Institute, and Employment Specialist with the International Labour Organization. He has been a consultant with the World Bank, Asian Development Bank, UN-ESCAP, UNDP and the Mauritius Research Council as well as to various agencies of the Government of India. He has also published extensively in academic and professional forums. His main areas of interest are labour and development studies.

Mukul G. Asher teaches Applied Public Sector Economics at the Lee Kuan Yew School of Public Policy, at the National University of Singapore. Mukul Asher has taught or researched in Australia, Malaysia, Sweden, India and the USA. He has held visiting positions at several institutions, including with the Fiscal Affairs Department of The International Monetary Fund, and Harvard Institute for International Development. He specialises in public finances of developing countries, social security arrangements in Asia and economic cooperation among nations. He has published several books and numerous articles in international journals. His most recent book (with Avijit Gupta) is entitled *Environment and Developing World*, published by John Wiley, London 1998. He has acted as a consultant to the World Bank, the Asian Development Bank, UN-ESCAP, Oxford Analytica, the Institute of Southeast Asian Studies (Singapore), the Malaysian Institute of Economic Research, Singapore's Trade Development Board and others. He was a member of the ASEAN-India Expert Group on Trade and Investment Relations in 1994–95.

Caroline Brassard has been teaching Development Economics and Statistics at the Lee Kuan Yew School of Public Policy, at the National University of Singapore since 2002. She obtained a B.A. in Mathematics-Economics at the University of Montreal, an M.A. in Economics at the University of Toronto, and a Ph.D. in Economics from the School of Oriental and

African Studies at the University of London. She began her career as an economist for the Government of Ontario and quickly moved into the field of international development. Over the next 10 years, she undertook research and long-term consultancy work on poverty reduction strategies for several international non-governmental organisations, including UNICEF in Madagascar, CARE in Bangladesh and Save the Children in Vietnam. Caroline taught empirical analysis techniques for business and economics at the University of London, and obtained a professional accreditation for teaching in higher education. Her current research focuses on the impact of the transitional process towards a market economy in Vietnam, on income distribution, poverty and inequality and more recently, on the development strategy being implemented in Bhutan.

Sean Cooney is Senior Lecturer and Associate Director (Taiwan) in the Faculty of Law at the University of Melbourne. He is also a member of the Asian Law Centre. He has studied at the University of Melbourne, Columbia University and National Taiwan University. He also spent several years as a lawyer practising mainly in the areas of employment and administrative law. His research interests are international and comparative labour law, with a focus on Asia, and Chinese law. He is currently working on new approaches to improving international working standards and is participating in an ongoing research project involving leading employment law scholars from Japan, Europe and the United States. He has published articles in major refereed law journals in the United States, China and Australia, such as the Comparative Labour Law and Policy Journal and Bijiaofa Yanjiu. He currently teaches Contracts, Chinese Law, Democracy at Work, and Issues in Transnational Labour Regulations.

Suzanne Jamieson is a Fellow of the Senate of the University, an advocate for the National Pay Equity Coalition before the NSW Industrial Relations Commission and Australian Industrial Relations Commission, and the Director of the Celtic Studies Foundation, University of Sydney. She is a member of the University of Sydney Staffing Committee (a committee of the Academic Board) and was an Executive Member, University of Sydney branch, National Tertiary Education Union until 1999. In 1998, she was appointed to the Operations Review Committee of the Independent Commission against Corruption, the NSW Anti-discrimination Board and Deputy Chair of the NSW Nurses Tribunal. Her main research areas are in equity in the workplace and she is currently involved in a major project, which look at international comparisons in the area of gender, occupational health and safety law. In addition, she has an extraordinary involvement within the University and the broader community.

Lucita Lazo is the Regional Programme Director of UNIFEM East and Southeast Asia Regional Office. She has extensive experience working in the UN system, as an independent consultant, and more recently for the government of the Philippines. Prior to joining UNIFEM in April 2003, Lucita was Director General of the Technical Education and Skills Development Authority then Under-Secretary of the Department of Labour and Employment in Manila. From 1988 to 1996 she was the Chief Technical Officer of ILO's Regional Office for Asia and the Pacific. Lucy has an M.A. in Psychology from the University of the Philippines, where she taught for 10 years.

Chris Manning is the Head of Indonesia Project and Senior Fellow, in the Division of Economics, Research School of Pacific Studies, at The Australian National University (ANU), Canberra. He has been at ANU for the past 13 years, and prior to that spent extended periods of teaching and research in Indonesia at Gadjah Mada University in Yogyakarta in the 1970s and 1980s, where he worked in the Population Studies Centre and Faculty of Economics, and at the Agricultural Research Institute in Bogor. He also worked for six years in Asian Studies and the Population Studies Programme at Flinders University (1985–1991). More recently (2001–2002) he spent 16 months working as a consultant to the National Planning Agency, Bappenas in Jakarta on leave from the ANU and funded by USAID. His specialist academic interest includes labour economics and labour policy, with a regional interest in East Asia and particularly Indonesia. He has recently been working on international labour migration issues in East and Southeast Asia, especially with reference to the movement of temporary workers within the region.

Pundarik Mukhopadhaya is a lecturer at the Department of Economics at Macquarie University. He obtained an honours and a master's degree in economics from Delhi University in India and a Ph.D. from the University of New South Wales in Australia. His current research interests include income distribution before and after the crisis in Indonesia; gender disparity in income; World Bank grants and development in third world countries; regional disparity in Australia; a stochastic dominance analysis and health, inequality and economic development in East Asian economies.

Haruka Urata is a Japanese pension expert and consultant at Towers Perrin Tokyo. He is an advisory member of the Japan Pension Research Council, an organisation bringing together researchers of various fields in order to generate debate on key issues of retirement benefits and corporate pensions. His work focuses on retirement benefits and corporate pensions in the period of drastic change, following the burst of the Japanese economic bubble.

Noriyuki Takayama teaches Economics and Social Security at Hitotsubashi University. Prior to joining Hitotsubashi University, he has worked as Assistant Professor in Economics at Musashi University, Tokyo. He is currently engaged in micro-data analyses of Japan's ageing and declining population. His particular interest is in the economics of pensions. He is also the Director General of a five-year research project on intergenerational equity that began in October 2000, the main theme of which is setting options for fair distribution of well-being among different generations. He has been a consultant on social security pensions for the World Bank, the European Commission, the Organisation for Economic Cooperation and Development, the Asian Development Bank and the International Monetary Fund.

Preface

The objectives of this book are to highlight upon the nature of regulation and deregulation process that some Asian countries have experienced in the recent decades. Such an exercise will help develop an interface of growth/development and its sustainability with welfare-distribution of gains. Based on individual country experiences, the book suggest ways to put in place, labour market regulations to foster fairer labour practises in some Asian countries.

This edited book is partly based on papers from the Wage and Labour Regulation Panel of the Regulation, Deregulation and Re-Regulation in Globalising Asia, at the Lee Kuan Yew School of Public Policy, previously the Master's Programme in Public Policy at the Faculty of Arts and Social Sciences, National University of Singapore, on March 22-24, 2004.

We would first like to acknowledge the financial support from the Lee Kuan Yew School of Public Policy for the organisation of the conference, and especially Dr. M. Ramesh, for his constant guidance and helpful suggestions.

Our thanks also go to the editors of the journal *Policy and Society*, from the University of Sydney, and of the journal *Economics and Finance* in Indonesia, from the University of Indonesia, who have published earlier versions of three of the chapters presented in this book. These papers are being published after obtaining due permission.

Individual writers wish to acknowledge the help that they received in preparing their papers. Sarthi Acharya thanks D.K. Srivastava, C. Brassard and Sandhya Iyer for comments on an earlier draft; Caroline Brassard wishes to thank the Faculty of Arts and Social Sciences Research Support Scheme at the National University of Singapore for funding her fieldwork in Vietnam; and Chris Manning wishes to thank participants at the Indonesian Study Group at the Australian National University for their comments, and participants at the Asian Studies

Association of Australia Annual Conference in Canberra where an earlier draft of the chapter was presented in July 2004, as well as Kelly Bird who has contributed to several of the ideas discussed.

Finally, we would like to thank our publisher, Academic Foundation, and Mr. Sanu Kapila in particular, for their support.

— Caroline Brassard and Sarthi Acharya

Part I

Introduction
and
General Context

1

Introduction and Overview

SARTHI ACHARYA
CAROLINE BRASSARD

This volume puts together research papers on labour regulation and deregulation and their impact on the countries in the Asia-Pacific region. These papers were presented at a conference on Regulation, Deregulation and Reregulation organised by the National University of Singapore in March 2004. The Conference discussed issues related to deregulation in different type of markets and sectors, of which one of the sessions was devoted to issues of labour. Subsequent to the seminar, it was felt that most of the papers presented, along with a few others commissioned to fill-in gaps, could be put together into a volume as they present the essence of the current debate on the topic. It is believed that the volume could bring to the reader, the present status of labour regulation along with an overview of the world of work in each of the countries. These issues are particularly important as they are related to the lives of common people—employment and unemployment, wages, work conditions and the like—especially at a time when the region is committed to improving the standards of living of its populace, and the countries are signatory to the Millennium Development Goals put forward by the United Nations. Many of these countries are grappling with options as to how a rapid and sustainable growth process could be combined with distribution of gains to the masses.

The papers, whose synopsis is discussed later in the text, present a picture of the current state of labour markets by describing and analysing the world of work, earnings, gender equity, social security, and so on; and then try to link these with the extant (or non-existent) regulatory regimes in specific country settings. Effort is made in this Introduction to find links between economic growth, regulation and workers' well-being to explicate the challenges that these countries are faced with in order to meet the twin objectives of growth and distribution. The coverage here is geographic—the Asia and Pacific region—and is not bound by the classification of a country by its being developed or developing. Hence, papers on Australia, Singapore and Japan too find place, along with those from Southeast Asian countries, and also Taiwan and India.

1.1. Deregulation: The Rationale

1.1.1. The Definition

Post the stagflation in the western economies in the 1970s–particularly with the need to readjust after the oil-crisis during the period, deregulation became the buzzword for a revival of the free economies. The message of deregulation addressed both capital and labour markets—do away with any form of restriction on free market activity and lower barriers on movement of goods and services across country boundaries. The point stated was that each factor of production must have full mobility in order to seek its most optimal use and markets must be open to all produce, which in turn would maximise the welfare of all the concerned societies. A consensus on the adoption of deregulated and totally market-oriented systems as against the interventionist ones was best articulated in the Washington Consensus in late 1980s. The World Trade Organization (WTO) and its predecessor the General Agreements on Trade and Tariffs (GATT), too have put forward agendas that closely resemble market-led economic systems, wherein there are regulations but they are meant to make markets, function more efficiently rather than meet some other ends like protection or factor price fixation.

Specifically, some prominent features of the proposition have been the removal or minimisation of tariff barriers[1], free mobility of capital, removal of restrictions on repatriation of profits or other kinds of accruals, rationalisation in the movement of commodities and manufactures, and of late, particularly within the WTO framework, recognition of (and payment for) intellectual property rights. In the context of labour, the proposals aim at making it more flexible and less expensive. It is maintained that enterprises must not carry the cost of labour when it is less than fully utilised in the process of value-addition, lest inefficiency creeps in. It further implies

---

1. Here tariff includes items like customs duties, taxes on manufacturing and the like. It does not refer to taxes on incomes or value-added tax.

that rigidities in wages should go: more specifically, downward movement in wages should be permitted. Geographical mobility of labour (as per labour demand) has not been explicitly mentioned, though there appears to be an implicit understanding on movement of highly skilled workers, particularly among the OECD economies.

1.1.2. The Driving Force

It is not too difficult to trace the reasons for the emerging demand for doing away with regulations that were actually put in place during and after the great Depression of the 1930s and later during the Second World War. The demand has been particularly loud since the 1970s and continued at least till the end of the 20th century if not beyond.

Among the first reasons is the excessive saving accumulated in some of the OECD countries that needs/needed investment in environments most conducive to profits. International mobility of capital—successfully achieved first in Latin America, later Southeast Asia, and China in recent years, resulting in a major industrialisation of at least the Southeast Asian countries—was the beginning point. The whole process got an additional boost with the need to recycle petro-dollars generated by the sudden spurt in petroleum prices in the 1970s. This trend has continued till date; both direct foreign investments (FDI) and institutional investments have never looked back in the last 3-4 decades, and run into hundreds of billions of dollars each year.

The next reason, which in a way could be found central to the advocacy for the deregulation argument, is the technological and managerial change that has permitted disaggregation of the production process (the so-called flexible production mode in contrast to the relatively rigid Fordian mode; in the latter the assignments of both workers and machines are rigidly defined) and in turn promoted more efficient and higher capital utilisation with lesser liability.[2] For example, large auto companies may find it cost-effective to source machine accessories from India, engines from Germany and compile a car say in Korea,[3] rather than manufacture all components under

---

2. Toyota Motors was probably among the first to get into sourcing parts and assembling automobiles rather than fabricating them within the same company. The more famous example in the literature, though, is about the flexible application of capital in northern Italy.

3. This is typically what Daewoo Motors did in the late 1990s.

one roof or in one country or even promote captive units. In fact such a process is more prevalent in the manufacture of products like home computers, where 2-3 companies make most of the memory storage devices (e.g. Seagate, Samsung) for meeting the global supply, 2-3 companies make processors (Intel, AMD), etc. while computer assembling companies (IBM, Tulip, Compaq, Toshiba and Dell, to name a few) assemble these parts to make computers of various configurations. The driving force becomes stronger when these core component-manufacturing companies spread themselves across several countries. Quick movement of products and high flexibility in factor markets are critical for maintaining these processes.

The third reason, which is perhaps a minor revolution in the finance world, is the financialisation of capital, which has permitted dismantling of expensive vertical integration processes, dispersing ownership of capital and permitting exchange of this ownership through financially splitting otherwise indivisible assets. Financialisation, coupled with the rapidly evolving telecommunications technology and internationally accepted norms of financial governance, has 'democratised' capital like never before, to the extent that pure social class categories of 'capitalists' and 'workers' have considerably diminished. Democratisation of capital globally necessarily requires deregulation of capital markets and banking operations to facilitate free movement of currencies and stocks for market-determined currency values to own capital (and repatriation of profits) through market operations anywhere, and so on. Hence, there was advocacy for deregulation.

What does this driving force for deregulation mean for labour markets? The answer, put simply is: both demand and price of labour should be market-driven with no restraints created by governments and unions.

1.2. Deregulation and Labour—Case For and Against

1.2.1. The Theory

Is the logic of deregulation as applied to other factors or products applicable to labour as well? There are two somewhat opposing positions taken in the literature, one backed by the neoclassical theory which follows the principles of a perfectly competitive market while the other follows the institutional logic wherein concern for workers' welfare assumes a paramount role, and it is believed that left to themselves, markets will not be able to achieve this goal.[4]

To first elaborate the neoclassical view: The neoclassical logic maintains that all markets, including that of labour, are alike, and should not be subject to distortions, lest markets get imperfect and less competitive. If intervention is resorted to, the consequent distortions created could result into the following:

(a) Misallocation of resources (labour): The claim to misallocation follows from the principles of microeconomics (theory of resource allocation under pure competition) that any rigidity in the price of labour would disturb the optimality, which is normally arrived through smooth market functioning, in turn result in factor substitution and reduction in employment.

(b) Wastage of resources through rent seeking: Transferring resources from one group (sector) to another through interventions could push productive resources towards rent seeking, which will typically result in deployment of these resources towards unproductive purposes.

(c) Slowdown in adjustments to shocks: A (downward) inflexibility in wages, typically in the event of a fall in production or profits might not permit possibility of adjustment to an external shock; and finally,

(d) Inhibition of investments and reduction in growth rates: A fall in returns to investment might deter investors from investing more and thereby reduce growth rates.[5]

The contrary view: Distinct from the neoclassical viewpoint, another logical frame of thought is put forth by institutional economists mainly espoused by multilateral organisations like the International Labour Organization (ILO), who maintain that the final aim of all economic activity is human welfare, which is best carried forward through ensuring better earnings to workers, guaranteeing liveable wages to them and permitting greater distribution of gains

---

4. There is a third, rather radical position taken by Marxist scholars, where the whole process of global capitalist development is seen as a conspiracy against the working class. This viewpoint, due to its waning acceptance in mainstream literature, is not presented here.

5. The neoclassical view described here is the principal position taken by the Bretton Woods institutions.

to the larger masses of the society.[6] They describe 'pure theorist' norms as unrealistic, and reject the focus on prices alone as efficiency bearing factors, maintaining that in actual market operation, a number of factors like collective bargaining, tripartite negotiation, minimum wages or labour standards could actually be improvements rather than being sub-optimal. In effect, the entry of a number of factors into the fray makes labour-related arguments in the neoclassical theory not necessarily tenable. Institutional economists further argue that managers need not necessarily feel obliged to cut costs through relaxing standards; in the same vein, they also tend to avoid facing the 'moral hazard' by maintaining lower than minimum labour standards.

In sum, it is found that the theory is neither strong enough to support, nor weak enough to reject, making an unambiguous case for or against intervention in labour markets. Hence, this situation calls for a closer empirical examination of the state of labour under different regulatory regimes.

1.2.2. Some Empirical Evidence

While it might be outside the scope here to present a representative survey of empirical literature on the subject, some evidences pertaining to the 1980s and 1990s are mentioned, which in a way summarises the findings from a wide range of countries:[7]

(1) In many countries in Africa and Latin America, despite wage regulations that could restrict labour flexibility, a wage reduction was experienced in the 1980s and 1990s. It might also be noted that the economies did not necessarily bounce back to high performance despite fall in both, the wage rate and share of wage bill in the national income.

(2) Studies in India and Indonesia in the 1980s and early 1990s show large wage differentials (larger enterprises pay more compared to the smaller ones, often to retain dextrous and trained workers) that cannot be linked to institutional rigidity in wage determination.

---

6. The most elaborate stand on this in the recent times is presented in the Report of the Director General of ILO in 1999, entitled *Decent Work*; though institutional labour economics has earlier as well, challenged the canons of neoclassical theory. ILO's World Employment Programme in the 1970s and 1980s has produced a large corpus of literature on this subject.

7. The survey here is restricted to literature obtained from research carried out by multilateral organisations: The World Bank, UN agencies, and the like.

(3) Empirical evidence on a large number of developed and developing countries suggests that labour market intervention (where it exists) reduces rather than increases wage differentials, implying that intervention reduces, and not increases, wage gaps. Thus, wage gaps are larger in (non-interventionist) US, and smaller in (interventionist) Scandinavia.

(4) Minimum wage promulgation affects employment in low-income countries where the prevailing wages are near to, or lower than, the prescribed minimum wages. The farther is minimum wage rate from the prevalent wage rate, lesser is the impact on employment.

(5) In India and Zimbabwe, adjustment process in the 1980s was rapid despite rigid labour laws. The adjustment process, however, reduced the overall rate of labour absorption, which might be attributed to the rigid labour laws. In the same vein, data suggest that jobs in Malaysia grew rapidly despite relatively high job security in that country.

(6) The public sector, in most settings, has generally been found to be a drag in effecting adjustment or cutting costs. However, even here there are exceptions, like Malaysia.

(7) Job losses in the US in the recent years to low-income countries (China, India) are not so much due to high wages or wage rigidity in the US. In fact the aggregate numbers of jobs have risen as a result of long term adjustment process in the country in which low productivity jobs are being phased out and relocated elsewhere.[8]

(8) Low employment growth outside the primary sectors in India in the 1950s until 1980s might have resulted from rigid labour laws (among other reasons), but the employment situation has not changed much in the post-1980s period despite liberalisation and relatively higher growth achieved in the period since the early 1980s. It is believed that the supply of skilled labour due to insufficient investment in human capital is partly responsible.

(9) Finally, while the Asian economic crisis created huge job losses in most countries in Southeast Asia, Malaysia where

---

8. Figures are seen from various issues of *Economist*, pertaining to 2003-04.

labour laws are relatively more rigid, recovered faster than Thailand where the labour market is very flexible.

Put succinctly, there is not enough evidence to unequivocally suggest a relationship between rapid growth, quick adjustment and a deregulated labour market. Some studies, however, are fairly critical of international comparisons as well, since each country is different and the databases are not perfect or comparable across countries. After conceding to these criticisms, among the more substantive reasons put forth to explain the above anomalies are; (a) Regulations might not be binding at the market equilibrium, e.g. minimum wages are considerably lower than those prevailing at equilibrium; (b) Even if regulations are binding, the relevant elasticities of supply and demand might be too small to impact efficiency; and (c) Even if the regulations are binding and elasticities not too small, compliance might be low.

What perhaps could also be deciphered from these evidences is that labour might be one of the factors but not the only one. Put alternatively, labour might not be the most important factor in specific settings for creating conditions for growth or undertaking rapid adjustment in the face of a changing external environment. In that case, what are the lessons that one could draw for a smooth functioning of the labour market as well as protecting labour? Contemporary country studies could be the best guide here.

1.3. Findings from Country Studies

The book is organised in three parts and includes nine chapters. In the first part following this Introduction, Chapter 2 presents the general framework to compare wage and labour market regulations in Asia. Part Two focuses on labour regulation impact on employment, wages and economic growth, with case studies from India, Vietnam, and Indonesia. Finally, Part Three emphasises upon the social impact of labour regulation by analysing the cases of Vietnam, Sri Lanka and Southeast Asia, in general. A synopsis of the country studies included in the book is presented next.

In Chapter 2, Sean Cooney addresses the importance of coverage of labour laws in the context of regulation and deregulation in Asia. His analysis includes the regulation of employment relations and working conditions by the state and private sector, as well as matters relating to the labour supply and quality, in terms of providing protection to labour organisations and workers. Given the relatively low level of collective bargaining in Asia, this comparative analysis brings forth the importance of the political context in which these laws are drafted and implemented.

Chapters 3 to 5 form the second part, which deal with the economic impact of labour regulation. In Chapter 3, Sarthi Acharya analyses the Indian experience of labour regulation and deregulation, addressing a wide-ranging set of issues. Based on the pattern of economic growth in India during the regulatory regime (1950-1980) and the gradual deregulation process since the 1980s, Acharya argues that as the economy moves towards more capital-intensive activities, the extant comprehensive set of labour laws will require substantial amendments to allow for more labour flexibility and mobility to address problems arising from the increasing labour surplus in India. He also argues for a stronger role of the state in providing social security and welfare to workers.

In Chapter 4, Caroline Brassard examines the extent to which wage and labour regulation can help in reducing poverty in Vietnam. Based on data from 120 rural communes from the Vietnam Living Standards Survey, she analyses the wage differentiation within sectors and between regions and genders. She finds highly significant regional differences which may be due to the different levels of development of the market economy between the northern and southern regions of Vietnam. Brassard concludes on the implication of wage regulation on employment, poverty and inequality within the sectors of agriculture and industry and between genders.

In Chapter 5, Chris Manning assesses the potential winners and losers from labour regulation in the formal sector in Indonesia. Since the liberalisation reforms in the late 1980s, Indonesia's labour market has been transformed. Manning finds that wages have grown more rapidly in Java-Bali, but labour in the outer island provinces has enjoyed large gains. He argues that this is the result of rapid economic growth that came during deregulation. Labour market outcomes have also been less favourable in the land-abundant provinces that received many assisted migrants during Indonesia's earlier oil boom. Manning concludes that export-led industrialisation concentrated in Java-Bali has helped in changing the labour market and income growth outside Java-Bali as well.

In the third part, Chapters 6 to 9 emphasise the social impact of labour regulation. In Chapter 6, Mukul Asher and Pundarik Mukhopadhaya compare the social security systems, in particular the severance pay policies in India and Sri Lanka. These policies are meant to provide short-term income support in case of loss of employment and to facilitate enterprise restructuring. The cases of India and Sri Lanka are particularly relevant for labour markets in countries, which have recently moved from an inward-oriented economic structure to an outward-oriented one. In the case of India, current severance pay arrangements are fairly small compared to international practices, yet a significant number of both public and private sector firms have failed to fully pay such statutory benefits. In Sri Lanka there is no statutory minimum severance pay, which gives unusually wide discretionary powers to the Commissioner of Labour and creates a lack of transparency, not to mention an uncertain business climate. They conclude that, in these two countries the labour laws are still inward-looking, which emphasise on existing jobs and enterprises. Since, this contrasts with their outward-oriented growth strategies, Asher and Mukhopadhaya argue that better alignment of the labour laws with a growth strategy will not only increase effective coverage of the labour force but will also have a positive impact on efficiency and growth and facilitate their integration with the world economy.

In the context of public policy, in Chapter 7, Suzanne Jamieson assesses health and safety regulation from a gender perspective. She analyses the legal cultures and legal policy makers' responses to the needs of women workers, comparing Australia with the Singaporean, Taiwanese and Vietnamese legal contexts. Jamieson argues that rapid industrialisation in the latter group of countries requires particular attention on issues of occupational health and safety. She warns against the gendered implementation and administration of gender neutral legislation and suggests ways to improve the position of women with the help of legal policies.

In Chapter 8, after reviewing the policy implications of labour regulation on the informal sector in Southeast Asia, Lucita Lazo asks as to what extent should the state be involved in the informal economy and whether attempts at regulating the informal sector should at all be done. She concludes that the state having a role in defining a policy mix reflecting the heterogeneity of the informal sector would best address the needs of the poor. Lazo argues that regulation should concentrate on addressing the lack of access to productive resources (credit, technology and market links) as well as provide social protection. She provides specific examples from Southeast Asia.

Finally, in Chapter 9, Urata and Takayama present the recent reforms in pension regulation and deregulation in Japan since the early 1990s and raise issues surrounding the breakdown of the lifetime employment model and the introduction of performance-based benefit plans. They explain the different types of employee pension funds in the context of a series of deregulation measures regarding investment for private pension plan assets. In Japan, corporate and individual defined contribution plans were introduced in late 2001, which gave wider options to employers for responding to fluctuations in financial and labour markets. The authors conclude their analysis by discussing some reregulation to protect participants' vested rights which has been unwelcome by employers and led to a lack of motivation to implement these reforms.

In conclusion, these country studies show the economic and social burden of extensive regulation in the labour market, in terms of reduced opportunities for income and employment growth as well as increased informality and corruption. At the same time they also suggest that in the absence of effective regulation, at least in the Asian context there would be significant loss in welfare of the workers. The questions, therefore, are not whether there should be more or less regulation, it should be: what should be the forms of regulation, in which geographic context, what is the coverage and what are the instruments of compliance.

2

Labour Market Regulation in Comparative Perspective

SEAN COONEY

2.1. Introduction

This chapter examines what we mean by 'labour market regulation' in the East Asian context and then considers the potential effectiveness of a particular form of regulation—state regulation—in ameliorating poor working conditions.

The chapter first note that 'regulation' has many forms, ranging from formal law to non-stated based conventions, and briefly discusses the main features of these various forms. The chapter then examines the effectiveness of state-based labour regulation (law) in the Asia-Pacific region, noting that there is wide variation in regulatory outcomes between and within countries. 'Effectiveness' here refers to law's impact—its capacity to influence outcomes—as well as to its content, although the two are obviously interlinked. Regulation can be ineffective (in the sense of failing to have influence) either because it does not apply to large classes of workers, or because although it purports to apply, it is dysfunctional or overridden by political, economic and/or social circumstances.

The chapter concludes by canvassing alternative regulatory strategies that may be deployed to improve working conditions across the region where traditional legal approaches fail.

2.2. What Regulates the Labour Market?

The term 'regulation' has a variety of uses (Baldwin *et al.*, 1998; Parker *et al.*, 2004). While it is commonly associated with laws produced by a legislature, the term can apply also to rules made by administrative agencies, policy directives and other state instruments. At a broader level still, regulation sometimes encompasses conventions established in the private and civil sector. Thus, even the informal economy could be said to be regulated by rules, albeit created by private actors rather than the state. In the Asia-Pacific context, we see all these forms of regulation operating in the labour market—legislation, governmental rules and policy, governmental incentives and non-governmental rules and practices (Cooney *et al.*, 2002).

2.2.1. Formal Regulation: Law

If we begin at the level of formal regulation constituted by legislation and judicial precedents, we can see that most nations in the Asia-Pacific have established relatively comprehensive legal frameworks for the labour market. As in other parts of the world, these frameworks are usually structured around the legal concept of the employment contract (a manifestation of the general law of contract) which regulates the individual relationship between the employer and employee. This relationship is used as a touchstone for public regulation through legislation dealing with matters such as minimum pay and leave, occupational health and safety, anti-discrimination, dispute resolution, trade unions, and collective bargaining (Johnstone and Mitchell, 2004).

However, formal regulation of the labour market is not confined to these matters and extends to laws affecting labour migration, vocational training and education, social security, privatisation and economic restructuring and taxation, all of which have an important impact on labour supply, demand and quality in the Asia-Pacific region (Cooney *et al.*, 2002; Mitchell, 1995).

In many countries in the region, including Australia, India, Japan, Malaysia, Singapore and South Korea, the core elements of the law regulating the labour market have been in place for at least half a century (albeit with significant amendments). These laws are generally derived from models in the industrialised Western societies (often imposed when the country was under the domination of a Western power) and from conventions of the International Labour Organization (ILO) (Deery and Mitchell, 1993; Mehmet *et al.*, 1999). Thus, the origin of core labour laws in Malaysia, India and Singapore can be traced back to British rule, while the Japanese, Philippines and South Korean industrial relations systems reflect strong American influence. Of course, these laws have been indigenised in response to domestic political and economical conditions, such as state development strategies (Kuruvilla, 1995), policies of union subordination (Deyo, 1989) and democratisation (Rodgers, 1990; Cooney, 1996). More recently, phenomena such as labour migration and increase in forms of non-standard employment have generated new legislative responses.

By way of contrast, in those countries where there has been a socialist revolution, such as in China and Vietnam, the continuity with imported Western labour law models has been broken. Now that these nations are making transitions to market economies, employment law (as it is understood in market economies) has had to be recreated. In both countries, the fundamental concept of the employment contract has been a feature of the legal system for less than 20 years. Governmental agencies, employers and employees are still coming to terms with what is often for them new ways of conceiving the employment relationship, a situation which may contribute to uneven compliance with the law (Zhu, 2002). Moreover, while the new systems reflect obvious Western and ILO influence (Kent, 1999), they also contain many features evincing the influence of the countries' communist parties.

2.2.2. *Subsidiary Rules*

In addition to the basic laws and judicial decisions providing the architecture for formal labour regulation, most nations have produced a plethora of subsidiary rules and policies; these are devised by bureaucracies such as labour departments. Frequently, these elaborate on the more general provisions found in legislation. For example, occupational health and safety laws impose duties on employers to provide safe work places. Subsidiary rules may then specify what this duty entails in particular kinds of workplaces—they may prohibit toxic chemicals, impose noise limits, prescribe the use of certain safety equipment, and so on (Gunningham and Johnstone, 1999).

In some cases, the subsidiary rules become so voluminous that it is very difficult for lawyers and administrators, let alone lay employers and employees, to determine which apply (for an analysis of the problems that may arise in this situation, see Bardach and Kagan, 1982). Sometimes they may even be inconsistent with each other and with the parent legislation, especially where the rules are made not only by different departments of the central government, but by regional and local governments as well. China is a case in point; owing to conflicting rules, it is unclear whether the ordinary working week is 40 or 42 hours long (Zhu, 2002).

2.2.3. *Non-state based Regulation*

The formal state framework operates alongside other systems of regulation which are not based in statutes or rules made by organs of government (Winn, 1994). In some cases, these other systems, while not mandated by the state, rely on the state legal infrastructure (Ginsburg, 2000). Thus, employers and employees may self-regulate their relationship through entering into private contracts, the enforceability of which is dependent on the state system of courts adjudicating disputes based on the general law of contract (Collins, 1999).

In other cases, there is less clearly a connection between non-formal systems of regulation and the state-established legal institutions. Non-formal systems may involve reproduction of customary practices, political organisations, clientalist arrangements, family and community networks, and networks based on corruption or violence (Lindsey and Masduki, 2002). The state is sometimes connected to these systems, but the connections are not mediated through the legal system. As many of the chapters in this book make clear, sometimes non-legal systems may have much more significance for work relations than formal employment regulation.

The diverse sources of labour market regulation mean that terms such as 'unregulated' labour or 'deregulation' are potentially misleading. These terms equate regulation with state rule-making, and, in the case of deregulation, even more restrictively to state regulation other than general laws pertaining to contract and property. If these narrow definitions are adopted, then one can speak of many workers—such as those in the 'informal economy'—as 'unregulated', in that they are not subject to state-generated employment rules. However, it does not at all follow that the relationships between those workers and the people who engage their services are ungoverned by rules, or that breach of those rules cannot be sanctioned. On the contrary, many workers in the informal sector are subject to extensive—often abusive—private disciplinary regimes, non-compliance with which may result in dismissal, or even physical violence (Chan, 2001). Thus, while labour laws should provide scope for employers and employees to make arrangements between themselves, it is desirable that there be public rules which prevent private ordering descending into violent coercion, misinformation and systemic discrimination. It is unfortunate that the labour law in many countries of the Asia-Pacific has an increasingly narrow sphere of application. Moreover, even where it purports to apply, it may have little impact.

2.3. Whom does Labour Market Regulation Apply to?

The various forms of labour market regulation just identified apply differentially to different categories of workers. To begin with, as several of the chapters in this book show, many, if not most workers fall outside of the sphere of application of the formal labour law framework. Usually only employees are covered. Western-derived legal systems construct many working arrangements not as employer-employee relationships but as contracts between 'independent' business people. This analysis can apply even where one party is clearly in a subordinate relationship to another, as is often the case with home-workers in the textile industry. If there is no employer-employee relationship, then much of the employment law will not apply (exceptions include some laws pertaining to health and safety).

Secondly, even if the legal requirements for identifying employment relationships are present, legislation may explicitly exclude certain categories of employees from the application of part or all of the legislation. Thus, the Employment Act in Singapore excludes managerial and domestic employees, while the equivalent law in Malaysia excludes workers earning above a specified sum.

Third, the scope of certain employment law provisions (such as severance pay) may be confined by reference to firm size. Commonly, a law may not apply to small and medium sized enterprises (SMEs) (see for example the discussion in this volume of severance pay in India and Sri Lanka). This exclusion may be very significant in countries with a large proportion of SMEs.

Fourth, employment legislation may extend some or all benefits only to persons engaged in regular or long-term employment. Casual or temporary employees in Australia, India, Japan and other countries are usually not entitled to legislatively-mandated labour conditions such as annual leave or sick leave.

These four limitations on the scope of employment legislation are becoming increasingly significant in many nations, including many nations in the Asia-Pacific, because of declines in firm size and in the proportion of the workforce constituted by 'standard' employees (Stone, 2004; Castells, 1996). As a result of technological changes in production processes, more extensive global supply chains, corporatisation and privatisation, work in many countries is being increasingly performed by part-time or casual workers (very often female), or is being contracted out to firms with few or no regular workers. This trend is problematic for the ILO-inspired regulatory framework developed during the 20th century. That framework was arguably predicated on the concept of the typical worker as a (usually male) regular worker in a large manufacturing enterprise (Cooney, 1999b). The decay of that working pattern means that many countries in the Asia-Pacific whose employment laws are influenced by ILO standards are finding that those laws are becoming less relevant to their work forces.

Certainly, many countries, such as Japan and Australia, are attempting to put in place more responsive forms of labour regulation (Sugeno, 2002: 305-316; Nossar *et al.*, 2003) which address non-regular working patterns or extend protections to non-standard workers. It is however unclear how much impact these can have, especially in developing countries.

2.4. Why Formal Labour Market Regulation be Ineffective?

To this point, we have been considering the various limitations in the scope of employment regulation created by laws themselves. However, there are further limitations in the employment framework which derive not from the wording of legislation or judgments but from their impact. Legislation may formally apply to certain workers but have no practical influence; workers cannot realistically invoke it. This may be because of internal deficiencies in the legal system as a whole, or because of law's interaction with the wider political, economic and social environment. Problems with the effectiveness of labour regulation are widespread in Asia-Pacific countries (for an extensive analysis see, Cooney and Mitchell, 2002; Frost, 2002). The phenomenon is particularly prominent in developing states such as Vietnam, the Philippines, China and India.

2.4.1. Deficiencies in the Wider Legal System

In order to be put into practice, law regulating the labour market needs effective institutions to implement it, such as courts and labour departments. If employers and workers do not have an expectation that the law will be reasonably interpreted and applied, then it will be discredited and ignored. Many countries in the Asia-Pacific have experienced periods during which legal institutions have been unable to implement the law in a predictable fashion. Two problems may be highlighted.

Firstly, courts and labour departments may be staffed by people without appropriate expertise. In Vietnam and China, for example, many judges do not have adequate technical expertise in the law, though the situation is improving (Nicholson, 2001: 43-44, 48-49; Peerenboom, 2002: 289-295). This means that they may often misapply important concepts of employment law.

This problem is compounded by the complexity of the law. As mentioned above, governments in most countries produce various forms of subordinate rules. Although it is often essential for labour agencies to clarify what legislation means, the difficulty with subsidiary rules is that they tend to become voluminous. Even in societies as different as China and Australia, there are hundreds of 'rules', 'regulations', 'guidance notes', directives, 'codes' (or similar terms in Chinese) and other documents that potentially pertain to employment relations. Even an experienced judge or bureaucrat may have difficulty in deciphering which provisions apply. It is often unclear what the legal statuses of these rules are, and sometimes they even contradict each other. This is especially the case where both central and local governments contribute to rule-making.

This complexity is not just a problem for courts and bureaucrats but also for the people who are the target of regulations. Even those employers who wish to comply with the law may be unable to do so because it is beyond them or they find it incomprehensive or inaccessible.

Secondly, there is strong evidence in many countries of corruption among judges and labour officials (Peerenboom, 2002: 295-298; Lindsey and Dick, 2002). Parties with superior connections and/or financial resources (usually the employer) will be able to obtain a favourable decision regardless of the merits of the case. This discourages weaker parties from attempting to enforce the law, so that important worker protections, for example, become a 'dead letter'.

Corruption can become systemic, extending from individual judges and officials to entire local bureaucracies (Peerenboom, 2002: 310-312). These may not wish to see labour law enforced because of 'kickbacks' from businesses, or because they believe they will attract more investment into their areas (Liu and Tan, 2002).

2.4.2. *Law and Politics*

In addition to constraints on the effectiveness of formal labour market regulation derived from weaknesses in legal institutions, formal regulation may also fail to have impact because of its interaction with its political, economic and social context.

Beginning with the political, periods of revolution, authoritarianism and emergency rule in many East Asian countries have contributed to destabilisation and marginalisation of formal labour market regulation. The recency of the regulatory framework in China and Vietnam is partly attributable to the Cultural Revolution in the former country (during which period the legal system was largely destroyed) and Civil War in the latter. As we have seen, legal institutions in both societies have yet to fully recover, and suffer from various systemic weaknesses.

Indonesia, the Philippines, South Korea and Taiwan are examples of non-communist societies which have experienced long periods of authoritarian rule. In all these societies, legal institutions were subordinate to, and reflected the interests of, governments which maintained close relationships with business at the expense of labour (Jayasuriya, 1999; MacIntyre, 1994). The effects of this on employment law are best illustrated by examining the regulation of trade unions and collective bargaining. During periods of military rule, the state imposed harsh restrictions on unions and effectively banned strikes (Deyo, 1989; Jiminez, 1993; Park, 1993; Cooney, 1996; Bacungan and Ofreneo, 2002; Lindsey and Masduki, 2002). In many cases, this was affected not by amending the basic labour statutes but by issuing administrative orders or decrees. The law was suspended or rendered irrelevant, except in purely private matters such as individual labour contract claims. As a consequence of this history, in all these countries, law's authority—its capacity to influence other social systems—has been greatly weakened.

Nonetheless, in many countries in the region, there are signs that law, including labour law, is gaining increased autonomy and, to some extent, credibility. This important development suggests that, as the subordination of law to authoritarian politics recedes, law may gain greater regulatory capacity.

In the 'socialist' states of China and Vietnam, there is growing state commitment to mediate the use of political power through the legal system (in China, reflected in the slogan *yifa zhiguo*) (Peerenboom, 2002). There is some scope for individual workers to invoke the legal system to pursue their interests against employers, although this does not of course extend to challenge state control of worker organisations. The number of labour law cases in the courts has dramatically increased. Given the deficiencies in the legal system identified above, the prospects for obtaining a just application of the law are often dubious. Despite this, workers persist in invoking the law as a standard against which to judge employers and the state— to call the state to account for its rhetoric. Commenting on her empirical work analysing labour dispute resolution in China, Mary Gallagher writes:

> "The invocation of laws is often not because these laws are meaningful in the sense that they represent reality, in fact most often they do not, but rather because the huge gap between reality and the potentiality of the law serves to highlight the systemic problems facing Chinese workers in their battle for better working conditions and effective interest representation" (Gallagher, 2003).

Law also appears to be gaining significance in the democratising societies of East Asia. In those societies, we see the restoration of representative law-making institutions (including, in South Korea and Taiwan, electoral success for parties with connections to worker movements), the repeal of the authoritarian measures and the emergence of an independent and assertive judiciary. This last point is especially important. In Indonesia, the Philippines, South Korea and Taiwan, courts enjoy increasing autonomy and clout in areas such as constitutional and administrative law, and collective labour law. All these societies have constitutions which protect basic rights, including worker rights. Courts are now empowered to invalidate laws that transgress those rights, and have done so, though usually in a cautious manner. These developments might be expected to confer greater legitimacy on the law in comparison to the previous authoritarian periods. Rather than law being subordinate to politics, it can now bind and restrain the state, protecting worker rights (because of constitutional protections of property-employer rights) against state incursion (Cooney, 1999a; Lindsey, 2002). This should mean that workers, employers and the state would be more willing to solve their disputes through the legal system.

However, it is difficult to judge how far democratisation has in practice increased adherence to law, and thus law's regulatory capacity. The question needs to be investigated empirically. Improvements in the Philippines and Indonesia, and perhaps even Taiwan may be modest at best (Bacungan and Ofreneo, 2002; Lindsey and Masduki, 2002; Wang, 2002), although the situation in South Korea may be more promising (Lee, 2002).

2.4.3. *Law and Economics*

Economic factors may also contribute to the ineffectiveness of law. A common criticism of labour law from some schools of economics is that it causes distortions in the labour market. Legislated minimum standards, in particular, impose outcomes on employers and employees that would not eventuate in a world of 'free' contracting, and this leads to undesirable social outcomes. A common contention is that where labour law prescribes a minimum wage that is too high, additional unemployment will be created. This claim needs to be assessed in specific contexts by empirical investigation (see, for example, some of the other chapters in this book).

An important assumption behind this economic analysis is that law does in fact affect labour market outcomes. However, economic considerations may contribute to blunting the law's regulatory reach. In other words, economics may undermine law rather than the other way round. Many employers do not simply obey the law for its own sake, but engage in some form of economic calculation balancing the benefits of evading the law (e.g. through paying below the minimum wage or extending working times above lawful maximum hours) against the costs of being sanctioned for breach of the law (such as being forced to pay a fine and/or back-pay). If it is generally known in an industry that the law is unlikely to be enforced, and that even if it is, sanctions are low, then many employers are likely to evade the law with impunity where the law imposes a significant cost. Even those who are minded to comply with the law will be under competitive pressure not to.

In most developing countries in the Asia-Pacific, there are not enough labour inspectors actively examining firms to deter employers from failing to comply with laws on minimum standards, occupational health and safety, and so on. And even when inspectors do visit firms, they may be bribed. Thus, non-compliance with the law is likely to go unpunished.

Moreover, private enforcement, the prospect of which might deter some opportunistic employers, is likely to prove impossible for the average worker. The complexity of the law and the legal process is extremely difficult for lay people to master. In addition, the transaction costs associated with litigation are frequently prohibitive. Writing of the Philippines, Bacungan and Ofreneo (2002:114) comment:

> "The legal complexity underlying the labour relations process... strongly favours the powerful and informed who are in a position to take advantage of and manipulate the dense and detailed [regulations]. In such cases, of course, in the very large sectors of the economy in which employees are unrepresented by labour organisations, there is very little chance of employees being aware of their legal rights or having the ability to have access to them."

In some instances, non-compliance results not only from poor enforcement but also from excessive costs imposed by labour legislation. The law sometimes sets a standard so unrealistically high that businesses have little alternative but to refuse to comply. This was the case in South Korea in the aftermath of the Korean War— standards more appropriate for a developed Western nation were adopted in a devastated society and proved unworkable (Porges, 1991: 344). A more recent example is provided by Indonesia, where, in the wake of the Asian financial crisis, more than 50 per cent of firms were insolvent, and around 90 per cent failed to pay the minimum wage (Lindsey and Masduki, 2002: 30-32). Again, tight production deadlines in the export-oriented clothing and textiles industry in China mean that hours of work legislation is routinely ignored (Liu and Tan, 2003: 83-85). Firms that attempted unilaterally to reduce working hours to the legal level would find that they were unable to meet orders with the same speed as their rivals, and would quickly lose customers.

One response to this problem—and certainly one which some labour economists would propose—would be to set more realistic standards (or indeed not to set standards in certain areas at all). However, even this were done to be on the basis of appropriate empirical analysis and modelling, the non-compliance problem would remain. This is because employers do not just violate standards which are arguably unrealistic and market-distorting. They also breach labour contracts and basic safety legislation. For example, non-payment of agreed wages is a widespread problem in East Asia. Chinese Vice-Premier Zeng Peiyan reported in August 2004 that US$ 43 billion was owing to workers in his country (*People's Daily Online*: 24 August, 2004). The weakness in state and private enforcement does little to prompt employers to keep their side of the bargain.

To be sure, where enforcement and dispute resolution institutions operate more effectively for employees, there is greater prospect of the law being taken more seriously. In China, for example, the number of labour disputes taken to formal institutions has risen significantly over the last decade (Gallagher, 2003). Some of these cases attract media attention, providing a reputational sanction to a firm often equal to or greater than penalties imposed by a state agency (see for example, the reports in China's *Gongren Ribao* (Workers' Daily). However, in countries such as China and Indonesia these cases seem to have little systemic impact in deterring breaches of the law.

2.4.4. Law and Social Practices

Another reason why formal labour market regulation may fail to have impact is that there are entrenched social practices which conflict with, and are more powerful than, legal norms (Cooney and Mitchell, 2002: 261-266). As stated earlier, labour markets can be regulated by informal systems. These may rely on customary practices (pertaining to gender roles, disciplinary measures and so on), networks of interest groups and/or violent and corrupt organisations. One example is provided by Indonesia where, during the latter years of Soeharto's rule, the labour market was regulated not only, or even not mainly, by law but by collusion between firms, the army and the state:

> "Industrial relations in Indonesia ... became a form of undeclared war between, on the one hand, grossly-underpaid employees working in appalling conditions, led by a tiny corps of labour leaders operating illegal or unrecognised unions, and, on the other, a loose and flexible coalition of employers, local governments, the Department of Manpower, the state intelligence services and the armed forces, most of whom were prepared to resort to criminal behaviour, interaction with criminal gangs and organised violence to achieve their aim of crushing labour organisation. ... Despite [Soeharto's] fall, much of this system remains intact, especially behind the scenes" (Lindsey and Masduki, 2002: 48).

It remains to be seen to what extent this 'shadow state' will be dismantled and its capacity to marginalise labour law reduced for a relatively optimistic assessment of Indonesia's prospects (Arnold, 2004).

A second example is the use of militaristic work practices by East Asian investors, such as the Taiwanese and South Koreans, in firms in China and Vietnam. Chan reports that some Taiwanese investors in China impose brutal disciplinary regimes in their firms, involving beatings, public humiliation (such as forcing workers to kneel and hanging weights around workers' necks) and control over bodily functions (water and toilet rations) (Chan, 2001: 46-81). Some firms have their own internal security departments equipped with batons and other weapons. Further, many firms unilaterally impose fines for alleged infractions, deducting them from workers' wages. These practices not only violate labour standards, especially occupational health and safety law, but criminal law as well.

By way of contrast, in their empirical investigation of labour practices in Chinese and Vietnamese firms, Chan and Wang (2003) report that Taiwanese investors in Vietnam are much less likely to resort to such practices, and more likely to comply with the labour law. Given the political and economic similarities between the two countries, this difference might be thought surprising. Chan and Wang attribute it to factors including greater constraints on mobility in China caused by the household registration system, the more frequent use of in-house dormitories in China and the much more assertive role played by Vietnamese unions in ensuring that their labour laws are complied with.

There are, then, a wide range of political, economic and social circumstances which can render labour market regulation ineffective. Importantly, the relationship between law and these circumstances is dynamic. The incapacity of law to regulate labour relations is not an inherent or permanent feature of the workplace in Asia-Pacific countries. It is a function of particular national or local contexts. If that context changes—for example, as a result of political reform, increased access to dispute resolution, or resistance to workplace disciplinary norms—then law's capacity to regulate is likely to change. However, it is difficult to predict in advance the extent and nature of change. This poses a severe problem for regulators seeking to improve the operation of the labour market, and the lives of vulnerable workers within it.

2.5. Can Labour Regulation be made more Effective?

Throughout the Asia-Pacific, labour market regulation fails to improve working conditions for many workers. First, at the level of content, we have seen that many aspects of labour laws apply only to certain categories of workers. Often the most vulnerable workers such as home-workers, casual and part-time staff are excluded from the scope of the law. Second, at the level of impact, even those workers covered by the letter of the law may see institutional shortcomings and political, economic and social forces attenuate it. For those concerned about improving the working lives of people across the region, both content and impact need to be addressed.

In terms of reform of content, I believe priority should be given to ensuring that workers, broadly defined, are protected from the most egregious forms of labour abuses (this view is elaborated in, Cooney, 1999b; Cooney, 2004). While labour economists and public policy analysts may engage in lively debate over minimum standards and benefits for regular workers, all can agree that forced labour, violence against workers, failure to implement even basic safety precautions, and the employment of children in dangerous occupations (as defined in ILO Convention 182) should not be tolerated. The law should address these wrongs regardless of whether a worker is technically an employee, works in a small or large firm, or is full-time or casual.

To be clear, I am not advocating that other aspects of labour law be downgraded. I am simply maintaining that when labour law is reformed, the worst abuses should be addressed first.

While content and impact are interrelated, refocusing content will not of itself render labour regulation more effective. To reiterate, it is not simply poorly constructed or overly ambitious labour law that fails to have 'bite'. We have seen that even those laws against egregious abuses, which are generally uncontroversial among labour scholars, are also violated and ignored. We have also seen that employers often default on agreed payments due under labour contracts, even though it is likewise uncontroversial that such contractual promises should be enforceable. How then can the law be given greater clout?

2.5.1. Diversified Enforcement Strategies

One approach is to develop more nuanced modes of enforcement (see, in the case of China: Cooney, 2003). Much labour legislation in East Asia takes the form of 'command and control' law—a statute mandates a standard and directs employers and employees to comply with it, or be subject to a sanction. For example, a law may direct that employees work no more than 48 hours a week. If an employer requires employees to exceed that limit, a fine may be imposed. Unfortunately, even in developed Western states, 'command and control' legislation can produce unanticipated or unproductive consequences (Bardach and Kagan, 1982; Teubner, 1987). This has led to an analysis of when command and control legislation is appropriate and when alternative forms of 'responsive' or 'reflexive' regulation may be preferable (Ayres and Braithwaite, 1992; Teubner 1983; Dorf and Sabel, 1998).

'Command and control' style law can be crucial in sanctioning egregious labour abuses (Gunningham and Johnstone, 1999). Violent and dangerous practices that risk serious harm to workers' health need to be criminalised. Enforcement can be strengthened through tough penalties and concentration of state inspection resources, so that destructive social practices are overcome through appropriate incentives for compliance.

On the other hand, where workers' immediate safety is not at risk, it is not always feasible or desirable to rely heavily on command and control style legislation to achieve social ends. Given limited numbers of labour inspectors, widespread breaches of the law and the large time and cost resources associated with prosecutions, developing states cannot realistically be expected to police enterprises to the extent necessary to secure compliance. And overly zealous policing can in any case lead to resistance by firms in the form of 'cheating' through provision of false information, coaching employees, or bribing inspectors (see the practices discussed in Liu and Tan, 2003). Labour enforcement agencies need, in those cases not involving serious safety issues, to adopt sophisticated enforcement strategies which do not simply rely on rigorous application of the law (see, e.g., the studies referred to in Gunningham and Grabosky, 1998).

One very useful concept in this context is Ayres and Braithwaite's (1992) 'enforcement pyramid' (Ayres and Braithwaite, 1992). Regulators need to design a range of strategies appropriate to the nature of the regulation they seek to implement and determine when those strategies should be used. Such sanctions can include persuasion and education, warning letters, fines, more serious penalties and, ultimately, termination of business. The capacity to escalate sanctions in the event that a firm fails to respond can be important in securing compliance. In other words, initial interventions may be less informal (and thus less costly), but they need to be backed up by credible threats of more serious interventions.

2.5.2. *Union as Enforcers*

While a greater range of regulatory strategies may improve the capacity of labour enforcement agencies, problems of resource limitation and corruption mean that improved regulatory sophistication is no panacea. Another major way of strengthening compliance with labour laws is through strong union involvement in monitoring and enforcement. There is considerable evidence that the presence of a union, at least in developed countries, leads to greater compliance with labour law, especially in relation to workplace health and safety (World Bank, 1995; Walters, 2003). The World Bank (1995:78) comments:

> "Individual workers may find it too costly to obtain information on health and safety risks on their own, and they usually want to avoid antagonising their employers by insisting that standards be respected. The benefits from compliance with standards are not limited to any individual but are enjoyed by all workers. A union can spread the cost of obtaining information on health and safety issues among all workers, bargain with employers on the level of standards to be observed, and monitor their enforcement without putting any individual worker at risk of losing his or her job."

Unfortunately, while trade unions in some parts of the region—South Korea for example—are well placed to perform this compliance function, in many other countries in the Asia-Pacific, they are not (Frenkel, 1993). There are at least three major difficulties. First, in several countries, the union density is extremely low. In India, Bangladesh, Indonesia and Thailand, union membership is around five per cent or less of the non-agricultural labour force (International Labour Organization, 1998). The overwhelming majority of workplaces are unorganised and unions cannot therefore play an effective monitoring role. Second, even where union density is much higher, union membership tends to be concentrated among 'regular' workers. This means that those workers who are most vulnerable such as casual workers and home workers—are less likely to receive protection from unions. Indeed, in some cases, unions may, in order to protect their 'regular' members act prejudicially to vulnerable staff. In these circumstances, the role of non-governmental organisations (NGOs) that organise non-regular workers becomes crucial. However, these organisations are often unable to access the legal rights accorded to traditional trade unions (for example, in relation to collective bargaining or occupational health and safety supervision).

Third, in some countries, unions are compromised by close links to management and/or the state. In China for example, union density is very high, especially in the state sector. Unions also have extensive legal powers to intervene when there has been a violation of labour law (see, the Trade Union Law of the People's Republic of China, as amended in 2001). However, they are subordinate to the party-state, and their base level governance structures commonly include firm managers (Gallagher, forthcoming; Chan and Wang, 2003). Thus, their willingness to enforce the law against firms is often in doubt.

2.5.3. *Self-regulation: Codes of Conduct*

Another approach to enforcement is to encourage firms to improve their internal compliance processes (Parker, 2002). Better self-regulation can be prompted by government (for example a state may indicate to firms that it will intervene unless they can demonstrate better compliance outcomes) or by industry and consumer pressure. In the area of labour standards, a well-known form of self-regulation is the code of conduct. Major multinational firms require their own management systems, and frequently their sub-contractors, to comply with stipulated labour standards. There is a very large literature on codes of conduct (Blackett, 2001; Murray, 1997; Liubicic, 1998; Pearson and Seyfang, 2001; Mamic, 2002; O'Rourke, 2002). The general thrust of this literature is that while codes of conduct may play some role in improving compliance with labour standards, especially in the more sophisticated forms developed by firms such as Reebok, they are plagued by problems of monitoring, evaluation and comparability.

Some scholars have proposed public regulatory frameworks which might increase the effectiveness of codes of conduct. (Sabel *et al.*, 2001). However, these frameworks have not yet been implemented and have in any case been criticised, particularly for allowing insufficient input from the affected workers themselves (Murray, 2001; Owens, 2004).

2.5.4. *Multi-stakeholder Regulation*

A more promising regulatory strategy for improving compliance with labour standards is to better integrate the enforcement work of state agencies, trade unions and other NGOs, as well as the self-regulatory efforts of firms (Cooney, 2003). There is some progress in this direction in relation to the activities of European corporations in the developing world (European Parliament, 2003). For example, the Ethical Trading Initiative (ETI) brings together major firms, unions, and community organisations, in order to devise practical strategies for improving workers' conditions. It is supported, but not controlled, by the British government and provides a potential model for developing countries (*www.ethicaltrade.org*), although there is as yet insufficient evidence as to the extent of ETI's success.

There would seem to be some scope for governments in the Asia-Pacific region to overhaul the enforcement of labour law not just through revising the way they approach their own regulatory strategies, but through facilitating and coordinating compliance initiatives by other stakeholders. The ILO and other international agencies can—and in some countries already do—assist states in these initiatives. The initiatives should be expanded.

2.6. Conclusion

Most nations in the Asia-Pacific now have elaborate formal regulatory frameworks governing the labour market. It is nevertheless obvious that these frameworks are only partly successful in influencing the conduct of firms, workers and state actors. Laws often focus on a narrowing band of relationships (employers and regular staff) at the expense of irregular or atypical workers, even though it is the latter who often suffer the worst working conditions. Moreover, the law is frequently marginalised by political, economic and/or social forces, although the relationship between law and these forces is rapidly changing throughout the region, and in some instances law is speaking with an increasingly powerful voice.

Addressing the deficiencies in labour market regulation is partly a matter of reforming the content of the law. I have suggested that reform needs to give priority to the worst forms of abuse, not least because it should be more straightforward to generate political and economic consensus around preventing such abuses. However, improving labour market regulation is not simply a question of better laws; it crucially involves better implementation. This entails the development of more sophisticated enforcement strategies by state labour agencies, more engagement of trade unions and NGOs in compliance, improved self-regulatory practices by firms and, most importantly, the coordination of all these approaches through multi-stakeholder initiatives.

References

Arnold, L. (1999). "Towards an Understanding of Labour Law and Practice in Post-Suharto Indonesia" in Timothy Lindsey, *Indonesia Law and Society*, The Federation Press, Sydney Melbourne.

Ayres, I. and J. Braithwaite (1992). *Responsive Regulation: Transcending the Deregulation Debate*, Oxford University Press, New York.

Bacungan, F. and R. Ofreneo (2002). "The Development of Labour Law and Labour Market Policy in the Philippines", in S. Cooney, T. Lindsey, R. Mitchell and Y. Zhu, (eds.) *Law and Labour Market Regulation in East Asia*, Routledge, London.

Baldwin, R., C. Scott, *et al.* (eds.) (1998). *A Reader on Regulation*, Oxford University Press, Oxford.

Bardach, E. and R. Kagan (1982). *Going by the Book: The Problem of Regulatory Unreasonableness*, Temple University Press, Philadelphia.

Blackett, A. (2001). "Global Governance, Legal Pluralism and the Decentred State: A Labour Law Critique of Codes of Corporate Conduct", *Indiana Journal of Global Legal Studies*, 9: 401-447.

Castells, M. (1996). *The Rise of the Network Society*, Blackwell Publishers, Oxford.

Chan, A. (2001). *China's Workers Under Assault: The Exploitation of Labor in a Globalizing Economy*, Armonk, M. E. Sharpe, New York.

Chan, A. and H. Z. Wang (2003). "Raising Labour Standards, Corporate Social Responsibility and Missing Links: Vietnam and China Compared". Paper presented at the conference The Labor of Reform: Employment Worker's Rights, and Labor Law in China, organised by the Center for Chinese Studies, the Insitute of Labor and Industrial Relations, the International Institute (Advanced Study Centre), University of Michigan, March 21-22.

Collins, H. (1999). *Regulating Contracts*, Oxford University Press, Oxford.

Cooney, S. (1996). "The New Taiwan and its Old Labor Law: Authoritarian Legislation in a Democratised Society", *Comparative Labour Law Journal*, 19: 1-61.

————. (1999a). "A Community Changes: Taiwan's Council of Grand Justices and Liberal Democratic Reform", K. in Jayasuriya (ed.), *Law, Capitalism and Power in East Asia*, Routledge, London.

————. (1999b). "Testing Times for the ILO: Institutional Reform for the New International Political Economy", *Comparative Labour Law and Policy Journal*, 20: 365-400.

————. (2003). "Towards More Effective Implementation of Labour Standards in China", *Wuhan International Law Journal*, 2: 64-93.

————. (2004). "A Broader Role for the Commonwealth in Eradicating Foreign Sweatshops?" *Melbourne University Law Review*, 28:291-342.

Cooney, S., T. Lindsey, *et al.* (eds.) 2002. *Law and Labour Market Regulation in East Asia*, Routledge, London.

Cooney, S. and R. Mitchell (2002). "What is Labour Law Doing in East Asia?", in S. Cooney, T. Lindsey, R. Mitchell and Y. Zhu (eds.), *Law and Labour Market Regulation in East Asia*, Routledge, London.

Deery, S. and R. Mitchel (eds.) (1993). *Labour Law and Industrial Relations in Asia: Eight Country Studies*, Longman Cheshire, Melbourne.

Deyo, F. (1989). *Beneath the Miracle: Labour Subordination in the New Asian Industrialism*, University of California Press, Berkeley.

Dorf, M. and C. Sabel (1998). "A Constitution of Democratic Experimentalism", *Columbia Law Review*, 98: 267-473.

European Parliament (2003). *Report on the Communication from the Commission concerning Corporate Social Responsibility: A Business Contribution to Sustainable Development* (COM (2002) 347-2002/2261(INI)), European Parliament , Brussels A5-0133/2003, P5_TA-PROV(2003)0200.

Frenkel, S. (ed.) (1993). *Organized Labour in the Asia-Pacific Region: A Comparative Study of Trade Unionism in Nine Countries*, ILR Press, Ithaca.

Frost, S. (2002). *Workers' Rights for the New Century*, Asian Monitor Resource Centre, Hong Kong.

Gallagher, M. (2003). "Providing Legal Clarity: Law and the Shaping of Workers' Grievances", *Reassessing Unrest in China Conference*, December 11-12, Arlington, Virginia.

————. (forthcoming). "Time is Money, Efficiency is Life: The Transformation of Labour Relations in China", *Studies in Comparative International Development*.

Ginsburg, T. (2000). "Does Law Matter for Economic Development? Evidence from East Asia", *Law and Society Review*, 34: 829-856.

Gunningham, N. and P. Grabosky (1998). *Smart Regulation: Designing Environmental Policy*, Clarendon Press, Oxford.

Gunningham, N. and R. Johnstone (1999). *Regulating Workplace Safety: Systems and Sanctions*, Oxford University Press, Oxford.

International Labour Organisation (1998). *World Labour Report 1997-98: Industrial Relations, Democracy and Social Stability*, ILO, Geneva.

Jayasuriya, K. (1999). "Corporatism and Judicial Independence within Statist Institutions in East Asia", in K. Jayasuriya (ed.), *Law, Capitalism and Power in East Asia*, Routledge, London.

Jiminez, R. (1993). "The Philippines", in S. Deery and R. Mitchell (eds.), *Labour Law and Industrial Relations in Asia*, Longman Cheshire, Sydney.

Johnstone, R. and R. Mitchell (2004). "Regulating Work", in C. Parker, C. Scott, N. Lacey and J. Braithwaite (eds.), *Regulating Law*, Oxford University Press, Oxford.

Kent, A. (1999). *China, The United Nations and Human Rights: The Limits of Compliance*, University of Pennsylvania Press, Philadelphia.

Kuruvilla, S. (1995). "Economic Development Strategies, Industrial Relations Policies and Workplace IR/HR Practices in Southeast Asia", in K. Wever and L. Turner (eds.), *The Comparative Political Economy of Industrial Relations*, Industrial Relations Research Association, Madison, Wisconsin.

Lee, C. S. (2002). "Law and Labour-Management Relations in South Korea", in S. Cooney, T. Lindsey, R. Mitchell and Y. Zhu (eds.), *Law and Labour Market Regulation in East Asia*, Routledge, London.

Lindsey, T. (2002). "Indonesian Constitutional Reform: Muddling Towards Democracy", *Singapore Journal of International and Comparative Law*, 6: 244-301.

Lindsey, T. and H. Dick (eds.) (2002). *Corruption in Asia: Rethinking the Governance Paradigm*, Federation Press, Sydney.

Lindsey, T. and T. Masduki (2002). "Labour Law in Indonesia after Soeharto: *Reformasi or Replay?*", in S. Cooney, T. Lindsey, R. Mitchell and Y. Zhu (eds.), *Law and Labour Market Regulation in East Asia*, Routledge, London.

Liu, K. M. and S. Tan (2002). *"Gongsi Xingwei Shouce Yundong dui Zhongguo Shehui de Yingxiang* (The Influence of Corporate Codes of Conduct on Chinese Society)", Academic Meeting on *International Labour Standards and Workers' Rights, and Business and Human Rights,* Wuhan University Research Institute of International Law, Wuhan, China.

—————. (2003). *Kuaguo Gongsi de Shehui Zeren yu Zhongguo Shehui* (Corporate Social Responsibility in China), *Shehui Kexue Wenjian Chubanshe* (Social Science Publishing), Beijing.

Liubicic, R. (1998). "Corporate Codes of Conduct and Product Labelling Schemes: The Limits and Possibilities of Promoting International Labour Rights through Private Initiatives", *Law and Policy in International Business*, 30: 111-158.

MacIntyre, A. (ed). (1994). *Business and Government in Industrialising Asia*, Allen & Unwin, Sydney.

Mamic, I. (2002). *Business and Code of Conduct Implementation: How Firms Use Management Systems for Social Performance*, International Labour Organization, Geneva.

Mehmet, O., E. Mendes, *et al.* (1999). *Towards a Fair Global Labour Market: Avoiding a New Slave Trade*, Routledge, New York.

Mitchell, R. (1995). *Redefining Labour Law*, Centre for Employment and Labour Relations Law, The University of Melbourne, Melbourne.

Murray, J. (1997). "Corporate Codes of Conduct and Labour Standards", in *Mastering the Challenge of Globalisation: Towards a Trade Union Agenda*, R. Kyloh. Geneva, ILO.

—————. (2001). "The Sound of One Hand Clapping? The "Ratcheting Labour Standards" Proposal and International Labour Law", *Australian Journal of Labour Law*, 14: 306-312.

Nicholson, P. (2001). "Judicial Independence and the Rule of Law: The Vietnam Court Experience", *Australian Journal of Asian Law*, 3: 37-58.

Nossar, I., R. Johnstone *et al.* (2003). *Regulating Supply-chains to Address the Occupational Health and Safety Problems Associated with Precarious Employment: The Case of Home-based Clothing Workers in Australia*, National Research Centre for OHS Regulation, Canberra.

O'Rourke, D. (2002). "Monitoring the Monitors: A Critique of Corporate Third-Party Monitoring", in R. Jenkins, R. Pearson and G. Seyfang (eds.), *Corporate Responsibility and Ethical Trade: Codes of Conduct in the Global Economy*, London.

Owens, A. (2004). "Testing the Ratcheting Labour Standards Proposal: Indonesia and the Shangri-la Workers", *Melbourne Journal of International Law*, 5: 169-195.

Park, S. I. (1993). "The Role of the State in Industrial Relations: the Case of Korea", *Comparative Labour Law Journal*, 14: 321-338.

Parker, C. (2002). *The Open Corporation: Effective Self-regulation and Democracy*, Cambridge University Press, Port Melbourne.

Parker, C., *et al.* (2004). "Introduction", in C. Parker, C. Scott, N. Lacey and J. Braithwaite (eds.), *Regulating Law*, pp.1-12, Oxford University Press, Oxford.

Pearson, R. and G. Seyfang (2001). "New Hope or False Dawn: Voluntary Codes of Conduct, Labour Regulation and Social Policy in a Globalizing World", *Global Social Policy*, 1(1).

People's Daily online (2004)."Zeng: Pay All Owed Wages to Migrants", People' Daily online, *www.english.peapledaily.com* 49-78.

Peerenboom, R. (2002). *China's Long March Toward Rule of Law*, Cambridge University Press, Cambridge.

Porges, J. (1991). "The Development of Korean Labour Law and the Impact of the American System", *Comparative Labour Law Journal*, 12: 335-359.

Rodgers, R. (1990). "An Exclusionary Labour Regime under Pressure: The Changes in Labour Relations in the Republic of Korea Since Mid-1987", *Pacific Basin Law Journal*, 8: 91-162.

Sabel, C., *et al.* (2001). "Realizing Labour Standards", *Boston Review* 2001, February-March.

Stone, K. W. (2004). *From Widgets to Digits: Employment Regulation for the Changing Workplace*, Cambridge University Press, Cambridge.

Sugeno, K. (2002). *Japanese Employment and Labour Law*, University of Tokyo Press, Tokyo.

Teubner, G. (1983). "Substantive and Reflexive Elements in Modern Law", *Law and Society Review*, 17: 239-286.

————. (1987). "Juridification: Concepts, Aspects, Limits, Solutions", in *Juridification of Social Spheres: A Comparative Analysis in the Areas of Labour, Corporate, Anti-trust, and Social Welfare Law*, G. Teubner. Berlin, de Gruyter.

Walters, D. (2003). "Workplace Arrangements for OHS in the 21st Century", *National Research Centre for OHS Regulation Working Papers*, Canberra.

Wang, H. I. (2002). "Taiwan's Labour Law: the End of State Corporatism?", in S. Cooney, T. Lindsey, R. Mitchell and Y. Zhu (eds.), *Law and Labour Market Regulation in East Asia*, Routledge, London.

Winn, J. K. (1994). "Relational Practices and the Marginalisation of Law: Informal Financial Practices of Small Businesses in Taiwan", *Law and Society Review*, 28: 193-232.

World Bank (1995). *Workers in an Integrating World*, Oxford University Press, Washington.

Zhu, Y. (2002). "Economic Reform and Labour Market Regulation in China", in S. Cooney, T. Lindsey, R. Mitchell and Y. Zhu (eds.), *Law and Labour Market Regulation in East Asia*, Routledge, London and New York.

Part II

Labour Regulation Impacts on Employment, Wages and Economic Growth

3

Economic Development, Deregulation and Employment Conditions

The Indian Experience

SARTHI ACHARYA

3.1. Introduction

Until the 1980s, India was one of the more heavily regulated market economies. High regulation along with an autarkic economic development model bred inefficiency, created wastages and kept growth rates low. Since the 1980s regulations have eased—in the early 1980s gradually and since 1991 more rapidly. This chapter discusses the process of regulation and deregulation in the labour markets in light of the overall liberalisation process in the economy initiated in the recent years. It then makes a case for higher flexibility in the labour market, with a proviso for better social and human security to compensate for any shocks that workers might face emerging from higher flexibility in the labour market.

Up to the 1970s, India was a largely agrarian economy—almost half its GDP (45 per cent) originated in the primary sectors (secondary sector: 22 per cent; tertiary sector: 33 per cent) and more than 70 per cent of the work force was engaged in it. With relatively higher growth exceeding 5-6 per cent in the later years (1980-2003) these proportions have changed. Agriculture in 2003 contributed about 22 per cent to the GDP (57 per cent work force, as per 2001 census), while the share of the secondary sector has risen to 26 per cent (18 per cent work force) and of services to about 52 per cent (25 per cent work force). The economy has primarily grown on the strength of services and modern industries—banking, transport, communication and telecommunication, computer-enabled services, software, auto-parts, automobiles, gems and jewels, chemicals and petrochemicals, pharmaceuticals and construction to name a few, though other sectors too have exhibited an upward trend.

Deregulation on the investment front provided the first boost to growth. Other factors contributing to the growth include the new demand for services in the international markets facilitated by technological advancement in the telecommunications sector, creation of rapid local demand as a consequence of deliberate state policy (of deficits and low interest rates), supply-side incentives, increased international capital mobility, and technology transfer.

Regulation and deregulation have alternatively impacted economic growth and its composition, which in turn have determined the nature and extent of employment, earnings and income distribution in the economy. What was the state of labour and employment in the (earlier) controlled regime, and what direction did it take under the (gradual) deregulation process that has been undertaken in the last two decades? This is the primary question pursued in this chapter. It then examines what it takes to expand the canvass of 'decent work' for workers, to borrow a phrase from the ILO.[1] The analysis is largely, though not exclusively, restricted to the non-agricultural sectors. The next section describes the earlier regulatory regime and economic development in that period, Section 3 portrays the pattern of growth under the (current) relatively more liberalised system, and Section 4 offers some stylised features of the labour situation. The chapter ends with a conclusion in Section 5.

3.2. Growth, Regulations and Deregulation

3.2.1 The Regulated Regime and Labour

India began industrialisation in the early 1950s on an already existing, albeit small, industrial base. Following a Soviet-style industrialisation model, the principal strategy was to establish capital goods industries under public sector ownership. The purpose was to instil forced savings (and investment), which was felt necessary at that time when the savings rate did not exceed 7-8 per cent of the national income. The private and multinational sectors nevertheless continued to produce a variety of consumer and capital goods and utilities alongside.

---

1. While the notion of decent work, as defined by ILO, is yet to be interpreted in the South Asian context, at least in India the most pressing engagement is with reducing poverty, i.e. reducing unemployment and raising wages.

However, India was (and is) a labour-surplus country and this form of industrialisation could not absorb labour to any significant extent. The planners, therefore, proposed promotion of small-scale industries, under private ownership, to grow in a protected market, produce consumer goods and create jobs. Special incentive packages were offered to them—product reservation, technical and market support, subsidised inputs.

The existing (large-scale) private sector was to grow under a licence regime; licences administered by the government, based on demand determined by input-output matrices (and consumption norms), and not market signals. The government regulated and channelled foreign exchange and other industrial inputs through quotas and end-use norms.

The regulated regime, in principle covered labour as well, and rather elaborately, albeit differentially across different groups of workers since there was huge segmentation, as is seen from the fact that only those workers who were engaged in the so-called organised sectors, i.e. in large industries, service establishments and the government (including government-owned industries and parastatal organisations) were recognised as 'labour'. For operational purposes, all enterprises outside agriculture employing 10 or more workers on a regular basis and using mechanical power (20 or more workers without power) were/are to be registered with the government—they form(ed) the organised sector. Others form the unorganised sector. A majority of small industries/services workers, tiny sector/single workers and workers engaged in agriculture were deemed to be 'in transition to becoming organised workers'.

The organised sector employed about 32 per cent of the non-agricultural workers in the 1970s (Table 3.1). One reason for the state to recognise only the organised sectors was political: trade unions of organised sector workers were patronised by left-of-centre political parties allied with the government(s) at that time. Unorganised sector workers were excluded, in part because of their status of work which made organisation difficult and expensive, in part because a chunk of these workers could not pay for memberships to support an elaborate infrastructure, and in part because the agenda set by trade unions did not serve the interests of unorganised sector workers. Agricultural workers as well, were kept outside the purview of 'labour' in the formal sense, and among the reasons why they were undermined was because this sector, being pre-dominantly agrarian, had an indistinguishable continuum between the self-employed and employees. Organised sector workers alone enjoyed actual legal protection.

Table 3.1

Total Organised Sector Workers in Non-agricultural Sectors and Aggregate

Year	Total Workers (in '000s)	Total Non-agriculture Workers (in '000s)	% of Non-agriculture Workers to Total Workers	Organised Sector Workers (in '000s)	% of Organised Sector Workers to Total Workers	% of Organised Sector Workers to Total Non-agricultural Workers
1961	188676	57527	30.49	12090	6.41	21.02
1971	180485	55066	30.32	17473	9.68	31.73
1981	222517	74494	33.48	22879	10.28	30.71
1991	278940	98044	35.15	26733	9.58	27.27
2001	402513	167446	41.60	27790	6.90	16.60

Source: Census of India (various years) and *Indian Labour Journal* (various issues).

3.2.2 Labour Regulation

Laws were enacted in regard to minimum wages and working conditions—wage-inflation indexing, working conditions, working hours, work rulings in mines, labour contracts, job protection, terminal benefits, arbitration, and the like, was each regulated to ensure a just living and working condition for the organised sector workers. Workers in relatively larger organisations were encouraged to form trade unions; and bipartite and tripartite mechanisms were set up for negotiation, training and dialogue on a range of issues spanning well beyond working conditions and earnings. Regional and national apex organisations were constituted, which affiliated enterprise-wise, industry-wise and city-wise unions to them. Several political parties allied with trade unions and their apex bodies to gain their favour (Chatterjee, 1980).

Due to legal protection coupled with political patronage, however, organised sector workers' trade unions soon became powerful labour aristocracies. They surely served the interests of their members but to an extent they became rent seeking; for example, wages and bonuses had to be paid by employers to their workers irrespective of whether or not their enterprises made profits, and such practices deterred healthy investments in the economy. Typical to what Freeman and Medoff (1984) would describe, these unions worked on keeping membership not too high and negotiated the wages to be at least as high as the productivity (see Tulpule and Datta, 1988 for a real wage series, 1967-84; also, Joshi and Little, 1994). Yet at the same time, there was little internal democracy within the unions (Bhattacharya, 1999).

The system officially did not differentiate between the organised and unorganised sector workers. In practice, however, neither the central nor provincial administrations had (or have until today) the wherewithal—finances, personnel or data—to regulate activities in the whole economy. Officials too were/are not clear enough whether to regulate activities outside the organised sector domain (Acharya, 1996). There was also a tacit recognition within the bureaucracy that higher wages cannot be sustained across all sectors in a low-income economy unless productivity also grew rapidly, which it did not.

Among the clauses in the industrial Act that had direct implications on the labour regulation system and was/is most contested till date, but is still largely in place, is the exit clause. It states that an enterprise beyond a certain size is not permitted to shut shop without government permission, and workers therein cannot be laid-off without adequate grounds (Industrial Disputes Act of 1947, which protects workers from 'unfair' dismissals, and an amendment to this Act in 1976, which requires government clearance before closing industrial units).[2] Industrialists had/have to offer explanations as to why a situation has arisen for retrenching staff, which could be contested by trade unions and government at several steps in a legal hierarchy, a process that could last well beyond a dozen years and cost a lot. In the earlier years such permissions were not always acceded (Bhattacharya, 1999), although now the courts have become more liberal.[3]

---

2. As in 2003, the enterprise size limit beyond which such permissions are needed is 100 workers.

3. E.g. Empress Mills, a textile factory established in 1880s, had to fight an elaborate lawsuit, lasting several years and receiving large publicity, in the 1980s, before it could be shut down.

3.2.3 Economic Performance

Industrial growth during 1950-80 was slow (3.2 per cent annually). The public sector lagged behind in making sufficient investments or operating plants successfully owing to excessive centralisation, bureaucratic decision-making and administered prices and many enterprises continuously made losses. At an annual aggregate profitability not exceeding 3 per cent on fixed capital, there was a gross waste of savings and investment; at this rate, the number of years for capital to replenish would be about 23 while the life of plant and machinery would often be lesser.

Next, the large-scale private domestic and multinational sectors thrived in protected markets because of which they became a high-cost, low-productivity, rent-seeking section of the industry. Paradoxically, the industry was also stifled; for one, the sizes of individual enterprises could not be raised lest such steps violated anti-monopoly laws, and next, the industry operated under rigid labour conditions. Managements therefore began to withdraw resources out of profit-making companies to put in other, new green-field ventures (lateral, not always above-board, transfer of resources), thereby making the older industries non-viable.

The unorganised sector was starved of capital, technology and markets. Modern small-scale industries—for purposes of labour protection most of them fell/fall outside the organised segments—too could not grow much since in an administered regime they could never get market-friendly. They also had no incentive to grow, lest they lose their special incentive packages. It is a different matter that the actual resource quantum earmarked for incentives was far too thinly stretched and poorly targeted—large numbers of firms were left unaided.

A heavily regulated regime created systemic inefficiency and perpetual resource shortage which did not permit any sector to grow.[4]

3.2.4 Labour and Employment

The growth of employment in the organised manufacturing and services sectors prior to 1980 was about 1 per cent a year, most of it during the 1950-67, originating in the public sectors. The share of the public sector in the industrial value added, however, has never

---

4. See for example, Chakravarty (1987); GoI (1997); Ahluwalia (1992); World Bank (1989).

exceeded 12-15 per cent of the total; hence its employment potential in the economy was not very large.

The licence-quota system, not being conducive to evolution of competition, yielded inefficient monopolies, which were conglomerations of not so large individual enterprises. At times these conglomerates could be as widely dispersed as having 40-50 enterprises under a single group; somewhat similar to the industrial conglomerates in South Korea, with the difference that in South Korea export orientation and no scale restriction permitted individual enterprises to emerge as global-sized companies. Many industrial houses had no core competence in several areas, and resultantly, they produced low quality products that sold at high prices in protected (local) markets (Das, 1999). Industrialists got rich due to their monopoly position and captive markets but industries and jobs did not grow (Piramal, 1998). Majority of the workers thus had to find livelihood in the unorganised sectors and small-scale industries (Table 3.1).

3.3. Patterns of Recent Development

3.3.1 The Growth Process

India has deregulated its economy in spurts since 1980. The largest spurt came in 1991; thereafter, a few clauses get modified every 2–4 years. India has also acceded to most clauses of the WTO. The country was not too seriously affected by the Asian financial crisis of 1997 because of its relatively minor monetary integration into the international financial markets at that time, but as in 2004, it is relatively more integrated.

The economic growth achieved since the early 1980s has been relatively more rapid compared to earlier (annual average growth, 1980-90: 5.5 per cent; 1991-97: 6.7 per cent; 1998-2002: 4.7 per cent; 2003-04: 8.3 per cent); it is more diversified and is also more export-oriented. There has been improvement in the quality of products and services and reduction in prices resulting from rationalisation of local and import taxes, relaxing regulations on investment and larger competition.

The managements of companies and businesses too are gradually changing—family-controlled managements are giving way to professional ones; enterprises are getting more competitive and those not, are forced to shut shop; markets are replacing patronage; expenditure on research and development is rising; etc. There is yet much to change, though; many companies in the so-called 'old economy' have yet to adapt, to meet the challenges of globalisation.

A reasonably high economic growth was achieved despite deregulation in the financial markets (in 1991) without adequate safeguards. A series of scams rocked the stock markets in the mid-1990s, which also, part contributed to reducing investment and economic activity during the late 1990s. For example, a number of (little-known) companies entered the primary markets to raise funds and then simply vanished. Another scam involved artificially raising stock prices through excessive betting on stocks—the resources coming from short-term borrowings from unsuspecting banks—and then suddenly off loading them, due to which the stock markets crashed. In the process, the savings of a large number of small investors were wiped out. Additionally, absence of adequate regulation has resulted in problems of undervaluation of state-owned companies during their disinvestment. A number of regulations and regulatory bodies are now being put in place so as to re-instil investor's confidence in the financial system, though some harm has already been done.

It needs explicit statement that while deregulation has occurred a great deal, the progress is more in the investment and trade regimes compared to that in labour.

3.3.2 *The Fate of Older Industries*

Among the first events resulting from liberalisation was the closure of many older and inefficient industrial and commercial establishments, which primarily survived due to protection, laying-off over a million workers (Bakshi, 1986; Bhaumik, 2000; Breman, 2001). These obsolete industries could neither compete with products from the modern enterprises nor with imported products. Long drawn court cases were fought between managements and trade unions/ government, some of which have continued into the new millennium.

Consequently, the organised labour in the private sector proportionately further decreased (Table 3.1) and along with it, the power of the organised trade unions has weakened. Older industries were located in Mumbai, Kolkata and Ahmedabad while the more recent enterprises have come up in other centres. Jobs lost in

Mumbai and Ahmedabad have been gained in other centres, but since labour in India is far less mobile compared to capital, localised unemployment has sharply risen [100,000 jobs lost in Ahmedabad (Breman, 2001)]. Also, since jobs in the unorganised sector have replaced those in the organised sector, the quality of jobs has been downgraded.

3.3.3 Diminishing Demand for Blue-collar Work

Economic activities of more recent origin have been growing in a different direction compared to those earlier. For one, the services industry has begun to assume a higher prominence (52 per cent of GDP, in 2003). Thus, computer software, banking and financial services, business process outsourcing (BPO), transport, communication, retailing and similar services have assumed a more leading status now (Figure 3.1). The composition of labour, however, is different: there are not necessarily many blue-collar workers employed here.[5] Next, even the newer manufacturing activities—pharmaceuticals, chemicals and petrochemicals, precision engineering and publishing—employ more white-collar than blue-collar workers.[6]

Figure 3.1

Organised Sector Employment by Industry Division (Million)

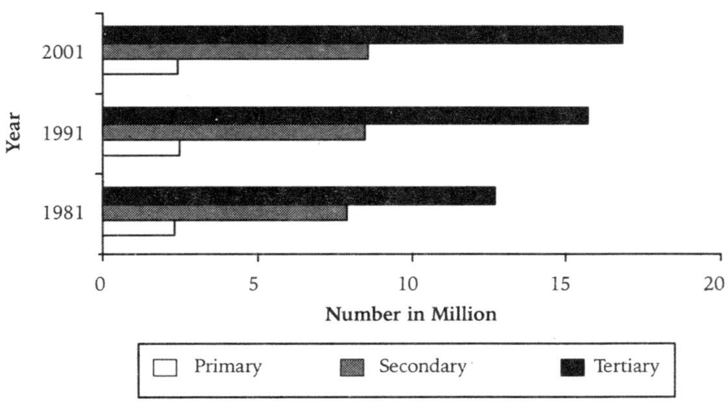

Source: Same as Table 3.1.

---

5. See for example, Unni and Rani (2000), and Madheswaran and Dharmadhikari (2000).
6. Data could be seen in Singh (2003), Bhatt (2003), and Deshpande (2003).

Thus, blue-collar workers proportionately get demanded in fewer numbers, in a country where there is a much larger number of semi-skilled and unskilled workers. The Indian government has until so far invested too little in education and human capital (about three per cent of GNP annually); the result is this evident mismatch (Mitra, 2003).[7]

3.3.4 Rising Capital Intensity

India continues to be identified to have comparative advantage in capital-intensive industries till date; a legacy from the past. The reason lies in the core competence earlier gained, part because many labour-intensive industries were reserved for small-scale sector until very recently (some continue even now)—a legacy of the reservation policies—and part also because of the history of rigid labour laws and militant trade unions.[8]

It is no coincidence that India is becoming an important manufacturing centre for automobile and auto part manufacture (over US$ 22 billion in sales, including export, fiscal 2003-04), petrochemicals (US$ 30 billion in investment, 1998-2003), etc., rather than for garments, shoes, leatherware, consumer electronics and other labour intensive industries. Chemicals, petrochemicals, pharmaceuticals, cement, metals and power-generation equipment, which also constitute important growth sectors, too are not labour intensive.

Even in the services sector labour intensity is not large. The computer software sector might be worth US$ 25-30 billion (in sales), but it directly employs only a little over a million workers. The much talked about business process outsourcing (BPO) industry presently employs less than 250 thousand workers directly. A detailed industry-specific break-up of the work force outside agriculture, given in Table 3.2, suggests that modern activities have not engaged enough workers so as to significantly alter the distribution.

---

7. Amartya Sen, in his comparative analysis of Indian and Chinese economic development, points out that China has been able to absorb far more labour per unit value added compared to India, which in turn has permitted a much better income distribution there (Dreze and Sen, 1997).

8. There are political hitches—compulsions arising from coalition politics—because of which the government is unable to enact far-reaching labour reforms.

Table 3.2

Per Cent Distribution of Workers in Non-agricultural Sectors, 1999-2000

S. No	Industry		Per Cent Workers
1	Mining and Quarrying		1.49
2	Manufacturing and Repairs		30.35
	2.1	Food	3.48
	2.2	Beverages and Tobacco	2.99
	2.3	Textiles	6.47
	2.4	Wood and Wood Products	3.48
	2.5	Leather and Leather Products	0.73
	2.6	Non-metallic Mineral Products	2.24
	2.7	Metallic Products	1.49
	2.8	Repairs	2.74
3	Electricity, Water and Gas		0.75
4	Construction		10.95
5	Trade		23.38
	5.1	Retail Trade	18.16
	5.2	Hotels and Restaurants	2.99
6	Transport, Storage and Business Services		9.20
7	Finance, Insurance and Banking		2.98
8	Community and Social Services		20.90
	8.1	Public Administration	6.72
	8.2	Education and Research	5.47
	8.3	Health	1.49
	8.4	Community Services	0.74
	8.5	Personal Services	5.97
9	Total		100.00

Source: NSS 55th Round, Ministry of Planning, Government of India.

3.3.5 Search for Labour Flexibility

Employers are increasingly looking for labour flexibility to gain greater competitiveness. Some examples:

Contract Labour

Contract labour is gaining ground across industries (Davala, 1992). It is finding acceptance because of the easing of the Contract Labour Abolition and Regulation Act of 1970. Contract workers are hired on short-term contracts—45 days, 90 days, 6 months—and their services could be terminated at one-day notice with no liability. There are no non-wage commitments, either. Workers hired on contracts are not members of trade unions; hence unions cannot take up their cause. Contracts are implemented mostly through third-party labour contractors. Much of the modern, computer-enabled service industry employs contract workers, directly or through third parties.

To an extent, even the government has begun to employ contract workers, directly or through contractors, on one-time or even recurrent short-term contracts; in dock, mines, and public enterprises or even in teaching institutions. In either case, employers cut costs and gain higher flexibility. A contract worker has no job security or any other benefit, and is paid no more than US$ 35-50 (PPP$ 150-220) per month for semi-skilled work, a school teacher could fetch US$ 65, an under-graduate college teacher US$ 80, and so on.[9] Thus, while the organised sector production (or service) is expanding, organised sector workers or wages are not.

Farming-Out Work

To seek other forms of flexibility necessary to be responsive to market demand, production itself—in full or part—is to an extent farmed out. Major mechanical, electrical or electronic companies and consumer goods industries farm-out part of the work, within and outside the country, and keep their operations restricted to core activities (Ramaswamy, 1999). Work is usually farmed-out or sub-contracted to smaller companies where enforcement of labour laws is minimal or slack, if at all, due to limited legal protection.

In effect, while jobs are created they are low paying and not necessarily secure. Also, there is dualism created in the market: there are protected workers in the main industry and then there are other, not so protected ones in the small-scale captive or ancillary units.

Regional Concentration

Some flexibility is sought by shifting the location of industries. Not all provinces in India have the same laws, regulations, implementation mechanisms and efficiency. Kerala, with 100 per

---

9. Examples of earnings and working conditions in the unorganised sector, with pictorial evidence, could be seen in Breman and Das (2000).

cent literacy, attracts no capital. This province, along with West Bengal has had a history of radical provincial governments for decades now, which have ensured relatively good governance but the comparatively more articulate labour keeps capital away. Investors find the business climate stifling; in fact during the 1980s, there was large-scale de-industrialisation in West Bengal. Even local Kerala-originated capital—and there is sufficient wealth there created from repatriation of money earned by immigrant workers in the Persian Gulf for almost three decades—keeps away from there, as other provinces promise higher private returns. Localised unemployment in several locales is high.

Capital shifts to places where it gets an environment of good governance, along with skilled and pliant labour at low cost. Some specific locations (a few cities and provinces in southern and western India) attract large volumes of investment, creating deep regional cleavages in incomes across provinces. The gap between the per capita income of Maharashtra and Bihar exceeds 5:1.

3.3.6 *The Status of Social Dialogue*

In the face of a changing labour situation, organised sector workers too have begun to respond differently from what they did earlier. There is a move away from apex trade unions as workers are increasingly opting for independent, enterprise-level trade unions. There was an increase in the number of registered trade unions from about 26 thousand in 1976 to about 58 thousand in 1999 and this could be possible only because of a rapid emergence of independent, enterprise-level unions since workers no more fancy their leaders to overtly politicise local issues (Bhattacharya, 1999). Enterprise level dialogues have shown positive results: the number of person-days lost due to striking work at the aggregate level has fallen by more than half between the early 1980s and late 1990s (Figure 3.2). Later data, for 2002, show that the total person-days lost were down to 6.21 million, from more than 10 times this figure in the early 1980s (GoI, 2003a).

In many public sector organisations, restructuring has been possible because of such dialogues. A computerisation drive in public sector banks and insurance companies, which was opposed in the 1980s, is now welcomed. Similarly, to downsize excess staff recruited in the past in a few public sector banks and manufacturing

Figure 3.2

Number of Person-days Lost due to Strikes and Lock-outs

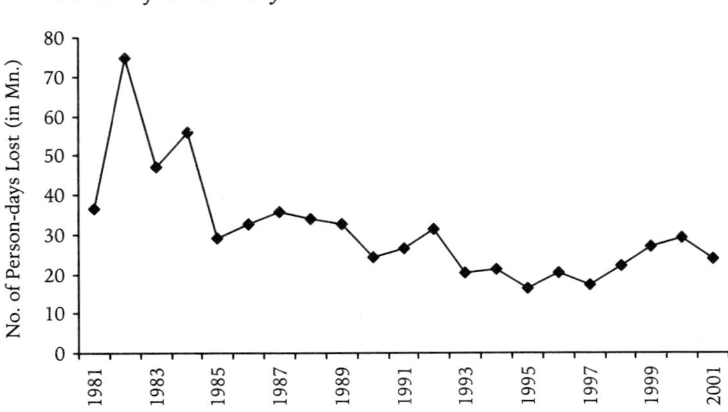

Source: Indian Labour Journal (various issues).

companies, there are agreements signed between workers and managements to pre-maturely retire a portion of the workers, with an understanding that the former will get generous retirement packages.

3.3.7 Work Outside Formal Sector

The unorganised sector contributed as high as 40-45 per cent of the total industrial production and 40 per cent of the total services in the country in 1997 (Table 3.3) (Kulshreshtha and Singh, 1999; GoI, 2003b). While a large segment in this sector is still composed of very small units, there are modern enterprises in it as well, providing high value-adding products and services. The sector is an important provider of jobs today, but the average monthly wage paid in it does not exceed US$ 30-60 (PPP$ 130-250) inclusive of all wage and non-wage payments (for low-skilled/semi-skilled, blue-collar work), and unionisation, social dialogue or collective bargaining are small to negligible. This is one of the reasons why it has gained some comparative cost advantage.

The government first gave tacit recognition to a relaxed labour law regime when it established an export-promoting zone in 1969. Eventually, such zones rapidly multiplied in the 1980s and 1990s, and there are over a dozen of them now. While there is some insistence on payment of minimum wages here—at least on paper—there is no compulsion on the employers to implement any other clauses.

Table 3.3

Share of National Income from the Unorganised Segments, 1996-97

Sector	Share of Unorganised Sectors (%)
Agriculture, Forestry and Fishing	96.30
Mining and Quarrying	8.74
Manufacturing	32.96
Electricity, Gas and Water	2.93
Construction	45.23
Trade, Hotels and Restaurants	85.49
Transport, Storage and Communication	53.15
Finance, Insurance and Real Estate	47.61
Community, Social and Personal Services	17.90
Total	60.27
Total Non-agriculture	42.56

Source: Kulshreshtha and Singh, 1999.

Work outside the organised sector (in the non-agricultural sphere) is large—2/5th of value added and 3/4th of workers—implying that proportionately, there are a large proportion of unprotected workers (2001 data).

3.3.8 Politics and Reality

The description so far, however, still does not provide the full picture: there is another side. Since the rigid labour laws of the yesteryears are technically even now largely in place, there is until date apprehension that India is a difficult place to put in money. Direct foreign investment (DFI) is low (<US$ 2-3 billion annual) and so is local investment in enterprises that have a genuinely large employment potential, and part of the reason for these is the labour law. Several investors are apprehensive of employing even highly skilled workers—often required in research-oriented production and services ventures—for fear of rigid labour laws. In many cases the fear is real: says the Chairman of a major industrial conglomerate about the downturn in the automobile industry during 2000-2002,

"We could, if we were in another country, have closed down the Jamshedpur and Lucknow plants and operated out of Pune. But in the Indian context one cannot do that, and also cannot lay people off" (Ratan Tata interviewed by *Business India*, Jan 19-Feb 1, 2004, p. 49).

Indian policy is caught in a political tug-of-war between a variety of vested interests: a section of industrialists champion globalisation, others plead for protection and still others want labour flexibility; the civil society cries for better justice for the unprotected workers (and farmers); trade unions demand a better deal for the organised sector workers; government-owned bank workers and teachers talk against excessive retrenchment, etc. The governments of the day claim to be market and reform friendly, but at the same time they are unwilling to displease any segment in the population that counts politically. In an attempt to preserve an image of a government wedded to 'pro-poor, yet pro-rich principles', the decision-makers drag their feet in taking decisions that have far-reaching implications. Change in labour laws is one example. Writes a prominent business magazine, "...the current economic boom seems distinctly unkind to workers. While most segments of the economy are shining bright, one large area of darkness is employment" (Business Section in, *India Today*, February 2, 2004; p. 48).

3.4. Regulation and Deregulation: Wither Labour Welfare?

3.4.1 A Synthesis

The unemployment rate in 1999-2000 was at an all time high of eight plus per cent of the work force (Dev, 2002), but then, the main joblessness has been among seasonal agricultural workers, low-skill urban, semi-urban and rural workers and those not having technical education, with concentration in specific pockets/areas where either growth has not occurred or there has been major restructuring or downsizing, implying that it is lack of growth rather than otherwise, that has led to higher unemployment. Next, over the last two decades, the proportion of those below the poverty line has dramatically reduced. In short, the growth process in the last two decades has certainly created jobs.

The work force covered by labour laws, however, has come down from 30 odd per cent earlier to 16.6 per cent of workers (Table 3.1). With a move to privatise public enterprises in full swing, there is likelihood of further protected job reduction, as many of them are over-staffed. During the 1980s, there was less than 0.5 per cent growth in the organised sector labour, which reduced to almost zero growth in the 1990s—it is not that the organised sectors are not recruiting, but they are recruiting contract and casual workers rather than permanent ones. The earnings (and social) gap between the modestly endowed workers (blue-collared operators, unorganised sector workers, the poor self-employed and small farmers) on the one hand, and the management staff, high-technology operators, professionals, capital owners, large land owners and the like on the other, is widening; the average profits and non-wage incomes are growing at more than 7-8 per cent annually (at least in the organised sectors), but wage incomes, especially of low-skill unprotected workers have been virtually stagnant in the recent years: primary sector—1.5 per cent growth in the 1990s; secondary sector—2 per cent; tertiary sector—1 per cent (*Frontline*, September 13, 2003, p. 5; NIRD, 2000; Sundaram, 2001).[10]

In short, organised sector activities have grown in a rather capital intensive fashion, and much of the labour intensive component of work is carried out through outsourcing and contract—in short unprotected conditions. There is trade-off between job creation (at low wages) and relatively high wage/social protection conditions.

3.4.2 The Theoretical and Comparative Position

Has deregulation been gainful to Indian labour? There is a long standing debate internationally on whether to deregulate labour markets, and whose interest does it serve. Does Indian data throw more light on this debate?

First the debate: The dominant school of thought maintains that no markets, including labour, should be subject to distortions, lest they get imperfect and less competitive because any rigidity in wage would disturb the optimal allocation of labour; in turn this would reduce employment. Labour market rigidity also promotes transferring resources from one group or sector to another (rent seeking), which deploys these resources in unproductive venues. Finally, wage rigidity slows down adjustments to shocks (World Bank, 1995; Freeman, 1992). Distinct from this neoclassical viewpoint, the

---

10. This relative widening of the gap is an important reason for forces of subversion to raise their not so amiable heads.

institutional thought, espoused by the ILO among others, rejects the supremacy of prices, and maintains that the welfare goals of workers and society are best carried forward through ensuring better earnings to workers, guaranteeing liveable wages to them and permitting greater distribution of gains to the larger masses in a society.[11] Thus, while the former advocates deregulation, the former advocates select intervention.

Empirical experiences from select countries in developed as well as developing countries in the 1980s and 1990s suggest that despite labour regulations and wage rigidity in those countries, adjustments in employment and wage have been observed (Freeman, 1992; Fallon and Lucas, 1991; World Bank, 1995). Next, some joblosses in the US recently, to low-income countries (China, India) have not been so much due to high wages or wage rigidity there, but to a long term adjustment process in that country, in which low productivity jobs are being relocated elsewhere.[12] Finally, while the Asian economic crisis created huge job losses in most countries in Southeast Asia, Malaysia, where labour laws are relatively more rigid, recovered faster than Thailand did, where the labour market is very flexible. In essence, labour market adjusts to market responses and business cycles in the economy, irrespective of hurdles in the form of rigidities that might exist.

How does the Indian experience contrast to that in other countries? India opened up in the 1980s to investment and trade and these continue to be the principal engines of growth. As elsewhere, the labour market here too has created a variety of ways to go past the rigid labour laws, so as to achieve investment and growth targets. The difference is that in sectors where the market could not go around the rigid labour laws it has left those sectors behind. Thus, most activities where large-scale labour intensive industries could have been set up—e.g. garments, leather products and consumer goods—have stayed stunted. Incomplete labour reform thus is certainly a reason for creating an image of 'unfriendly labour environment' which in turn has promoted capital intensive growth.

Deregulation in labour markets has provided opportunities for employers to cut excess costs and avail of low cost advantages. The

---

11. The most elaborate stand on this in the recent times is presented in the Report of the Director General of ILO in 1999, entitled *Decent Work;* though institutional labour economics has earlier as well, challenged the canons of neoclassical theory. ILO's World Employment Programme in the 1970s and 1980s produced a large corpus of literature on this subject.

12. Figures could be seen from various issues of *Economist,* pertaining to 2003-04.

resultant higher profit has permitted them to grow fast and provide more employment, albeit at low wages and at uncertain terms. Why low wages and uncertain terms? The answer lies in the excess labour supply of a not too skilled work force, which drives/keeps wages low.[13]

3.4.3 How to Promote Employment and Better Work Conditions?

Rapid growth is a necessary condition for achieving better well being of a society; however, this need not always be a sufficient condition for betterment of workers. Next, workers engaged in activities outside the protected sectors are at the edge of the labour market as they are unprotected against business cycles, downturns, or even abuse.

The position taken in this chapter is closer to the ILO stand, that the starting point of any policy is the quest to achieve minimum acceptable work conditions and wages for all (ILO, 1999). There are four options about labour discussed here.

Labour Flexibility

It is now well recognised that the era of lifetime job security is bygone since product demands are globally determined and are highly variable, and product cycles have become shorter. Notions of income security and continuity in work, therefore, must shift from employers to the state/social security systems. For rapid job creation it is vital to enable maximum production (and labour) flexibility, including the exit clause. Under such a regime, the comparative advantage of a nation would emerge and employers would be less hesitant to employ more workers.

Labour Standards

It might be useful to replace the multiples of minimum wages extant presently with a minimum wage, at which workers could subsist at a modest, above poverty line standard of living (more aptly referred to as a living wage). Next, for enforcing labour

---

13. Recent researches suggest that while the old industry shutdown in the 1980s did initially impact workers adversely, rapid growth in the 1990s more than compensated for this loss (Hirway and Mahadevia, 2000; Dutta and Batley, 1999; Unni, 2000). Breman (2001), however, finds that informal sector wages are too low for families to subsist above poverty line, and that these workers get employment for so few days that even if minimum wages are paid, it does not suffice. He says that the market is moving in the direction in which everyone is becoming unprotected and vulnerable. These data really confirm the thesis put forward in this chapter.

standards, social dialogue (bipartite, tripartite or any other) is an important means. Trade unions are vital partners in social dialogue; hence enterprise-level trade unions might be a useful option. Last, quick, inexpensive and simple methods to arbitrate and adjudicate are desirable propositions.

Social Security

To define a social security package for all workers, irrespective of whether they work in large or small enterprises or services, is an important step towards achieving a better deal for labour. For one, social security should be a function of the state. Its elements should include limited support for those who lose work temporarily due to closure (of industry or economic activity), health insurance, small loans for making adjustments or meeting emergency needs, and pensions for those who get incapacitated due to accidents at work. Additional anti-poverty and nutrition programmes could also find place. Presently the Indian government spends only 1.8 per cent of its GDP on social security, social safety nets and social assistance, while Sri Lanka spends 4.7 per cent and many developed countries spend up to 40 per cent. There is therefore sufficient scope to augment the resource base for this purpose. There are a number of success stories of how decentralised and community-based systems could provide extremely efficient and cost-effective services. They could provide clues for framing state policy.[14]

Human Capital

Human capital assumes a central position in today's economy. The government should redeem its promise to spend at least six per cent of GDP on human resource development (including education) to up-scale the general level of education and skills, and hence employability at a living wage. It is also vital that functional and vocational education finds complementarity with general education for creating direct links of education with employment and labour market. In the same context, facilities to retrain and up-scale skills of workers in mid-career (as a part of the human resource development strategy) could be put in place.

---

14. There is a large corpus of literature on this subject. See for example, Jhabvala, Sudarshan and Unni (2003).

3.5. Conclusions

This chapter attempts to examine economic development in India, first under the regulatory regime (1950-80) and then under a gradual deregulation process (1980-until date) in the perspective of labour and employment. The chapter finds that irrespective of the growth rates achieved (or not achieved) and eras when these growth rates occurred, the employment potential, particularly in the large scale organised sectors, has been low, and that there has been high differentiation in the work place by both earnings and labour standards.

Labour legislation in India encompasses a vast span of laws, which at one level comprehensively protect organised sector workers' interests, but they also act as hindrance to investment and employment. With the opening up of the economy since the 1980s, employers have devised ways to go around the rigid laws and do business, but the rigidity in the laws has created a general impression of 'labour-unfriendliness', as a result, capital-intensive activities have sprouted, against the country's natural advantage of abundant labour. Thus, while in the earlier years capital intensity was built-in by design; later it became a natural advantage.

International comparison of experiences in labour markets suggests that labour market adjusts to the natural laws of demand and supply, irrespective of labour laws—laws might slow or somewhat shift the pace, but cannot change the natural tendencies. The Indian experience too suggests that industry tends to seek natural advantage in its inexpensive work force (low costs). However, in those sectors where the industry is not able to surmount the rigid laws, it bypasses them, resulting in these sectors remaining at growth levels far lower than their potential.

The view subscribed in this chapter is that the era of permanent lifetime jobs is now relegated to the past, and the present (and future) periods would require larger labour flexibility and mobility. Laws should be accordingly amended. To protect the interest of workers, social security, labour standards should be enforced to ensure a living wage, health insurance and possibility of training and redeployment of workers in mid-career. Last, investment in human capital is non-negotiable.

References

Acharya, S. (1996). "The Equal Remuneration Act of 1996", Report prepared for ILO, Geneva.

————. (2000). *Report of the Proceedings of the National Workshop on the Strategic Approach to Job Creation in the Urban Informal Sector in India*, Surajkund, 17-19 February, *http://www.ilo.org/public/english/region/asro/newdelhi/surajrep.htm.*

Ahluwalia, I.J. (1992). *Productivity and Growth in India Manufacturing*, Oxford University Press, New Delhi.

Bakshi, R. (1986). *The Long Haul: The Bombay Textile Workers Strike of 1982-83*, BUILD Documentation Centre, Bombay.

Breman, J. and A.N. Das (2000). *Down and Out: Labouring Under Global Capitalism*, Oxford University Press, New Delhi.

Bhatt, P.R. (2003). "Changes in Workforce Structure in India", *The Indian Journal of Labour Economics*, 46(4).

Bhattacharya, D. (1999). "Organised Labour and Economic Liberalisation: Past, Present and Future", *Discussion Paper* DP/105/1999, Labour and Society Programme. International Institute of Labour Studies, Geneva.

Breman, J. (2001). "An Informalised Labour System, End of Labour Market Dualism", *Economic and Political Weekly*, 36.

Chakravarty, S. (1987). *Writings on Development*, Oxford University Press, New Delhi.

Chatterjee, R. (1980). *Unions, Politics and the State: A Study of Indian Politics*, South Asia Publishers, New Delhi.

Das, G. (1999). *India Unbound*, Penguin, New Delhi.

————. (2003). *The Elephant Paradigm*, Penguin, New Delhi.

Davala, S. (ed.) (1992). *Employment and Unionization in Indian Industry*, FFS, New Delhi.

Deshpande, S. (2003). "Changing Employment Structure in Large States of India: What do the NSSO Data Show?", *The Indian Journal of Labour Economics*, 46(4).

Dev, M. (2002). "Pro-Poor Growth in India: What Do We Know About the Employment Effects of Growth 1980-2000?", *Working Paper* 16, Overseas Development Institute, London.

Dreze, J. and A. Sen (1997). (eds.). *India: Economic Development and Social Opportunity*, Oxford University Press, New Delhi.

Dutta, S. and R. Batley (1999). "Urban Governance, Partnership and Poverty: Ahmedabad", *Working Paper 16*, International Development School, University of Birmingham.

Fallon, P.R. and R. Lucas (1991). "Impact of Changes in Job Security Regulations in India and Zimbabwe", *World Bank Economic Review*, 5(3).

Freeman, R.B. (1992). "Labour Market Institutions and Policies: Help or Hindrance to Economic Development?", *Proceedings of the World Bank Annual Conference on Development Economics*, Washington.

Freeman, R. and J. Medoff (1984). *What Do Unions Do?*, Basic Books, New York.

GoI (Government of India) (1997). "Report of the Expert Committee on Small Enterprises", Ministry of Industries.

————. (2002). *The Tenth Five-Year Plan*, Planning Commission, New Delhi.

————. (2003a). *Economic Survey:* Ministry of Finance, New Delhi, *http://www.indiabudget.nic.in/es2002-03/chapt2003/chap711.pdf.*

————. (2003b). *National Income Accounts*, Ministry of Planning, New Delhi.

Hirway, I. and D. Mahadevia (2000). *Gujarat Human Development Report 1999*, Gandhi Labour Institute, Ahmedabad.

ILO (International Labour Organization) (1999). "Decent Work", Report of the Director General, Geneva.

Jhabvala, R., R.M. Sudarshan and J. Unni (2003). *Informal Economy Centrestage—New Structures of Employment*, Sage Publications, New Delhi.

Joshi, V. and IMD Little (1994). *India: Macroeconomics and Political Economy: 1964-1991*, The World Bank, Washington.

Kulshreshtha, A.C. and G. Singh (1999). "Gross Domestic Product and Employment in the Informal Sector of the Indian Economy", The *Indian Journal of Labour Economics*, 42(2).

Madheswaran, S. and A. Dharmadhikari (2000). "Income and Employment Growth in Service Sector in India", *The Indian Journal of Labour Economics*, 43(4).

Mitra, S. (2003). "New Technology and the Indian Labour Market", *The Indian Journal of Labour Economics*, 46(4).

NIRD (National Institute of Rural Development) (2000). "India Rural Development Report", Hyderabad.

Piramal, G. (1998). *The Business Maharajas*, Penguin, New Delhi.

Ramaswamy, K.V. (1999). "The Search for Flexibility in Indian Manufacturing, New Evidence on Outsourcing Activities", *Economic and Political Weekly*, 36(6).

Singh, A.K. (2003). "Changing Workforce Structure in India, 1981-2001: An Inter-state Study", *The Indian Journal of Labour Economics*, 46(4).

Sundaram, K. (2001). *Employment-Unemployment Situation in the 1990s: Some Results from the 55th Round of the NSS, http://www.cdedse.org/papers/work95.pdf.*

Tulpule, B. and R.C. Datta (1988). "Real Wages in Industry", *Economic and Political Weekly*, 23, October.

Unni, J. (2000). "Urban Informal Sector: Size and Income Generation Process in Gujarat", *SEWA-GIDR-ISST-NCAER: Report #2*, National Council of Social Science Research, New Delhi.

Unni, J. and U. Rani (2000). "Globalisation, Information Technology Revolution and Service Sector in India?", *The Indian Journal of Labour Economics*, 43(4).

World Bank (1989). *India Country Memorandum: Poverty, Employment and Social Services*, Washington.

————. (1995). *World Development Report*, Washington.

4

Impact of Wage and Labour Regulation in Vietnam

CAROLINE BRASSARD

4.1. Introduction

Since 1986, Vietnam officially began its transition from a centrally-planned economy towards a market-oriented economy. In parallel to drastic economic reforms, the regulatory environment was improved and enhanced, in order to facilitate this transition. One of the most prominent challenges in a developing country such as Vietnam is the fight against poverty, which both influences and is influenced by the success of these reforms.

This chapter analyses the extent to which current wage and labour regulations can help reducing poverty levels in Vietnam. Since Vietnam is planning to join the World Trade Organization (WTO) in 2005, this study timely coincides with the preparatory process. It identifies some of the remaining regulatory gaps necessary to protect the poorer segment of the population. The approach for this study is based on the belief in the human right to have decent employment, including adequate minimum wage and labour standards.[1] For this purpose, the chapter evaluates the depth of infiltration of wage and labour regulations in the labour market, using commune level data on wages released in 1998.

The minimum wage is defined as the legal minimum level of payment for work performed. The purpose of minimum wage is to protect vulnerable low wage labourers from exploitation and poverty. It usually applies to unskilled adults and is legally enforceable. The minimum wage should be set such that it is sufficient to attain a basic standard of living.

---

1. See Prasch and Sheth (1999) for an analysis of ethical issues related to minimum wage legislation.

However, two major factors play against the use of the minimum wage as a policy tool to combat poverty. The first is the level of under-employment and unemployment in the economy. The second is the extent of informalisation, as workers move out of the formal sector and into the informal sector. Therefore, this chapter also identifies the extent of wage differentiation between sectors and genders, and the potential impact of wage and labour regulations on the poor.

The chapter is organised into six sections. Following this introduction, the second section presents a background on trends in population and pattern of employment since 1990. Annexe A-4.1 gives detailed indicators to complement this background. The third section reviews the wage and labour market regulations. The fourth presents the Vietnamese labour market in context and discusses the poverty alleviation strategy. The fifth presents the results of the empirical analysis based on the Vietnam Living Standard Survey of 1998. The final section presents the regulatory options to be explored and concludes on the extent to which they can be integrated into the poverty alleviation strategy.

4.2. Population and Employment since 1990

Since 1990, the population growth rate has slowly been declining from 1.92 to 1.32 per cent in 2002.[2] The total population of Vietnam nearly reaches 80 million and the labour force participation rate is about 71 per cent (ILO, 2001). This participation rate is amongst the highest in the Southeast Asian region.

During the last decade, the level of urbanisation, in terms of percentage of total population living in urban areas rose from 19.5 to above 25 per cent.[3] The agriculture share of employment has declined from 73 per cent in 1990 to 67 per cent in 2001, whereas the corresponding figures for industry increased from 11 to 13 per cent and for services it increased from 16 to 20 per cent.[4] Due to the transitional process in Vietnam, this structural change process has been accelerating in the last five years, despite the impact of the Southeast Asian financial crisis.

---

2. See Table A-4.1.1 in Annexe A-4.1.

3. In addition, according to the World Bank Indicators (2003a) for Vietnam, in 2002, the fertility rate was 2.1, life expectancy was nearly 70 years, and the level of illiteracy (in terms of percentage for individuals aged 15 and above) was only 7.1 per cent.

4. See Table A-4.1.2 in Annexe A-4.1.

The level of employment between the state and non-state sector shows that, since the financial crisis in Southeast Asia, the formal private sector has been expanding quickly, and accounts for nearly 2.5 million jobs, which is higher than the entire public sector (World Bank, 2003b).[5] Moreover, Nicholson (2002) finds that there is an increased level of unionisation in the state sector, whilst it is nearly inexistent in the private sector. This implies a different degree of wage inflexibility in both sectors.

The rate of unemployment in urban areas in Vietnam has maintained around six per cent in the last five years, whilst the rate of working time in rural areas has been estimated as nearly 75 per cent in 2001.[6] This indicates a high level of underemployment in rural areas. Since 1996, unemployment rates in urban areas have been highest in the Red River Delta and lowest in the Central Highlands, which is amongst the least urbanised region.[7] Finally, the rural areas in the Northwest region of Vietnam has the lowest rate of working time with 71 per cent, whereas the Central Highlands (the poorest region in Vietnam) has the highest rate of working, with nearly 78 per cent.[8] Complementing this background, the next section presents an overview of wage and labour regulation in Vietnam.

4.3. Wage and Labour Regulation in Vietnam

The Vietnamese Labour Code of 2002 provides the regulatory framework for the rights and obligations of workers and employers, labour standards and labour utilisation. This overview of wage and labour regulation indicates some of the gaps and inconsistencies in the Labour Code. This section presents the most recent amendments in the 1994 Labour Code, focusing on regulation relating to minimum wages, to labourers on farms and to female labourers, which is especially relevant to combat poverty for day labourers.

In theory, the Labour Code applies to urban and rural labourers who have signed a labour contract or a labour agreement, or who have obtained a verbal agreement. However, the Labour Code does not directly impact all of the Vietnamese labour market; for example,

---

5. As at 2003, there were nearly 5000 state-owned enterprises in Vietnam.

6. See Table A-4.1.3 in Annexe A-4.1.

7. See Table A-4.1.4 in Annexe A-4.1.

8. See Table A-4.1.5 in Annexe A-4.1.

labourers below the age of 15 and labourers who have not signed a labour contract or agreement or a verbal agreement, including most of the self-employed. These labourers usually form a large part of the vast informal sector in developing countries and are—more often than not—poor.

4.3.1. Recent Key Amendments to the 1994 Labour Code[9]

The 1994 Labour Code was amended in April 2002, to be effective from January 1, 2003 (Labour and Social Affairs Publishing House, 2002: 110). In particular, chapters on Labour Contract, Collective Labour Agreement and Wages were amended. The amendments partly reflect the new priorities and requirements arising from the transition towards a market economy. However, the Labour Code regulation on wages falls short of establishing a market-based system of wage fixing. Some of the key amendments for each chapter are analysed below.

Chapter IV on Labour Contract, Article 27, was supplemented with the definition of different kinds of contract, such as indefinite term, definite term and seasonal work. There was also an amendment on new contract after contract expiration. Article 37 was amended such that in case of insufficient employment for all existing employees, there will be a proposal for the utilisation of the labour force. If workers must terminate the labour contract as pursuant to that article, they shall be entitled to the allowance of work loss. Chapter V on Collective Labour Agreement, Article 48 was amended such that the provincial labour authority shall have the right to declare collective agreement void.[10]

Chapter VI on Wages, Article 57 was amended such that, with consultation from Vietnam General Confederation of Labour and representatives of employers, the Government shall stipulate the principles for developing wage scales, wage tables and labour norms. The Government shall determine wage scales and wage tables for state-owned enterprises. When developing wage scales, wage tables and labour norms, the employers have to consult the Executive Committees of enterprise trade union and the wage scales and tables

---

9. The following chapters were not significantly amended: (I) General Provision, (II) Employment, (III) Vocational Training, (VII) Working Time and Rest Time, (VIII) Labour Discipline and Physical Responsibility, (IX) Labour Safety and Labour Hygiene.

10. Vietnam has not ratified the ILO conventions on collective bargaining, freedom of association and protection of the right to organise.

shall have to be registered. Article 61 was amended such that on public holidays and holidays with payment, workers shall be paid an amount at least equal to 300 per cent. Finally, Article 64 was amended such that grant bonuses to workers shall have to be based on annual results in production and business activities and workers' performance. The rule of bonus system shall be determined by the employers with consultation from the Executive Committee of the enterprise trade union.

Chapter X on separate provisions on women labourers, Article 111 was amended to include provision for time off during pregnancy, maternity leave or when nursing a child under 12 months old. The female employee shall be exempt from unilateral termination of her labour contract. However, the Labour Code contains no such provisions applicable to male labourers nursing children under 12 months old.

Finally, Chapter XI on separate provisions concerning junior workers and other categories of workers, Article 121 was amended such that the employment of junior workers in work and workplace which may give bad influence to their personality, as determined in a list issued by the Ministry of Labour, Invalids and Social Affairs (MoLISA) and the Ministry of Health. The next section focuses on minimum wage regulations in the agricultural, services and industrial sectors.

4.3.2. Farms Labourers

Labourers working on farms are also theoretically protected by the Labour Code. Based on Decree no. 03/2000/NQ-CP dated February 2000, the MOLISA Circular No. 23/2000/TT-BLDTBXH of September 2000 provides orientation on the application of policies towards labourers working on farms (Statistics Publishing House, 2001: 536-541). However, although the circular states that "The farm owner has the authorisation to recruit an unlimited number of labourers and without distinction of area of living of the labourer" (p. 536), there are inherent constraints to the migration of labour in Vietnam. For example, migrant status comes with problems in access to basic services, and to social safety nets.

In addition, the circular states that "The Government encourages the farm owner to recruit labourer of peasant family, lack of work (unemployed), poor people, female labourer, with priority for local labourers" (p. 537). This prioritisation, though not officially enforced legally, is supported by incentives which again contradict a free labour market. Moreover, these migrants are unlikely to be accounted for in census data or household data based on these censuses. This remains an unresolved and under-researched issue, as none of the household surveys collected information on the registration status of migrants. This means that there is likely to be an underestimation of poverty and inequality.

The World Bank (1999: 12) estimates that, each year, between 1.5 and 2.5 million people migrate. Using the VLSS household data, Nguyen, Tran, Bui, Ngo and Vo (1999: 197) conclude that nearly a third of the urban population was born in rural areas. Furthermore, it has recently been estimated that approximately one million individuals move into urban areas each year (World Bank, 2003a: 122). Part of the reason for the different patterns of migration (including the gender-based migration) between the North and the South may be reflected in the wage differentials between regions, within the industrial and agricultural sectors, as discussed later.

In addition, according to the circular, the farm owner and the labourer arrange the wage according to the workload, load of products, or arrange the level of wage according to daily, weekly or monthly wage, based on the kind of job and the complexity of the job. For relatively simple work in 'normal' work conditions, the circular states that 'it is not permitted to pay under the minimum or common salary stipulated by the government. The minimum salary applied from January 2000 is 180,000 Dong per month' (p. 538). This is the equivalent of 7,500 Dong per day or less than 12 US Dollars per month[11] and falls far below the level of subsistence, leading labourers to undertake multiple jobs.

Finally, with regards to working time and rest, the circular states that the maximum number of hours worked should not exceed eight hours per day. However, overtime can be arranged if it does not exceed four hours per day. Within a 30 day month, the circular indicates that working time should be six days work and one day rest. Moreover, if the duration of the job is one year or above, the worker is entitled to 12 days leave with wage per year worked. Problems related to enforcement of the Labour Code for this leave entitlement, especially in remote areas, can pose a serious challenge to the efficiency of the regulation in protecting the poor.

---

11. One US Dollar is equivalent to 15,800 Vietnamese Dong (as at end of 2004).

4.3.3. Minimum Wage Regulation in Enterprises

A decree of the government (No. 03/2003/ND-CP) in January 2003 and effective since February 2003 was proposed by the Minister of Internal Affairs and Minister of Labour, War Invalids and Social Affairs and the Minister of Finance on adjusting salary and social subsidies and reforming the salary management mechanism. Article 1 stipulates that the minimum salary is raised to 290,000 Dong per month (up from 210,000 Dong from Decree 77/2000/ND-CP), applicable to persons who are entitled to salary and allowance financed by the State budget and employees working in enterprises, with the exception of foreign-invested enterprises. This salary is based on a maximum of eight hours per day, six days per week and is equivalent to a daily salary of 12,080 Dong.

Decision No. 708/1999/QD-BLDTBXH of June 1999 stipulates that the minimum wage levels applicable to unskilled/untrained Vietnamese labourers in foreign-invested enterprises would be no less than 626,000 Dong per month for foreign-invested enterprises located in urban districts of Hanoi and Ho Chi Minh City (HCMC), no less than 556,000 Dong for foreign-invested enterprises located in the rural districts of Hanoi and HCMC and urban districts of Hai Phong, Bien Hoa and Vung Tau cities. For foreign-invested enterprises located in urban and rural districts of other provinces and cities, the minimum wage level shall be no less than 487,000 Dong per month. Finally, foreign-invested enterprises located in difficult geographical areas with poor infrastructure, the minimum wage level shall be no less than 417,000 Dong per month.[12]

In sum, foreign invested enterprises are required to pay their employees minimum wages that are more than twice that of their domestic counterparts. Various macroeconomic factors can influence the level of competitiveness of industries, such as exchange rates and productivity levels. However, this dual wage system, which serves to protect domestic industries, can lead to pervasive government control of the labour market, and seriously challenge a smooth transition towards a market economy. The last section discusses the particular case of female and junior labourers in all economic sectors.

---

12. Nhan Dan newspaper, legal article on decision on minimum wage levels, August 21, 1999. Available at *http://www.nhandan.org.vn/english/legal/19990821.html.*

4.3.4. *Female and Junior Labourers*

Based on Decree No. 23/CP dated June 1996, circular No. 03/LD-TBXH-TT of January 1997 provides instructions on the execution of some articles stipulated toward female labourers (Statistics Publishing House, 2001: 288-295). This circular states that female labourers should be at least 15 years old, as in the case of male labourers (p. 288). According to the circular, female labourers working at home are also subject to the Labour Code. However, the current labour law stipulates that female labourers are prohibited to work night shift (p. 289). The usually higher wages for working night shift are thus reserved for their male counterpart.

Section I of Chapter XI of the 2002 Labour Code presents separate provisions concerning junior labourers. Under the Labour Code, junior workers consist of workers less than 18 years of age. The admission to work of children under 15 years of age is prohibited, except in certain categories of occupations and works, as determined by the MoLISA (p. 56-57). This list was not available at the time of writing this chapter. More importantly, it appears that the application of the Labour Code is unclear for workers between the ages 15 to 18.

Thus, in theory, according to the Labour Code, wages should be agreed between the employees and employers (Article 7). This suggests that female and junior labourers are entitled to market-based wage rates. However, that there is no reliable data on the economic variables taken into consideration whilst fixing the minimum wage rates. As discussed in the next section, the application of the Labour Code faces many significant challenges, mainly resulting from labour market imperfections. Moreover, the indirect impact of wage and labour regulation on the informal economy should also be considered, as part of the poverty alleviation strategy.

4.4. The Vietnamese Labour Market in Context

The regulation of the Vietnamese labour market has to be put in context. For this purpose, this section begins with an analysis of the imperfections in the labour market. Then, it presents the overall strategy for poverty alleviation in Vietnam. This will be used to explain how wage and labour regulation can and should be integrated in the long term strategy.

4.4.1. Labour Market Imperfections

Within the transitional process towards a market economy, pressures for greater access to free markets come from various sources. For example, lack of funds invested in labour-intensive projects during the socialist period has led to declining income distribution which reinforced the need to reform the stagnating Vietnamese economy (Beresford, 1989: 145). However, labour market imperfections reduce the scope of change brought by reforms and vary greatly between the formal and informal sectors.

Labour market imperfections may be due to lack of incentives, lack of labour mobility or lack of information. This may result in inadequate wages, underemployment and bad labour conditions. In Vietnam, the most vulnerable group is undoubtedly the large informal sector, with very little protection against economic downturns. This consists mainly of the self-employed and small farmers, mostly engaged in subsistence agriculture, small trading and handicraft activities.

In contrast, as a result of state owned enterprises reform, most of the reduction of labour employment in the public sector was done in the first few years of the reform period between 1989 and 1992. State owned enterprise (SOE) labour force was reduced by nearly 30 per cent, with over one million employees retrenched. In the early 1990s, when SOEs were able to formulate their own wage policies, wage scales were not increased but reduced (Lu, 1996: 413). By 1998, Bales (2000) estimates that the state sector still accounted for about 40 per cent of all wage employment. This could be explained by relatively higher wage rates in SOEs. Indeed, Bales and Rama (2002) estimate that should SOE workers earn from the private sector, their total earnings would fall by over 20 per cent.[13]

In Vietnam, economic growth is largely due to the intensification of labour production. However, concerns over the sustainability of Vietnam's development and integration to the world economy lie in its growth pattern, where labour-intensive industry has declined in share from 58 per cent to 51 per cent in the last few years. Despite the migration of labour from agricultural sector to industry and manufacture, according to Bales (2000), one-third of newly created

---

13. They also indicate that their results are likely to underestimate the extent to which SOE workers are overpaid (Bales and Rama, 2002: 23).

jobs in the rural areas are in the agricultural sector. Yet, only 18 per cent of all wage jobs are in the agricultural sector. Consequently, there is a very high degree of underemployment in the agricultural sector, compared to other sectors.[14] In addition, many new jobs in this sector do not necessarily ensure adequate living standards over time, as evidenced by household living standards data in Vietnam.

4.4.2. Poverty Alleviation Strategy

Although poverty has declined sharply over the last decade, nearly 30 per cent still live under the poverty line according to the World Bank poverty line (World Bank, 2003b). Like in most developing countries, poverty in Vietnam is concentrated in the rural areas, where 35.6 per cent of the population lives under the poverty line (World Bank, 2003b: 9). Amongst the most severely affected are ethnic minorities and residents of isolated areas, located mainly in in the Central Highlands, the Northern Mountains and the North Central Coast.

The Hunger Eradication and Poverty Reduction (HEPR), initiated in 2001, headed by the (MoLISA) is one of the first attempts at providing concrete objectives for poverty alleviation for the period 2001-2010. The main objectives are to eliminate chronic hunger and falling back to hunger. One of its main components is to provide subsidised loans to the poor for income-generating activities without requiring collateral. However, a report (World Bank, 2000: 75) indicates that only 20 per cent of the loans have been disbursed to the poorest 40 per cent, whereas the better-off 40 per cent received 30 per cent of all loans, which highlights that the programme is not pro-poor in its loan component.

In parallel, since 1999, governments in low-income countries receiving concessional lending from the World Bank through the International Development Association or from the International Monetary Fund (IMF) through the Poverty Reduction and Growth Facility must develop their own Poverty Reduction Strategy Papers (PRSPs). Written within a participatory process between governments and donors, the aim is to strengthen the coordination between partners to reduce poverty more effectively.[15]

---

14. Bales (2000: 9) estimated that the number of hours worked in the agricultural sector is less than 15 hours work per week.

15. So far, nearly 30 countries have developed their Poverty Reduction Strategy Papers, available at *http://www.worldbank.org/poverty/strategies/index.htm.*

More than 80 per cent of the poor are low skilled farmers with little access to productive resources. Hence, one of the major policies of the Comprehensive Poverty Reduction and Growth Strategy (CPRGS) in Vietnam is to diversify agricultural production and increase investments in agriculture. It also calls for the development of labour-intensive industries using domestically produced inputs (SRV, 2002). The impact of these strategies on the poor are intrinsically linked with labour market imperfections discussed earlier, and need to pay close attention to the structure of employment in general and to the wage system in particular.

As part of the fights against poverty, construction of the poverty profile in Vietnam is based on the Vietnam Living Standard Survey (VLSS) implemented since 1993. Based on the household data, Bales and Phung (2001: 55-56) show that the share of employment in agriculture was 62 per cent in 1998 (compared to 66 per cent in 1993), and that 55 per cent of hired labourers in agriculture still live below the poverty line, compared to 47 per cent for self-employed farmers in 1998. These are the two sectors where poverty is most severe in Vietnam. Yet, when decomposing changes in poverty Bales and Phung (2001) find that 55 to 60 per cent of the reduction in poverty between 1992 and 1998 was due to higher agricultural incomes.

Finally, Wiens (1998) argues that rural poverty is associated with lack of productive resources (land, savings, liquid assets and physical capital), low quality of basic infrastructure (irrigation and transport), lack of access to markets (especially to inputs, credit and off-farm markets), and a high number of dependents. He also concludes that, "Agriculture development is not the route out of poverty for the individual rural household" (Wiens 1998: 95). His research suggests that off-farm employment and non-farming enterprises are most likely to boost incomes and relieve poverty. He concludes (1998: 96) that:

> "Raising the productive capacity of the rural poor is not enough—the market for their goods and services must be expanded through regional development and labour-absorbing structural change in the rural economy. This strategy can be thought of as one of bringing the market to the poor, as opposed to bringing the goods and services of the rural poor to (a distant) market."

In sum, the legacies for the centrally-planned years are still felt at various levels in the labour market. The historical development of the northern and southern regions of Vietnam meant that the development of a market-oriented economy has been achieved at different degrees.[16] The recently available data on living conditions also includes commune level data that can shed some light on the degree of disparity between the northern and southern labour conditions. For this purpose, the following section provides some evidence of the differences in wages between the two regions and between genders for the agricultural and industrial sectors.

4.5. Analysis of Commune Level Data

Valuable information on the agricultural informal sector can be obtained using commune level data from the Vietnam Living Standard Survey of 1998. As a background on the larger socioeconomic environment of these households, the community questionnaire includes over 200 general information questions on demography, the economy, basic infrastructure, education, health and agriculture in each rural commune (GSO, 2000). In the follow-up survey, separate school and health centres questionnaires were implemented to increase the quality of the community data. Few empirical studies have made full use of this community level information.

4.5.1. Vietnam Living Standards Survey Commune Data

This data is collected over a two-week period, based on interviews with various community leaders.[17] Unfortunately, the community questionnaire was collected only for the 120 rural communes because it was considered that "many of the questions are more relevant for rural than urban areas".[18] Due to this rural bias, it is not possible to include variables concerning community endowment when analysing poverty in urban areas. Also, due to the relatively small sample size, it is not possible to disaggregate beyond the northern and southern regions. Note that the northern region includes the Red River Delta,

---

16. For an in-depth discussion of the legacies from the past on the Vietnamese economy, see Brassard (2005).

17. Community leaders include—the chairperson, deputy chairperson, party secretary, chief or deputy chief of police, finance officer, statistical officer, head of cooperative, school director, health worker, women's union cadre, farmer's union cadre, fatherland front cadre or the village leader. (GSO, 1997a).

18. Quoted from the introductory notes for the *VLSS Statistical Abstract* 1997/1998, (GSO, 1997b: 2).

Northeast, Northwest and Northcentral Coast regions, whereas the southern regions covers the Southcentral Coast, the Central Highlands, the Southeast and the Mekong River Delta.

Inferential analysis is also done using independent and paired tests on sample means of particular aspects of the commune data. The statistical tests focus particularly on finding out whether significant differences exist between northern and southern communes in terms of wages, land use and commune budget. The two-sample tests of hypothesis on the difference between the means of two independent samples is given by:

$$t = \frac{\overline{X}_n - \overline{X}_s}{\sqrt{s_p^2 \left(\frac{1}{n_n} + \frac{1}{n_s} \right)}} \quad \text{where} \quad S_p^2 = \frac{(n_n - 1)S_n^2 + (n_s - 1)S_s^2}{n_n + n_s - 2}$$

and $\overline{X}_n$ is the mean in the northern commune sample, $\overline{X}_s$ is the mean in the southern commune sample, n_n is the number of communes in the North n_s is the number of communes in the South and s_p^2 is the pooled estimate of the population variance. For example, independent t-tests are used when comparing between northern and southern regions.

In contrast, when the two samples are paired, the following t-test is used to test the difference in means and is given by:

$$t = \frac{\overline{d}}{s_d / \sqrt{n}} \quad \text{where} \quad S_d = \sqrt{\frac{\sum d^2 - \frac{\left(\sum d \right)^2}{n}}{n-1}}$$

and $\overline{d}$ is the mean of the difference between the paired observations, n is the number of paired observations and S_d is the standard deviation of the differences between the paired observations. For example, the paired t-test is used for comparisons between genders within the northern and southern regions. However, there are often less than 30 communes by category of answer so that these tests cannot always produce statistically significant results due to small sample sizes. Nevertheless, these descriptive statistics can provide insights concerning some of the legacies from the past on differences between the two regions affecting their economic development. The analysis presented below tests whether there are significant differences in salary between males and females in the agricultural and in the industrial sectors, and between northern and southern communes for unskilled workers.

4.5.2. Agricultural Wages

Daily salary figures were obtained based on the average wage that a commune resident earns if he/she does a particular type of work (GSO, 1997a). Table 4.1 indicates the gender differences in daily wages within regions between the different types of agricultural work for the main staple food crop, namely, preparation of land, planting crops, tending crops and harvesting crops. According to the minimum wage regulation for farm labourers (discussed in Section 3) the minimum daily salary is 7.5 thousand Dong. The mean daily salary received by these respondents is about double that amount and is incommensurate with the regulation.

Table 4.1

Daily Salary of Males and Females for Different Types of Agricultural Work for the Main Staple Food Crop (in Thousands of Dong)

Mean Salary (Standard Deviation in Parentheses)	Males	Females	Paired t-test
Northern Communes			
Prepare Land (N=38)	15.60 (4.94)	14.73 (4.62)	3.045 **
Plant Crop (N=32)	13.87 (4.33)	13.97 (4.36)	-0.680
Tend Crop (N=25)	13.36 (4.29)	13.24 (4.39)	1.365
Harvest Crop (N=49)	15.81 (4.68)	15.40 (4.74)	2.478 **
Southern Communes			
Prepare Land (N=41)	22.68 (7.38)	18.63 (7.13)	7.096 ***
Plant Crop (N=47)	20.45 (5.73)	18.0 (6.35)	2.715 ***
Tend Crop (N=49)	18.94 (5.24)	16.32 (4.13)	4.913 ***
Harvest Crop (N=63)	24.57 (7.04)	20.22 (6.07)	7.452 ***

Source: Author's calculation (VLSS, 1998).

Note: ***, **, * Significant at the 0.01, 0.05, 0.1 level, respectively.

In addition, in the northern communes interviewed, there is a statistically significant difference in daily salary wages between males and females for land preparation and crop harvesting, but no significant difference for planting and tending crops. In comparison, in the southern communes interviewed, there is a significant difference in salary between males and females for all types of agricultural work, and this difference is also statistically more significant than in the North. Part of the explanation may stem from the socialist legacy of the cooperative system, which included a relatively egalitarian system in the North.

In contrast, Table 4.2 indicates the differences in daily wages by gender and between regions for the different types of agricultural work for the main staple food. Once again, information on children relate to those under the age of 15. All results are statistically significant and suggest that in addition to gender differences shown in the previous table, there exist significant regional differences. The existence of a large seasonal labour surplus in the North may exert downward pressure on wages and explain these statistically significant differences in daily wages between regions.

Table 4.2

Daily Salary of Northern and Southern Communes for Different Types of Agricultural Work for the Main Staple Food Crop
(in Thousands of Dong)

Mean Salary (Standard Deviation in Parentheses)	North	South	Independent t-test
Males			
Prepare Land	16.75 (6.45)N=53	24.36 (7.25)N=61	-5.878 ***
Plant Crop	13.87 (4.33)N=32	21.39 (5.93)N=58	-6.299 ***
Tend Crop	13.36 (4.29)N=25	18.94 (5.24)N=49	-4.585 ***
Harvest Crop	15.78 (4.58)N=51	24.57 (7.04)N=63	-7.682 ***
Females			
Prepare Land	14.73 (4.62)N=38	18.63 (7.13)N=41	-2.856 **
Plant Crop	14.75 (4.63)N=52	18.0 (6.35)N=47	-2.927 **
Tend Crop	12.84 (4.04)N=33	16.68 (4.27)N=57	-4.183 ***
Harvest Crop	15.33 (4.73)N=52	20.22 (6.02)N=64	-4.782 ***
Children			
Prepare Land	10.00 (3.55)N=7	16.69 (9.71)N=16	-1.752 **
Plant Crop	10.72 (4.47)N=11	13.0 (3.11)N=20	-1.663 *
Tend Crop	9.611 (3.46)N=9	12.67 (3.92)N=18	-1.978 **
Harvest Crop	10.28 (3.29)N=11	16.00 (5.39)N=22	-3.218 ***

Source: Author's calculation (VLSS, 1998).
Note: ***, **, * Significant at the 0.01, 0.05, 0.1 level, respectively.

These results suggest that, in the northern part of Vietnam, wages tend to be more equal between males and females than in the southern part, except for work that requires more physical strength, such as preparing land and harvesting. At the same time, average wages for these types of work are significantly lower than in the southern part of Vietnam. These results apply for all types of labourers, whether male, female or children. Children's wages in the North are about 70 per cent of female wages in that region, compared to nearly 80 per cent in the South.

More importantly, it appears from Table 4.2 that children's daily salary in the South for the preparation of land and harvesting are actually above those of adult males and females in the North. These two types of agricultural work are usually physically more demanding than planting and tending crops. These results suggest that there may be some extra incentives for poorer households in the South to send their children to work instead of school. Finally, the additional income from the children's work allows for increased expenditure, used as a proxy for income. Therefore, this is likely to lead to an underestimation of the poverty level of households sending children to do agricultural work, mainly located in the South.

Table 4.3 presents similar statistics for the main industrial or fruit crop. Results show a highly statistically significant difference in

Table 4.3

*Daily Salary of Males and Females for Different Types of
Agricultural Work for the Main Industrial or
Fruit Crop (in Thousands of Dong)*

Mean Salary (Standard Deviation in Parentheses)	*Males*	*Females*	*Paired t-test*
Northern Communes			
Prepare Land (N=12)	16.58 (8.54)	16.33 (8.66)	*1.393*
Plant Crop (N=11)	14.09 (5.17)	14.0 (5.19)	*1.000*
Tend Crop (N=11)	14.09 (5.30)	14.00 (5.31)	*1.000*
Harvest Crop (N=11)	15.64 (6.78)	15.36 (6.87)	*1.399*
Southern Communes			
Prepare Land (N=30)	22.40 (5.29)	18.47 (4.09)	*5.745* ***
Plant Crop (N=33	21.12 (5.05)	18.15 (4.02)	*4.400* ***
Tend Crop (N=41)	20.58 (4.19)	17.09 (3.87)	*5.635* ***
Harvest Crop (N=44)	24.20 (5.97)	20.34 (5.38)	*6.215* ***

Source: Author's calculation (VLSS, 1998).

Note: ***, **, * Significant at the 0.01, 0.05, 0.1 level, respectively.

wages between genders within the southern communes. However, there are no significant differences in wages between genders in the North. The sample size for northern communes is two-thirds smaller, but may suggest that the level of diversification in the northern communes is much lower. This may stem from the legacy of market orientation in the South and the fact that the southern part of Vietnam is more land-abundant than the northern part.

Table 4.4 presents tests for whether wages for different types of agricultural work for the main industrial or fruit crop are significantly different between regions. Wages for children (under 15) are included even though the sample size is very small. They serve as a rough indication of the extent of difference between adults' and children' wages.

Table 4.4

Daily Salary of Northern and Southern Communes for Different Types of Agricultural Work for the Main Industrial or Fruit Crop (in Thousands of Dong)

Mean Salary (Standard Deviation in Parentheses)	North	South	Independent t-test
Males			
Prepare Land	16.58 (8.54)N=12	23.58 (5.77)N=41	*-3.297* **
Plant Crop	14.09 (5.17)N=11	21.8 (5.19)N=40	*-4.361* ***
Tend Crop	14.09 (5.30)N=11	20.58 (4.19)N=41	*-4.31* ***
Harvest Crop	15.64 (6.78)N=11	24.20 (5.97)N=44	*-4.142* ***
Females			
Prepare Land	16.33 (8.66)N=12	18.47 (4.09)N=30	*-1.091*
Plant Crop	14.0 (5.19)N=11	18.5 (4.45)N=34	*-2.798* **
Tend Crop	14.00 (5.31)N=11	17.41 (4.14)N=43	*-2.302* ***
Harvest Crop	15.36 (6.87)N=11	20.34 (5.38)N=44	*-2.593* **
Children			
Prepare Land	10.20 (4.44)N=5	14.33 (3.42)N=12	*-2.088* **
Plant Crop	10.0 (4.19)N=6	12.84 (2.47)N=13	*-1.87* **
Tend Crop	10.17 (4.11)N=6	13.71 (3.51)N=14	*-1.968* **
Harvest Crop	10.40 (4.56)N=5	15.24 (3.23)N=17	*-2.687* **

Source: Author's calculation (VLSS, 1998).

Note: ***, **, * Significant at the 0.01, 0.05, 0.1 level, respectively.

Similar to the main staple food crop, the preparation of land and harvesting are associated with the highest wages, though the difference is slightly less statistically significant for the main industrial or fruit crop. This may be due to the relatively smaller sample size in the northern communes. But, there is again a similar pattern for children, where significant differences in wages are found between the two regions, for similar types of work.

Finally, data from Table 4.4 shows that children in the North earn less than 70 per cent of female wages in that region. However, in the South, the proportion is only about 55 per cent. This contrasts with the findings from Table 4.2, where children earn higher wages for work related to the main staple food crop. The smaller sample sizes also reflect the fact that children are less likely to do agricultural work for the main industrial or fruit crop. In order to understand these differences further, the next section presents data analysis focusing on land use and land tenure between the two regions.

4.5.3. Industrial Wages

Monthly salary figures in different types of industries are obtained based on the average wage received by male and female adults in factories belonging to the state and private sectors, but outside the foreign sector. Table 4.5 shows the difference in salary between males and females and within regions for three types of industries—food and beverage, textile and garments and glass, ceramics and cement industries. Note, that of all the communes interviewed in the North, none mentioned the presence of a food and beverage industry.

Recall from Section 3 that according to the regulation, the minimum monthly salary in enterprises outside the foreign sector is 290 thousand Dong. According to Table 4.5, the average monthly salary in the textile industry in the Northern communes falls below this stipulated minimum threshold. For all other industries, including the southern textile industry, the average monthly salary is clearly above the stipulated minimum wage.

Within the northern communes, the results indicate a statistically significant difference in monthly salary between males and females in the glass, ceramics and cement industry. Within the southern communes, the only significant difference in monthly salary between males and females is in the food and beverage industry. In other southern industries, the small sample size does not allow robust comparisons.

Table 4.5

Monthly Salary of Males and Females in Different Industries (in Thousands of Dong)

Mean Salary (Standard Deviation in Parentheses)	Males	Females	Paired t-test
All Communes			
Food and Beverages (N=40)	512.75 (209.21)	401.5 (194.34)	*3.264* ***
Textiles and Garments (N=20)	331.5 (120.31)	314.5 (113.8)	*1.952* *
Other Non-metal Mineral Products (Glass, Ceramics, Cement) (N=15)	496.7 (148.1)	410.0 (127.0)	4.516 ***
North			
Food and Beverages (N=0)	N/A	N/A	*N/A*
Textiles and Garments (N=13)	288.5 (79.46)	273.8 (62.4)	*1.891* *
Other Non-metal Mineral Products (Glass, Ceramics, Cement) (N=13)	492.3 (159.2)	396.1 (131.43)	4.63 ***
South			
Food and Beverages (N=40)	512.7 (209.2)	401.5 (194.3)	*3.264* **
Textiles and Garments (N=7)	411.4 (147.5)	390.0 (151.7)	*1.000*
Other Non-metal Mineral Products (Glass, Ceramics, Cement) (N=2)	525.0 (35.3)	500.0 (0)	1.000

Source: Author's calculation (VLSS, 1998).
  n/a no valid pairs available.
Note: ***, **, * Significant at the 0.01, 0.05, 0.1 level, respectively.

Finally, comparisons between genders in all communes reveal that all industries show a statistically significant different salary between males and females, although this difference is less pronounced in the textile industry. Although the sample sizes are small, these findings suggest that rural industries hiring unskilled labour tend to provide significantly different wages between males and females. This has important implications for labour absorption and the increased income inequality resulting from the development of rural industries. The implications of these findings are discussed in more detail later.

In contrast, Table 4.6 shows the difference in salary within each gender for the three types of industries. The results indicate that the disparity within genders and regions in the textile and garment industry is most pronounced. This is important when considering the promotion of equitable income generation and diversification and when looking at the impact of foreign direct investment by sector. Since some results are not statistically significant due to the small number of observations, further research is required to determine the gap between salaries in the two regions. For example, it is not possible to draw conclusions for the food and beverages industry due to lack of data from the northern communes.

Table 4.6

Monthly Salary of Males and Females in Different Industries between the Northern and Southern Communes (in Thousands of Dong)

Mean Salary (Standard Deviation in Parentheses)	*Food and Beverages*	*Textiles and Garments*	*Other Non-metal Mineral Products (Glass, Ceramics, Cement)*
Males			
North	n/a n=13	288.5 (79.46) n=13	492.3 (159.2)
South	505.6 (196.7) n=48	411.4 (147.5) n=7	525.0 (35.3) n=2
Independent t-test	n/a	-2.45 **	-0.281
Females			
North	n/a n=13	273.8 (62.4) n=13	396.1 (131.43)
South	401.5 (194.3) n=40	390.0 (151.7) n=7	500.0 (0) n=2
Independent t-test	*n/a*	*-2.44 ***	*-1.083*

Source: Author's calculation (VLSS, 1998).

n/a no valid pairs available.

Note: ***, **, * Significant at the 0.01, 0.05, 0.1 level, respectively.

Table 4.7 compares the daily salary between adult males and females and children, focusing on the textile industry. It shows that there are statistically significant differences in adult male and adult female salaries between regions. Since, the sample size for children is small, it does not indicate significant differences in children's wages between regions. Compared with other industries (Table 4.5), southern wages in the textile industry vary much more than in the North.

A possible explanation for the wider wage variability in the South is that the skills required within the southern textile industry are of higher levels and more varied than in the North. This is consistent with the use of more modern equipment and technology. However, further research is required to understand if there are other underlying causes and their effects.

Table 4.7

Daily Salary of Adult Males and Females and Children in the Textile Industry (in Thousands of Dong)

Mean Salary (Standard Deviation in Parentheses)	Adult Males	Adults Females	Childern
North	6.4 (4.3)n=5	8.6 (3.8)n=7	5.5 (5.0)n=6
South	20.0 (10.4)n=6	19.2 (10.7)n=6	5.0 (7.07)n=5
Independent t-test	-2.67 **	-2.46 **	0.136

Source: Author's Calculation (VLSS, 1998).
Note: ***, **, * Significant at the 0.01, 0.05, 0.1 level, respectively.

In addition, Table 4.7 indicates a large difference in mean daily wages between children and adults, where children are defined as individuals below the age of 15. The difference in daily wages between adults and children in the southern communes is much more significant than within the northern communes.[19] Although daily salaries are quite low in the North, children tend to earn 70 per cent of adults salaries, whereas in the South, children earn less than in the North, and only 25 per cent of adult salaries. This might suggest the presence of a larger pool of semi-skilled labour in the South compared with the North, and hence, a smaller need for child labour. However, the validation of this finding requires further field research, since data on children's wages are sparse.

The questionnaire does not differentiate between male and female children. But given the difference between adult males and

---

19. Section I of Chapter XI of the 2002 Labour Code presents separate provisions concerning junior labourers. Under the Labour Code, junior workers are workers who are under 18 years of age. Work by children under 15 years of age is prohibited, except in certain categories of occupations, as determined by the MoLISA (SPH, 2001: 56-57). However, this list was not available at the time of writing this chapter.

females, more research could be necessary to see whether there is also a gender differentiation between children. Finally, although the difference within regions and between genders is not large, when comparing between regions, the differences in wages for males and for females are highly significant in the textile industry. Two reasons for this disparity may be brought forward—the first is the use of female labour for less skilled jobs in the textile industry; the second is the failure to implement wage regulation for female labourers. These need to be taken into consideration when investing in rural industries, to understand the impact of wage regulation on female labourers. The policy implications of the results of this data analysis are discussed next.

4.6. Policy Implications and Conclusion

Once Vietnam joins the WTO in 2005, the impact on employment will depend not only on sound regulation of minimum wages and labour conditions, but on their implementation between sectors and across regions. Despite the current limitations of the commune level data, the analysis reveals important trends at the regional level, which have relevance for policy makers. Indeed, analysis of the commune level data indicated significant differences in salary between males and females and between the northern and southern regions of Vietnam.

This can partly be explained from the varying degree of development of the market economy in both regions. Moreover, it also highlighted a disparity in the implementation of minimum wage regulation between the different regions. For example, it showed that the average wage in the textile industry in the northern communes is well below the minimum wage prescribed in the Labour Code.

It is often argued that minimum wage regulation as a policy tool for protecting the poor is ineffective as it only applies to the formal economy due to constraints on enforcement. On the other hand, weak enforcement means a small disemployment effect due to minimum wage regulation (Rama, 2003). In addition, there is a widely debated view that the minimum wage can become a 'trap' in local enterprises. However, this chapter argues that, in order to ensure a minimum living standard, the poor must be protected from exploitation. More specifically, policy implications can be drawn at many levels, in the perspective of poverty reduction.

The importance of considering regional and sectoral characteristics in the labour market cannot be overemphasised. Priority should be set to provide incentives towards an increased formalisation of the agricultural sector, such that labour contracts would ensure protection of farm labourers. Linking pay with performance must be carefully balanced with the type of work undertaken. For example, as shown in Table 4.1, in the northern region of Vietnam, wage differentials are significantly larger for farm work requiring more physical strength. However, in the southern region, wage differentials between genders were significant irrespective of the type of work.

In addition to differing opportunities for work between the two areas, wage scales are significantly lower in the North, in both the agricultural and industrial sectors. Although the difference in price indices between the two regions is about 6 to 7 percent (World Bank, 1999a: 153), according to the independent t-tests, southern wages are significantly higher than northern ones. In addition, according to the paired t-tests, gender differences are particularly pronounced in the South, as wages for males are significantly higher than those of females in nearly all types of work.

In the agricultural sector, the wage discrepancy between genders is more significant in the southern area, although wages are generally higher. Within both regions, inequality is particularly high for more physically demanding work, such as land preparation and crop harvesting. In addition, although the commune data include only a relatively small sample of observations on children's wages, a similar trend can be identified.

Within the industrial sector, the commune data has also raised serious problems with the formulation and implementation of wage and labour regulation. According to the Labour Code, foreign invested industries and domestic industries are regulated differently. Foreign invested industries are subjected to a minimum wage that is more than double that of domestic industries. This particular example of regulation shows how regulation can play against policies aimed at fostering private sector development in Vietnam and reducing poverty.

In addition, in the domestic textile industry, the commune data indicate that adult labourers in the North (both men and women) tend to earn less than 70 per cent of their counterparts in the South. However, within both regions, women's wages are about 95 per cent of men's wages. Moreover, as noted before, the mean wages in the northern textile industry fall below the minimum wage stipulated in the labour code, itself insufficient to meet basic needs.

In the domestic food and beverage industry and non-metal mineral product industry, the gender difference in wages is more pronounced, as women tend to earn only about 80 per cent of men's wages. These findings highlight the importance of considering regional and gender differences when analysing the impact of rising wages on the reduction of intra-household poverty and inequality.

Problems due to gender differentiation of wage income for similar type of work have great implications in the poverty alleviation strategy. In a recent study on gender wage differentials between 1993 and 1998, Liu (2003) concludes from the VLSS household data that improving the understanding of equity practices in the workplace and deregulation of markets to encourage the development of the private sector would encourage competitiveness and may lead to an increase in the cost of discriminatory practices.

In Vietnam, gender-related problems occur within and outside the household. Amongst the common problems mentioned by poor women are disproportionately heavy workloads, unequal decision-making power in the household and lack of access to and voice in institutions (World Bank, 1999). These problems deepen the issue of inequitable salary found in the commune level data analysis. Regulation and enforcement of regulation on equitable salary can have a significant impact on poor females but should not impede women's access to wage income in rural areas.

Lastly, child labour issues and the challenges to regulation also need to be addressed in Vietnam. According to the ILO definition, children under the age of 18 who are working in areas that are exploitative, hazardous or detrimental to their schooling are considered as child labour. This includes underpayment, as widely seen in all sectors of the Vietnamese economy, based on the commune level data.

In conclusion, this chapter demonstrates the extent to which regulatory tools can be used as part of the poverty alleviation strategy but also shows their limitations. Clearly, regulation can offer great opportunities to relieve poverty, including child poverty and gender discrimination and should be better integrated with the policies included in the CPRGS. Increasing access to wage labour is part of a sustainable solution to poverty, but the large informal sector, indirectly affected by these regulation, also requires protection.

This chapter demonstrated some of the regulatory gaps and illustrated the unequal implementation of wage regulation using commune-level data from the Vietnam Living Standard Survey of 1998. Understanding the impetus for an accurate implementation of wage and labour regulation is one of the key to successful poverty alleviation. The central state, as legislator needs to collaborate with lower level governments in order to reduce inequalities at the regional level. The determination of minimum wages should involve the interplay of market forces and collective bargaining power at various levels in the economy. In parallel, civil society is required to monitor (even informally) the implementation of sound wage and labour regulation. Without such monitoring, efforts to improve the legislation will be ineffective.

References

Bales, S. (2000). "Vietnam's Labour Situation and Trends–Analysis based on 1992-93 and 1997-98 Vietnam Living Standards Data", *Background Paper to the Vietnam Development Report 2000*, Hanoi.

Bales, S. and M. Rama (2002). "Are Public Sector Workers Underpaid? Appropriate Comparators in a Developing Country", *World Bank Working Paper on Labour and Employment* No. 2747, Hanoi.

Bales, S. and Phung Duc Tung (2001). "Sectoral Changes and Poverty", in D.J. Haughton and Nguyen Phong, (eds.), *Living Standards During an Economic Boom: The Case of Vietnam*, pp. 47-61, Statistical Publishing House, Hanoi.

Beresford, M. (1989). *National Unification and Economic Development in Vietnam*, MacMillan Press, London.

Brassard, C. (2005). *Poverty and Inequality in Vietnam: Legacies from the Past*, Doctoral Dissertation, School of Oriental and African Studies, Department of Economics, London.

GSO (General Statistics Office) (1997a). *Handbook for the Commune Questionnaire of the Living Standard Measurement Survey 1997-1998*, General Statistics Office, Hanoi.

————. (1997b). *Statistical Abstract of the VLSS 1997/1998*, General Statistics Office, Hanoi.

————. (2000). *Vietnam Living Standards Survey 1997-1998*, General Statistics Office, Hanoi.

————. (2003). *Statistical Yearbook 2002*, General Statistics Office, Hanoi.

ILO (International Labour Organization) (2001). "World Employment Report", International Labour Organization, Geneva.

Labour and Social Affairs Publishing House (2002). *Labour Code of the Socialist Republic of Vietnam (Amended and Supplemented in 2002)*, Hanoi.

Liu, Amy Y. C. (2003). "The Gender Wage Gap in Vietnam 1993-1998", forthcoming in the *Journal of Comparative Economics*, revised draft 4th Sept.

Lu Ding (1996). "Labour Reform and Human Resource Management in Transitional Economies", in Anthony T.H. Chin and Hock Guan Ng, (eds.), *Economic Management and Transition Towards a Market Economy: An Asian Perspective*, pp. 407-432, World Scientific, Singapore.

MoLISA (Ministry of Labour, Invalids and Social Affairs) (2001). *Major Socio-Economic Information Obtained From Ten Large Scale Surveys in Period 1998-2000*, Statistical Publishing House, Hanoi.

Nguyer Hoong Bao, TranThiBen, Bui ThiHong, Ngo Thi Loan and vo ThiKim Sa (1999). "Internal Migration" in Haughton, Dominigue, Jonathan Haughton, Sarah Bales, Thuong Thi Kim Chuyen and Nguyen Nga (eds.) (1999), *Health and Wealth in Vietnam: An analysis of Households Living Standards*, Institute of Southeast Asian Studies, Singapore: 183-201.

Nicholson, P. (2002). "Vietnam's Labour Market: Transition and the Rule of Law", in Sean Cooney, Tim Lindsey, Richard Mitchell and Ying Zhu (eds.), *Law and Labour Market Regulation in East Asia*, pp. 122-156, Routledge, New York, London.

Prasch, Robert E. and F.A. Sheth (1999). "The Economics and Ethics of Minimum Wage Legislation", *Review of Social Economy*, LVII (4): 466-487.

Rama, Martin (2003). "Globalisation and Workers in Developing Countries", *World Bank Policy Research Working Paper 2958*, Development Research Group, World Bank, Washington, DC.

SRV (Socialist Republic of Vietnam) (2002). *The Comprehensive Poverty Reduction and Growth Strategy*. Socialist Republic of Vietnam, Hanoi.

Statistics Publishing House (2001). *Labour Code and Ordinance on the Procedure of Settling Disputes on Labour*, Hanoi.

Wiens, Thomas B. (1998). "Agriculture and Rural Poverty in Vietnam", in D. Dollar, P. Glewwe and J. Litvack, (eds.), *Household Welfare and Vietnam's Transition*, pp. 61-98, World Bank Regional and Sectoral Studies, Washington, DC.

World Bank (1999a). Vietnam Development Report 2000, *Attacking Poverty*, World Bank Country Operations Divisions Report No. 19914-UN, Washington, DC.

World Bank (1999b). *Voices of the Poor*, Joint Report from the World Bank, DFID (UK) in partnership with Action Aid Vietnam, Oxfam (GB), Save the Children (UK) and Vietnam-Sweden Mountain Rural Development Program, Hanoi, Vietnam.

————. (2000). "Vietnam Managing Public Resources Better: Public Expenditure Review 2000", Vol. 1 Main Report and Vol.2 Annexes, *Report No. 21021-VN*, Washington, DC.

————. (2003a). *World Development Indicators 2003*, Washington, DC. World Bank: 122.

————. (2003b). "Vietnam Development Report 2004: Poverty", Joint Donor Report to the Vietnam Consultative Group Meeting, Hanoi.

Annexe A-4.1

Demographic and Employment Indicators

Table A-4.1.1

Demographic Indicators of Vietnam (1990-2002)

Year	Population (million)	Urbanisation (% of Total Population)	Growth Rate
1990	66.02	19.51	1.92
1991	67.24	19.67	1.86
1992	68.45	19.85	1.8
1993	69.64	20.05	1.74
1994	70.82	20.37	1.69
1995	71.99	20.75	1.65
1996	73.16	21.08	1.61
1997	74.31	22.66	1.57
1998	75.46	23.15	1.55
1999	76.6	23.61	1.51
2000	77.64	24.18*	1.36
2001	78.69	24.74*	1.35
2002	79.73	25.11*	1.32

Source: GSO, 2003.

Note: * Since 2000, some rural communes of provinces changed into precincts and towns.

Table A-4.1.2

Employment Share by Sector (1990-2001)

Unit: Thousands of Persons

Year	Total	Agriculture	Industry	Service
1990	29412.3	21476.1	3305.7	4630.5
1991	30134.6	21907.3	3390.3	4837
1992	30856.3	22339.5	3473.9	5042.9
1993	31579.4	22755.5	3561.9	5262.0
1994	32303.4	23155.5	3654.6	5493.3
1995	33030.6	23534.8	3755.7	5740.1
1996	33760.8	23874.3	3887.7	5998.8
1997	34493.3	24196.4	4020.7	6276.2
1998	35232.9	24504.1	4157.1	6571.7
1999	35975.8	24791.9	4300.4	6883.5
2000	36701.8	25044.9	4445.4	7211.5
2001	37676.4	25304.9	4712.3	7659.2

Source: GSO, 2003.

Table A-4.1.3

Employment by Sector and Unemployment Rate in Rural and Urban Areas (1990-2001)

| Year | Employment | | Unemployment Rate in Urban (%) | Rate of Working Time Used by Employment in Rural Area (%) |
| | Total (Millions Persons) | Of which | | |
		State (Millions of Persons)	Other (Millions of Persons)		
1990	29.41	3.42	25.99	n/a	n/a
1991	30.13	3.14	26.99	n/a	n/a
1992	30.86	2.98	27.88	n/a	n/a
1993	31.58	2.96	28.62	n/a	n/a
1994	32.3	2.93	29.37	n/a	n/a
1995	33.03	3.05	29.98	n/a	n/a
1996	33.76	3.14	30.62	5.88	72.28
1997	34.49	3.27	31.22	6.01	73.14
1998	35.23	3.38	31.85	6.85	71.13
1999	35.97	3.43	32.54	6.74	73.56
2000	36.7	3.5	33.2	6.44	74.18
2001	37.67	3.6	34.07	6.28	74.26

Source: GSO, 2003; and MoLISA, 2001.

Table A-4.1.4

Unemployment Rate in Urban Area by Region (1996-2002)

Regions	1996	1999	2000	2001	2002
Whole Country	5.88	6.74	6.44	6.28	6.01
Red River Delta	7.57	8	7.34	7.07	6.64
Northwast	6.42	6.95	6.49	6.73	6.1
Northwest		5.87	6.02	5.62	5.11
Northcentral Coast	6.96	7.15	6.87	6.72	5.82
Southcentral Coast	5.57	6.55	6.31	6.16	5.49
Central Highlands	4.24	5.4	5.16	5.55	4.92
Southeast	5.43	6.33	6.2	5.92	6.31
Mekong River Delta	4.73	6.4	6.15	6.08	5.52

Source: GSO, 2003.

Table A-4.1.5

Rate of Working Time Used by Employment in Rural Areas
(1996-2002)

Regions	1996	1999	2000	2001	2002
Whole Country	72.28	73.56	74.18	74.26	75.3
Red River Delta	75.88	73.88	75.66	75.36	75.38
Northeast	78.3	71.72	73.01	73.05	75.9
Northwest		72.62	73.44	72.78	71.08
Northcentral Coast	73.43	72.28	72.12	72.52	74.5
Southcentral Coast	70.93	74.02	73.92	74.6	74.85
Central Highlands	75.05	78.65	77.04	77.18	77.99
Southeast	61.83	76.2	76.58	76.42	75.43
Mekong River Delta	68.35	73.16	73.18	73.38	76.55

Source: GSO, 2003.

5

Potential Winners and Losers from Labour Regulation in the Formal Sector

The Case of Indonesia

CHRIS MANNING

5.1. Introduction

With the spread of globalisation, there has been considerable attention on labour standards in poor countries. Inadequate standards have been highlighted in the context of charges of 'unfair' trade advantages gained by some Third World countries, in part through the 'exploitation' of hapless workers by multinationals.[1] Whether in pursuit of a protectionist or humanitarian cause, threats of trade and consumer boycotts are frequently linked to the failure of companies or countries to meet minimum absolute standards, the benchmark for which is often set in more developed countries.[2]

In this chapter we approach the subject of labour standards in a quite poor developing country, Indonesia, from a different perspective. Labour standards are assessed primarily from the standpoint of domestic labour market circumstances rather than international norms. We examine several aspects of labour standards from a broad perspective of basic, civil, survival and security rights. Minimum wages, the rate and principles regulating severance pay, and clauses legislation in dealing with contract labour were the main policy issues in the Indonesian context in 2003-2004. We assess government approaches to improving these standards in the context of Indonesia's

---

1. For two alternative views on subject by well-known economists, see for example Rodrik (1996), in favour of greater international efforts to regulate standards, and Bhagwati (2004) strongly against such actions, especially if they are linked to trade access. For general treatments see Moran (2002) and Elliot and Freeman (2003).

2. By far the greatest attention in both professional literature and advocacy has been focused on the employment of child labour as both morally repugnant and a key element of the unfair advantage held by Third World countries, even though the issue is of minor significance in terms of employment or abuse of rights in many countries.

daunting 'employment challenge'—providing more productive and better paying jobs for over half the work force in low paid, informal and marginal jobs, as well as for new job seekers.

Under Soeharto, Indonesia was in the international spotlight for abuse of rights and standards. At the same time, it was a country where the take-off in export-oriented manufacturing had a significant impact on employment and wages in the modern sector (Manning, 1998). Since the fall of Soeharto, enormous changes have occurred in the regulatory environment, with regard to both rights and standards. Three major Acts were passed by Parliament in 2000-2004, and Indonesia has ratified all core ILO conventions. At the same time, labour market circumstances have worsened. Economic growth has slowed and export industries struggled in a less favourable domestic and international environment for business (Van and Basri, 2004).

It is useful to think of these reforms as occurring in two stages in the post Soeharto period—reforms that deal mostly with labour freedoms and rights, and those that cover material standards and welfare. We look at the interaction of each of these developments with employment and wages. It is argued that protection of labour freedoms is long overdue. However, while legislation setting labour standards rigidly in the modern sector benefits the few with better jobs, it has the potential to penalise many less fortunate Indonesians.

Section 5.2 of the chapter asks how we might usefully define labour standards for analytical purposes. It examines issues of implementation capacity and institutions, and the nature of relationship between economic structure and growth, on the one hand, and labour standards on the other. We then look briefly at the economic and labour market context in which labour reforms have been pursued in the post-Soeharto era. In Sections 5.4 and 5.5, the main part of the chapter, the discussion of recent reforms is divided into two parts—the affirmation of basic rights and freedoms, and legislation for the protection 'Survival' and 'Security' Rights in Indonesia since the fall of Soeharto.

5.2. Labour Standards and Employment: General Considerations

The delineation of the boundaries between labour standards and basic rights, as well as the relationship of both to employment, earnings and labour welfare is both complicated and difficult to test empirically. The discussion first draws attention to several of these issues. In addition, we set the stage for a discussion of the Indonesian case by looking briefly at the range of instruments and institutions that are important for setting standards, and how they might relate to economic structure and growth.

5.2.1 Defining Labour Standards and Rights

First, how might we usefully define labour standards and distinguish them from basic rights? Among the various classifications, we have adapted the typology developed by Singh (2003: 111).[3] Drawing on the work of several other authors, Singh suggests four broad groups all of which he terms as 'rights'—Basic Rights, Civic Rights, Survival Rights and Security Rights (Table 5.1). The first group consists of basic standards or fundamental rights. Most observers agree that all should be incorporated in labour laws, even if precise definition and implementation is problematic—freedom

Table 5.1

A Classification of Labour Standards as Rights

Type of Standard/Right	Description
Basic Rights	Right against involuntary servitude/forced labour.
	Right against physical coercion.
	Right against discrimination.
	Right against (exploitative use of) child labour.
Civic Rights	Right to free association.
	Right to collective representation.
	Right to free expression of grievances.
Survival Rights	Right to a living wage.
	Right to full information about work place hazards.
	Right to accident compensation.
	Right to limited hours of work.
Security Rights	Right against arbitrary dismissal.
	Right to severance and long service pay.
	Right to retirement compensation.
	Right to survivor's compensation.

Source: Adapted from Singh (2003: 111).

---

3. An alternative grouping is 'core' and 'cash' standards (Elliot and Freeman, 2003:11).

from forced labour and coercion, abolition of child labour and non-discrimination in hiring, firing and remuneration. The second, civic rights, related to rights of collective bargaining and action, and expression of grievances, are also regarded by many as fundamental to modern labour codes.

These two groups together constitute, with minor differences, what ILO refers to as core labour rights that should be enshrined in national laws and open to monitoring by national and international bodies (ILO, 2000). Importantly for our later discussion of Indonesia, affirmation of these two sets of rights has little direct relationship to labour costs.

The third and fourth group, Security and Survival Rights, "relate to conditions of work that affect workers' well being, but do not necessarily directly affect freedom of choice" (Singh, 2003: 110).[4] Survival Rights are most problematic in that they are not always covered in labour codes and may vary significantly according to levels of development. The fourth group, termed Security Rights, is typically covered in national legislation, dealing with rights against arbitrary dismissal, retirement and separation payments (severance pay) and survivors' compensation.[5] The most obvious example is the level of wages or compensation, which increases with economic progress (World Bank, 1995).[6]

5.2.2 Implementation and Institutions

A second issue relates to the mechanisms for setting standards either in place of or in addition to government legislation, and what institutions tend to facilitate or, alternatively, to hinder the setting of socially acceptable ˜tandards. Aside from regulation of basic standards, some countries such as the USA set many labour standards through collective bargaining at the establishment level, rather than through legislation. This results in much greater variation in labour

---

4. In some discussions the distinction is often made between process and outcomes, where process relates to basic freedoms or rights and outcomes to standards which correspond to a given level or pattern of development.

5. We have added severance pay to the list of standards compiled by Singh, as comprising Survival Rights.

6. Although to this author's knowledge there has not been systematic research on the subject, there also appears to be a clear (positive) relationship between the level and form of several other labour standards (hours of work, amounts of accident compensation and health and safety conditions, and a country's stage of economic development).

standards across firms and industries, in accordance with the economic and labour market conditions. In contrast, many European countries (especially in Scandinavia) have legislated many of the basic standards mentioned above, or allow them to be set through centralised collective bargaining processes.[7] The latter centralised bargaining and arbitration system has historically been a key feature of setting labour standards in Australia and New Zealand.

Legislation by national governments has been by far the dominant mode for regulation of labour standards in Third World countries, including East Asia (Nayyar, 1995; Lee, 1996). Other channels for regulation of labour standards have emerged in recent years, although their application is still limited to small groups of consumers and multinational corporations. These include certification of sub-contracting arrangements by large multinationals such as Nike and compliance labelling by first world consumer groups who seek to restrict the imports of goods produced in low wage and 'exploitative' settings (Golub, 1997; Moran, 2002). The ILO has played a more active role in disseminating information and advising on policy in recent times.[8] But international efforts to enforce labour standards have had limited success, and country proposals that have sought to utilise the World Trade Organization to impose better labour standards have fared little better.[9]

Political and legal institutions play an important role in supporting the implementation of standards. Countries with democratic traditions or newly established democratic systems of government have tended to give greater reign to trade unions. In the Asia-Pacific region, the Philippines, South Korea and Taiwan are outstanding examples, all of which have seen greater freedom go to the labour movement after democratic reforms in the 1980s. Legal institutions also play an important role in dispute settlement (even if excessive litigation in

---

7. See especially Engerman (2003) and Moene and Wallerstein (2003) on the origins of present labour standards legislation in the USA and Scandinavia, respectively. Historically, those standards regulated by government have tended to be the responsibility of the central authorities. The USA is again an exception, where the setting of basic labour standards has been under the jurisdiction of state governments. More recently, regional governments in some developing countries such as the Philippines have begun to assume responsibility for minimum wage regulation.

8. See Elliot and Freeman (2003: Chapter 5).

9. Moran (2002:103) notes that the ILO has only been successful in recommending a cut in international links with one country, Myanmar (over the issue of forced labour). Elliot and Freeman (2003:116-119) discuss the role of the ILO in helping implement the US-Cambodian Textile and Apparel Agreement, although they do not assess the potential effects of a new minimum wage regime on employment.

countries like the Philippines can hamper resolution of labour disputes).

At the same time, implementation of the national labour code is a problem in several Asian countries (Hutchison and Brown, 2001). Autocratic governments and security organisations that override the rule of law, either through direct intervention or indirect mechanisms, have been able to neutralise labour protests and trade union action. In addition, an underpaid bureaucracy is likely to support extensive regulation often to the detriment of both employers and workers— local officials accept bribes in return for turning a blind eye to labour law transgressions, thus raising the cost to business and penalising employment.

5.2.3. *The Importance of Economic Structure and Growth*

Before turning to the Indonesian case, we look briefly at some general dimensions of the interaction between economic structure and growth, and labour standards (bearing in mind that the country experienced rapid economic growth and structural change in three decades before the crisis, but a major turnabout in fortunes since). Three points are relevant. First, with regard to economic structure, less open trade and investment regimes (often associated with both more dualistic economic structure), have tended to be associated with greater protection of modern sector workers through labour legislation. It is no accident that the most protective labour codes have been in countries where the modern sector has been insulated from international competition, such as in much of Latin America, and also in India in Asia.[10] At the same time, the pressures to protect workers in modern sectors outside enclave industries are likely to be particularly intense in protected economies, and also resource rich yet labour abundant countries like Indonesia. In such economies, the gap in wages between the capital-intensive, enclave modern sectors, and the rest of the economy tends to be large. This leads to upward pressure on wages through regulation, or collective bargaining, in other less protected modern sectors, and especially in large export-oriented and labour-intensive, manufacturing plants (Berg, 1969; Manning, 1998). Under such circumstances, employment will be a major casualty.

---

10. See especially Cox-Edwards (1997).

Second, the rate of economic growth and employment expansion is also important for labour standards. Worker demands for protection are likely to be greater in relatively stagnant than in rapidly growing industries, regions and countries. Witness the calls for protection of standards in declining industries such as textiles, footwear and garments in developing countries, or the persistently high level of protection afforded to workers in the slow growing modern sector in India over many decades. Similarly, calls for labour protection from developed countries through international trade sanctions have been most strident in support of sunset industries in those economies such as garments, that are most threatened by imports from developing countries.

As Srinivasan (2003: 183) has rightly noted, "Many types of labour standards such as caste discrimination [in the case of India] in employment and wages tend to disappear in a tight labour market and with urbanisation, both of which are associated with rapidly growing economies." Similarly, he notes (p. 184) that issues of child labour have received most attention in countries like India and Pakistan where slow employment growth in the modern sector has denied parents access to better and more stable jobs, and low levels of education have offered children little alternative to work. We shall see that slow growth, in particular, would seem to feature strongly in the call for greater protection of workers in Indonesia in the post-Soeharto period, notwithstanding the greater pressure for worker rights associated with more democratic processes.

Third, with regard to trade reform, liberalisation has been opposed, especially by protected workers fearful of loosing their jobs. And complaints among both domestic and foreign NGOs and labour groups about labour exploitation have been strongest with regard to wages, working conditions and labour rights in the newly emerging export industries, where employment growth has tended to be most rapid. Some of these complaints are well justified where foreign direct investors have lobbied to undermine labour laws, especially in the case of rights to form trade unions and strike in export processing zones.[11] But the weight of evidence suggests that even in the labour-intensive garment and footwear industries, wages have tended to be at least as high (and to rise more quickly) in foreign firms and their

---

11. Moran (2002:59-60) documents specific cases of such lobbying in the Philippines and the Dominican Republic.

sub-contracting agents than in many other industries, and especially compared with smaller scale firms.[12]

To sum up, a wide range of labour standards are regulated in national labour legislation in most developing countries. This has been the main mechanism for setting standards in environments where labour unions are weak, and where excess demand exists for jobs in the modern sector. The impact of labour standards on employment depends in part on the economic structure and the rate and pattern of economic growth. The need for, and advocacy of, extensive protection for workers is likely to be less pressing in rapidly than in slow growing economies. But we have suggested that trade and economic growth are not always 'complementary' with labour standards.[13]

As noted in the Introduction, there have been two waves of labour legislation in Indonesia since the Soeharto era. First was affirmation of basic labour rights and freedoms culminating in a Trade Union Act (*Undang-Undang*) in 2000 and, second, efforts to improve labour standards culminating in the passing of the Manpower Protection Act of 2003.[14] We trace the main elements of reform in both labour rights and standards, and their relationship to employment and wages in Sections 5.4 and 5.5 of the chapter, drawing attention to parallels and contrasts with labour standards and rights and their implementation before the downfall of President Soeharto in 1998. First, however, it is necessary to look at the labour market context which changed dramatically during the economic crisis year of 1998, and has remained much less favourable than in the Soeharto period.

5.3. The Economic and Labour Market Context

Three features of the Indonesian labour market are important in helping interpret the implications of recent changes in labour

---

12. See especially Rama, (2001: 14-18) on the effects of globalisation on employment, wages and equity. Moran (2002) has marshalled impressive evidence on wages and working conditions among FDI firms and their sub-contractors, drawing attention to the substantially improved working conditions and skill levels in EPZs that have begun to shift into higher-tech industries.

13. This is notwithstanding Elliot and Freeman's (2003:139) more optimistic description of the relationship at the end of their informative book: "Globalisation and labour standards are not mortal enemies but complementary ways—Siamese twins, in our analogy—to make modern economic growth work better for all."

14. The Basic Laws were No. 21, 200 and No. 13, 2003 respectively. A further Act governing dispute resolution was passed by the Parliament in early 2004.

legislation and their implementation in Indonesia. With a GDP per capita of around $ 600-700 in 2002-2003, it is still a low income country (World Bank classification). The economy and the structure of employment display the features of an underdeveloped country. GDP per capita is well below that of middle income countries such as Thailand and Malaysia in Southeast Asia. Low productivity agriculture and services still played a major role in the economy, and are of even greater importance for employment (Table 5.2). A small proportion of both agricultural and non-agricultural workers are employed as wage employees, and hence potentially affected by labour regulations,

Table 5.2

The Structure of Indonesian GDP and Employment and Output per Workers, 1986-2002

	1986	1996	1998	2000	2002
Share of GDP					
Agriculture	24.6	16.5	18.0	17.7	16.9
Industry	35.5	43.0	42.7	43.6	43.6
Manufacturing	17.9	25.0	25.6	26.7	27.0
Services	40.0	40.6	39.3	38.7	39.4
	100.0	100.0	100.0	100.0	100.0
Share of Employment					
Agriculture	55.1	44.0	45.1	44.3	44.3
Manufacturing	8.2	12.6	13.0	13.2	13.2
Services	36.7	43.4	41.9	42.4	42.4
	100.0	100.0	100.0	100.0	100.0
Wage Employees	45.8	50.0	48.9	49.2	47.9
Non-wage Employees	54.2	50.0	51.1	50.8	52.1
Output Per Worker (Rp. Million)*					
Agriculture	1.5	2.1	2.0	2.1	2.1
Manufacturing	7.5	11.3	11.5	10.8	11.2
Other**	5.4	7.7	6.6	7.0	7.3
Total**	3.4	5.7	5.1	5.2	5.5

Source: *National Accounts* and *National Labour Force Surveys* (various years).

Note: * At constant 1995 prices. Includes services and other industry.

   ** Includes all services, mining, utilities and construction.

---

15. Although labour laws apply to all wage workers, in practice workers of most small and cottage establishments (some 60 per cent of the total in the case of manufacturing and a higher share in other sectors) are outside the ambit of regulations. See SMERU (2001) for a discussion of the coverage, in practice, of minimum wage legislation.

although many are not covered in practice.[15] While not a particularly useful indicator of short or longer term labour market imbalance, unemployment rates (around 10 per cent) were quite high by Third World and regional standards.[16]

Second, as in other countries, wages and labour productivity are very much higher in the formal sector—in manufacturing, for example, average wages were several times higher in large and medium than in small enterprises, even before minimum standards legislation began to be implemented more intensively in recent years. Differences in value added per worker were of a similar magnitude (Table 5.3).[17] Moreover, of relevance to our later

Table 5.3

Employment, Wages and Value Added in Large and Medium and Small Firms in Indonesian Manufacturing, 1995-2002

	No. of Firms	Employ-ment '000	Wage Costs Rp.b.	Value Added Rp.b.	Average Wage Rp.m/wkr.	Value Added Per Worker Rp.m	Ratio of Wages to Value Added	Ratio of Small of L and M Firm Wages Per Worker
				Large and Medium				
1995	21551	4174	13627	73909	3.26	17.71	0.18	0.29
1996	22997	4215	15752	93332	3.74	22.14	0.17	0.24
1997	22386	4170	18642	100900	4.47	24.20	0.18	0.19
1998	21423	4124	28642	154651	6.95	37.50	0.19	0.23
1999	22070	4234	30438	191393	7.19	45.20	0.16	0.25
2000	22851	4371	36085	222112	8.26	50.81	0.16	0.19
				Small				
1995	190767	1598	1498	3888	0.94	2.43	0.39	
1996	228978	1915	1715	4612	0.90	2.41	0.37	
1997	241169	2077	1774	4802	0.85	2.31	0.37	
1998	194564	1507	2420	6923	1.61	4.59	0.35	
1999	225564	1779	3240	8182	1.82	4.60	0.40	
2000	256823	2005	3127	8380	1.56	4.18	0.37	

Source: BPS-Indonesian Statistics, *Indonesian Statistical Yearbook*, various years (data from the Annual Survey of Large and Medium Manufacturing, and periodic surveys of small scale industry).

---

16. Relatively high rates may be partly explained by a broader definition of unemployment in Indonesia. According to the official definition, a significant share of all unemployed workers (around 40 per cent in 2002) consisted of 'discouraged' workers, who were not involved in job search activities.

17. The table shows data for large and medium and small firms only which accounted for around 60 per cent of total manufacturing employment.

discussion of minimum wages policy, wages per worker rose faster in the modern sector, despite slow employment growth, after the economic crisis in 1998.

This large absolute difference in earnings is of direct significance to discussion of the impact of labour market regulation on the welfare of workers. More rapid expansion of the formal sector offers major opportunities for better jobs among informal sector workers, especially if the greater stability of jobs among the former is taken into account. From this standpoint, legislation that discourages inter-sectoral movements of labour penalises job seekers from small-scale and informal sectors.

Third, job creation in the modern sector emerged as a major problem in the post economic crisis era. GDP growth slowed significantly, and most observers highlight the slowdown in investment, both domestic and international, as Indonesia's key development problem (Hill, 2004). As a consequence, whereas the share of output and employment in non-agricultural sectors, and wage employment rose quite rapidly before the economic 'crisis' of 1998, both slowed once Indonesia had regained economic stability after 1999 (Table 5.2). Even though unemployment did not rise much, wage employment outside agriculture declined by around 10 per cent from 1996 through to 2003, after growing by some 50 per cent and creating just under 60 per cent of all new jobs created in the previous decade.[18]

A similar pattern was apparent in labour manufacturing. Before the crisis, wages and employment in the labour-intensive and export-oriented textile, clothing and footwear (TCF) industries (in which foreign investment played an important role), increased quite substantially and rose more quickly than in all industries (Table 5.4). In short, although average wages were lower in labour-intensive activities compared with more capital-intensive activities, widespread repression of labour rights was not synonymous with wage repression. However, after the crisis, employment in the TCF industries barely increased, and real wages fell and remained below pre-crisis levels in 2001. Thus, the introduction of new labour legislation and institutions should be viewed in the context of a

---

18. Estimates based on data from the National Labour Force surveys, 1986-2003.

labour market under stress, and particularly a modern sector which has performed well below its potential in terms of creating new and better jobs for Indonesia's large and growing population.[19]

Table 5.4

Growth of Employment, Value Added and Wages in TCF, and All Industries 1986-2001 (Per Cent Per Annum)

	Textiles, Clothing and Footwear	All Industries
Employment		
1986-1991	16.9	11.4
1991-1996	8.0	6.8
1996-2001	1.0	0.7
Value Added		
1986-1991	24.1	29.8
1991-1996	25.3	16.2
1996-2001	22.1	21.7
Real Wages		
Growth		
1986-1991	5.3	4.6
1991-1996	5.3	3.5
1996-2001	-2.1	-1.3
Index (1996=100)		
1986	59	67
1996	100	100
1998	70	70
2001	90	94

Source: CBS, *Statistical Yearbook*, 2001 (data from Survey of Large and Medium Manufacturing, various years). Real wages are calculated by deflating average nominal wages by the national CPI Index.

5.4. Labour Reforms Stage I: Affirmation of Basic Labour Rights

The fall of President Soeharto in 1998 ushered in a new period for labour rights and standards in Indonesia. Under Soeharto's New

---

19. One favourable development, however, has been a slowdown in growth of the working age population, owing to the age structure effects of past declines in fertility, which had begun to significantly affect the number of new entrants into the labour force by the year 2000.

Order, labour freedoms were tightly controlled, the above-mentioned increases in wages and employment notwithstanding (Hadiz, 1997; Manning, 1998).[20] The rights of organised labour were kept under control through one official trade union (SPSI) that was closely aligned to the ruling party. Collective bargaining was encouraged in legislation, and strikes permitted by law (outside essential industries), and the latter increased in periods of greater political openness and economic stress. However the rights to air grievances and participate in dispute resolution were limited. In practice, labour complaints were dealt with harshly by local police and military, which were commonly on the payroll of the larger companies (Hadiz, 1997). Labour disputes that were taken to local and central government Disputes Councils either dragged on for long periods, or were frequently settled in favour of employers through bribes to council members. It was an open secret that labour inspectors and local officials were also on the payroll of private companies.

With the downfall of President Soeharto in 1998, and the emergence of a more open democratic system, the government could no longer continue to publicly suppress labour rights. As Indonesia experienced its worst economic crisis in three decades, political change permitted a freer trade union movement and several important labour reforms.

First, the government ratified several key ILO Conventions, including rights to compete without discrimination and freedom of association. Four conventions were signed in 1998-2000, dealing with Basic Rights (minimum age of employment, worst forms of child labour, abolition of forced labour and freedom from discrimination).[21] Ratification of the key ILO convention on the Freedom of Association (Convention No. 87), which provides for the right of workers to establish unions of their choosing, effectively ended the long period from 1973, some 25 years, in which workers could only join one, government sanctioned, trade union.

---

20. Although, formal controls were relaxed somewhat in the last years of the regime, when the government passed legislation permitting the formation of independent unions at enterprise level.

21. The four conventions and their date of ratification by Indonesia were No. 138 (1999), No. 182 (2000), No. 105 (1999) and No. 111 (1999) respectively. Previously the government had ratified two conventions—No. 28 on forced labour (ratified in 1950) and No. 98 (1958) on the right to organise and bargain collectively.

Second, more importantly, the right to organise was enshrined in law through the Trade Union Act in 2000, setting the minimum size of trade unions (10 members), conditions governing multiple unionism in single establishments, and rules for the formation of union federations and confederations. The Trade Union Act has contributed to a proliferation of unions across the country. From just one trade union, a total of 61 federations were reported to be in place across the country and (according to official estimates) as many as 10 million or more members from a total number of non-casual wage workers of some 26 million in April 2001, 24 million outside agriculture, including 8 million in manufacturing (SMERU, 2002). A study by a social research institute, SMERU, of industrial relations in major industrial areas in 2002 found that over half of all enterprise unions had been set up after 1997. The study also found that the process of signing collective agreements had accelerated at enterprise level.

For employers, this was a major change in the industrial relations framework. Many were shocked by the 'big bang' nature of the reforms, doubting that firms would be able to deal with multiple unionism. But in reality the opening up of the industrial relations system appears to have had little negative effect on employment and did not result in a significant increase in employer complaints. Jobs and wages in large and medium scale firms which fell during the crisis, subsequently grew, albeit slowly, in the new industrial relations environment in the period 1998-2001.

However implementation of new legislation related to both Survival and Security Rights was another matter. We argue that it was these reforms, much more than the reforms to basic rights, that have threatened to slow the expansion of employment in the modern sector. We now turn to these reforms, giving special attention to minimum wages, new rates of severance and the employment of contract workers.

5.5. Labour Reform Stage II:
Extending Survival and Security Rights[22]

Before the crisis in 1998, governments had legislated for quite comprehensive set of labour standards covering both Survival and

---

22. Some of the material presented in this section overlaps with material discussed in Manning (2004: 238-245).

Security Rights, most of which had been introduced through Basic Laws (Acts) in the 1950s and 1960s before Soeharto came to power.[23] However, there were problems in ensuring that these were guaranteed even in the small modern sector, owing to shortcomings in the political, bureaucratic and institutional framework for implementation and supervision. In part, this can be attributed to the above-mentioned tight formal and informal controls over the trade union movement which limited the capacity and right of appeal by workers in cases of disputes over standards. By East Asian standards, the Labour Acts (some based on legislation in force in Holland after World War II), were quite favourable to labour, providing for a 40 hour week (compared with 48 hours in many other countries in the region until quite recently), generous overtime provisions, 12 days annual leave and two days menstruation leave.[24] All dismissals and retrenchments had to be approved by Labour Disputes Councils.

Following the passing of the Trade Union Bill in the year 2000, labour protection shifted to top priority on the labour reform agenda in the populist Wahid government (1999-2001), and the subsequent government under Megawati Sukarnoputri (2001-2004). Ex-union leaders appointed as Ministers of Manpower championed reforms on the grounds that Indonesian workers had suffered in terms of both Survival and Security Rights in the past. In particular, raising minimum wages and providing better protection for laid-off workers was viewed as essential, given that workers were seen to have suffered on both counts under Soeharto and during the Asian economic crisis.

Although preceded by stand-alone regulations, the passing of the Manpower Protection Act in early 2003 embodied the new, more interventionist approach to labour standards. It covers almost every conceivable aspect of labour protection—manpower planning, employment of child, female and foreign workers, wages and condition of work, contract employment, dismissals, collective bargaining and settlement of grievances—in large and small enterprises in some 18 chapters and nearly 200 articles. The Act provided greater certainty

---

23. Most of the early labour protection legislation was passed shortly after independence in the 1950s and 1960s, although limitation of several key rights (including the right to strike) were imposed even in this period as the 'left' leaning labour unions began to pose a political and economic challenge to the government during a period of economic decline.

24. The main laws were Act No. 14, 1969, Law No. 12, 1964. See Manning (1998: Chapter 8) for details on labour law and rights under Soeharto, and Nayyar (1995) for some comparative data for East Asia.

for both business and labour.[25] But at the same time, the basic law had the potential to undermine efforts at collective bargaining and the role of the newly empowered union movement, which was now in a much stronger position to bargain with employers than had been the case for several decades. It also had the potential to break any nexus between productivity and labour standards, which might be established in the work place, through collective bargaining in different firms, industries and regions.

We now look at several examples of articles in relation to both Survival and Security Rights in the Manpower Protection Act, and their potential impact on wages and employment.

5.5.1. Survival Rights: Minimum Wages

Minimum wages (MW) are regulated in the Act that provides for annual revisions to wages through provincial government decrees, based on the recommendation of district governments.[26] The criteria for setting MW are to be based on a 'decent' or 'suitable' standard of living (*kehidupan layak*), defined in detail by subsequent regulations issued by the Ministry of Manpower.[27]

Minimum wages regulation had already been a key element in labour policy under Soeharto. An index of minimum living needs (KHM—*Kehidupan Hidup Minimum*) had become the main basis for assessing minimum wages relative to the needs of workers, at the provincial level, before the crisis in 1996.[28] However, even under Soeharto, the MW was never viewed as a social safety net for lower paid workers, as is commonly the case in many other countries. Rather it was regarded as a standard for unskilled wages throughout

---

25. Although there remains considerable uncertainty, given that many issues were not sufficiently resolved in the legislation and depend on implementing legislation and machinery, which will take several years to put in place.

26. The MW is to be set at either District or Provincial level for all industries and also according to specific sectors (see Articles 87-98 of the Manpower Protection Act of 2003). 'Bipartite' negotiations between employers and worker representatives or trade unions are required to make recommendations to the district governments.

27. The Act also stipulates that firms must set wage and salary scales according to level (*golongan*), job, years of service, education and competency, to be regulated further by the ministerial decree (Article 92).

28. Five other overlapping criteria including the interests of business, were recommended by the Ministry of Manpower as relevant to recommending minimum wage increases at the provincial level. However, clear guidelines were never established as to how information on these other criteria might be collected and applied.

the modern sector. The absolute value of the KHM was high by most criteria of disadvantage in Indonesia (for example, it was more than twice the level of per capita poverty line in 2001), and included several items that were not regularly consumed by low income families.[29] While minimum wages had remained well below average wages much of the New Order period, SMERU (2001) found that they were much closer to the prevailing wages of majority of workers by 2000 and were 'bunched' around the minimum wage. Compliance with the minimum wage had steadily increased over time and the MW was 'binding' for most workers in the formal and urban sector. In comparison to wages outside the modern sector, the MW could not be described as a 'survival' wage (Bambang, 2003).

Related to the high level of the KHM, and through the efforts of an ostensibly pro-labour Ministry strongly in support of raising standards, the MW was increased steeply after the crisis.[30] Even though employment conditions were difficult, the Central Government encouraged rapid minimum wage growth from 1999, resulting in a complete recovery in real rupiah terms by 2001 and significant growth in the major industrial areas in 2002, compared with the pre-crisis period (Figure 5.1). In dollar terms, the minimum wage had recovered to pre-crisis levels, the large rupiah depreciation notwithstanding (Manning, 2004).[31]

What was the impact of rising minimum wages on employment? Several researchers found a strong negative relationship between minimum wages and employment in the modern sector, especially affecting unskilled, less educated and female workers (SMERU, 2001). The relationship was much stronger in the post-crisis period (Bird and Manning, 2002).[32] As we have seen, the impact was partly

---

29. The KHM was calculated according to regular estimates of the prices of a basket of 43 items. According to the Manpower Act, the basket of goods was to be expanded to provide a decent standard of living, which according to Ministry of Manpower calculations would raise the standard of basic needs by around 20 per cent above prevailing absolute value of the KHM.

30. It was used to restore wage levels after a substantial decline in real terms owing to high inflation (a close to 100 per cent increase in the CPI) during the economic crisis in 1998.

31. The new MW probably helped the recovery in the index of textile, clothing and footwear wages by 2001, after they plummeted in 1998 (Table 5.4).

32. Several other studies have found little relationship between minimum wages and employment in the pre-crisis period when output and investment were growing rapidly, and minimum wages were not binding on the wages for most workers. See Islam and Nazara (2000), and Alatas and Cameron (2001).

Figure 5.1

*Real Minimum Wages in Major Industrial Centres
and All Indonesia, 1992-2002 (Rp., '000 Per Month, 1996 Prices)*

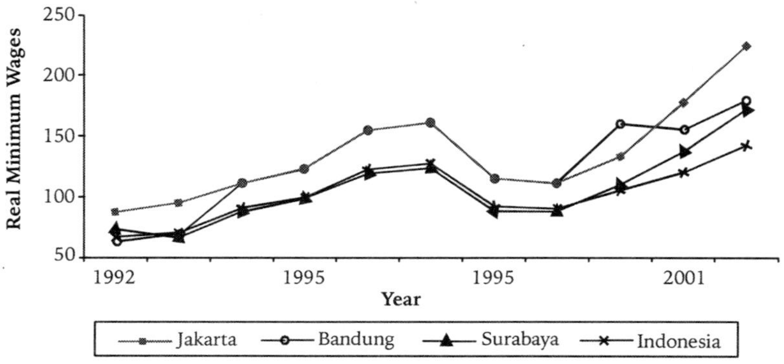

Source: Indonesia, Ministry of Manpower, unpublished data, various years

hidden. Labour was absorbed into the informal sector rather than resulting in higher unemployment rates in a country where there were no unemployment benefits. Unemployment rates were not significantly affected, although they did rise in 2002.[33]

Two other potential effects are also worth noting. First, wage differentials by skill and years of experience were likely to be compressed, as firms reacted to steeply rising minimum wages and labour costs by narrowing the margins for skill and experience. Individuals were now likely to have less incentive to invest in human capital. Second, a range of other labour costs tied to minimum wages were also likely to rise. This was the case with severance pay to which we now turn.

5.5.2. Security Rights I: Severance Pay

As we have seen, the economic crisis created a major challenge for modern sector employment in Indonesia. Manufacturing employment alone declined by over 10 per cent and over a million wage jobs were also lost in other sectors outside agriculture in 1998. Although there was some subsequent recovery in employment, large

---

33. National unemployment rates rose only very slightly during the crisis and remained stable at around 5 per cent in 2001 (or around 8 per cent according to the new definition employed in the national labour force surveys). By 2003, they had risen to 10 per cent, according to the new definition.

numbers of both educated and less educated people lost their jobs in the modern sector, in an environment where there are no publicly funded unemployment benefits and few people had private unemployment insurance. There was strong pressure on firms to give generous payouts to their workers and more severance than required by legislation, even though rates had already been increased substantially by government regulation several years earlier.

Minimum rates of severance pay and long service pay have subsequently been regulated in detail in the Manpower Protection Act of 2003. As in other countries, a distinction is made in the rights to severance depending on the cause of separation, and in rates of severance and long service payments: different coverage is mandated for quits and dismissals, and in the latter category for dismissals for economic reasons (including downsizing and bankruptcy), minor violations of company regulations or, lastly, major violations or offences (Table 5.5). Unlike in many other countries where rates of severance are lower for dismissals due to economic cause, the maximum rates apply according to the new Act in Indonesia.

Reflecting rates already raised several years earlier, in a controversial earlier Ministerial Decision, the new Manpower Act increased the rate of severance and long service pay by 30-40 per cent.[34] Business had cause for concern. It had initially protested strongly regarding increases in severance and long service pay in the year 2000.[35] Comparative data reveal, moreover, that severance pay was now several times higher in Indonesia compared with most neighbouring countries. The number of months of pay which firms had to give in severance for employees who were dismissed for economic cause was three to five times more than in China, India, Korea and Malaysia in 2003-04.[36] The difference was smaller with Philippines and Thailand (1.5-2.5 times higher in Indonesia). But absolute costs were probably as high or higher for firms in Indonesia than in both these countries, despite much higher wage rates in both the Philippines and Thailand.

---

34. Although there were some important changes, mainly in response to lobbying from business, the rates of severance remain the same in the Manpower Act as in the Ministerial Decision of 2000 (Decision No. 150), and most articles in Ministerial Decision were incorporated in the Act.

35. Larger changes introduced in 1996 (Ministerial Decree No. 3, 1996) caused less of a stir when the economy was still booming, dismissals for economic cause were rarer, and compliance was low.

36. See Hill (2004), citing data compiled by Dr. Kelly Bird (USAID) in Jakarta.

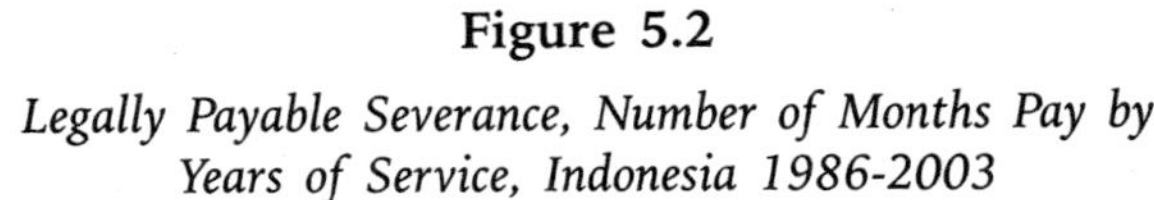

Figure 5.2

*Legally Payable Severance, Number of Months Pay by
Years of Service, Indonesia 1986-2003*

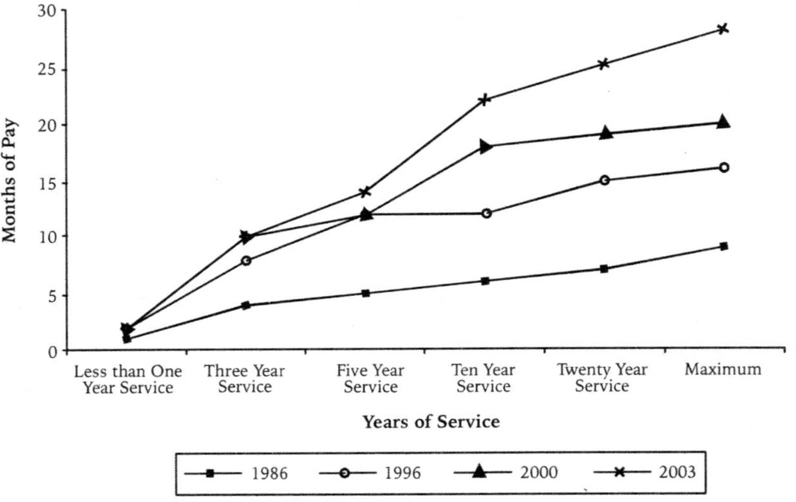

Source: Indonesia, Ministry of Manpower, *Ministerial Regulation* No. 4 1986, *Ministerial Decrees* No. 3, 1996 and 150, 2000, and the *Manpower Protection Act*, (Act No. 13 2003).

Aside from increasing the overall rate of severance by some 200 per cent over the past 20 years (Figure 5.2), and more than 50 per cent for workers with longer years of service since 2000, these changes have had a two-fold effect on the incentive structure with regard to severance.

- First, it has raised the cost of dismissing workers with longer years of service (10 years or more) relative to workers with fewer years of service. The steeper lines for total severance (including payments for years of service, also regulated in the Act) according to the regulations in 2003 and 2000 compared with earlier years (1986 and 1996) shown in Figure 5.2 indicate this advantage accruing to more experienced workers.

- Second, it has raised the total relative cost of dismissing workers for economic cause, precisely at a time when many firms were under pressure to lay-off workers. Figure 5.2 demonstrates that severance pay for workers dismissed for

Table 5.5

Months of Severance and Long Service Pay, according to the Cause of Separation, Indonesia, 2003

	Basic Rates	Cause of Separation							
					Change of Firm Status		Dismissal		Voluntary Quit
		Economic Cause	Bankruptcy	Retirement/ Death/ Illness*	Dismissed	Quits	Minor Offence	Major Offence	
		Months of Pay							
Severance Pay									
Less than One Year Service	1 mth.	2	2	2	2	1	1	0	0
Three Years Service	4 mth.	8	8	8	8	4	4	0	0
Five Years Service	6 mth.	12	12	12	12	6	6	0	0
Ten Years Service	9 mth.	18	18	18	18	9	9	0	0
Twenty Years Service	9 mth.	18	18	18	18	9	9	0	0
Maximum	9 mth.	18	18	18	18	9	9	0	0
Long Service Leave									
Less than One Year Service	0	0	0	0	0	0	0	0	0
Three Years Service	2 mth.	2	2	2	2	2	2	0	0
Five Years Service	2 mth.	2	2	2	2	2	2	0	0
Ten Years Service	4 mth.	4	4	4	4	4	4	0	0
Twenty Years Service	7 mth.	7	7	7	7	7	7	0	0
Maximum	10 mth	10	10	10	10	10	10	0	0
Total Severance									
Less than One Year Service		2	2	2	2	1	1	0	0
Three Years Service		10	10	10	10	6	6	0	0
Five Years Service		14	14	14	14	8	8	0	0
Ten Years Service		22	22	22	22	13	13	0	0
Twenty Years Service		25	25	25	25	16	16	0	0
Maximum		28	28	28	28	19	19	0	0

Source: The Manpower Protection Act No. 13, 2003, Clauses 156-167.

Note: * In lieu of a company financed pension scheme. Prolonged illness for 12 months or more.

economic cause had more than doubled for most years of service from 1986 to 2003, and nearly tripled for workers who had been employed with the same firm for 10 years or more.

Even though increases in severance and long service pay were much larger several years earlier, they were likely to have quite a significant effect on labour costs and hence employment in the post-crisis period. Greater pressure for higher levels of compliance and slow growth in demand were particular problems. This was especially true in larger labour-intensive establishments in competitive industries, such as garments and footwear, where profit margins are slender and job-hopping is common. Further, the large recent minimum wage increases discussed above were one additional factor contributing to higher costs of severance.[37] Thus for example, the costs of dismissal for economic cause of a worker, earning the minimum wage and with 10 years experience, in Jakarta was approximately Rp. 3.4 million in 2000 (around US$ 400) prior to issue of the Ministerial Decree in 2000. The cost rose to just over Rp. 5 million after the decree was issued in the same year. But it had ballooned to Rp. 13 million ($ 1450) by the time that the Manpower Protection Act was passed in 2003 for the same category of worker, with the increase being wholly due to the rise in minimum wages.

In short, the reforms act as a tax on employment and discourage firms from dismissing older workers. Further, they are likely to encourage industrial disputes. Neither employers nor employees are required to 'invest' in severance pay up front, and hence firms are often not in a position to pay severance at times of unexpected difficulty. Higher rates of severance pay are likely to compound the effects of higher minimum wages by encouraging firms to employ fewer permanent workers. It would be hardly surprising if many prefer outsourcing jobs or other forms of temporary contract. However, this too has been another area where the Manpower Protection Act would seem to be heavily penalising new job seekers.

5.5.3. Security Rights II: The Employment of Contract Workers

One strategy for conserving labour costs in light of higher severance pay rates (especially for workers with longer periods of service) is the substitution of regular employees on permanent contracts for workers on fixed term contracts. Another possibility is greater outsourcing of

---

37. Severance is calculated as a multiple of monthly salary at the time of dismissal, depending on years of service.

activities, especially where production tends to fluctuate owing to seasonal work or unpredictable variations in demand, such as variations in orders from domestic and overseas buyers.

However, the Indonesian government has also sought to regulate contract work and outsourcing, at the same time as it has increased the rates of severance pay. With regard to fixed term contracts, the Manpower Protection Act permits contract work for one-off production activities, production runs which extend for no longer than three years, seasonal work and work associated with the introduction of new products which are still of a temporary or experimental nature (see Clause 59).[38] Such activities are only permissible for up to three years (two years initially, plus one year extension) initially, and for a further two years under a new contract. The Act limits labour outsourcing to 'non-core' activities (that are outside the production process), which support the company 'as a whole' and do not inhibit production processes. Typical examples are service activities such as cleaning, catering or security (Article 64).

The provisions in the Manpower Protection Act are not overly restrictive compared with regulations in many other developing and developed countries. Limitations on fixed-term contract work are consistent with modern labour codes, although they are likely to exacerbate problems for modern sector firms under difficult labour market conditions, such as those experienced by Indonesia in the post-crisis period.

The attempted regulation of outsourcing is probably more serious for employment. In practice, the limitations on outsourcing seek to remove putting-out activities to households or companies, which may be called on by a company to produce extra output at times of peak demand, such as regularly occurs in industries like garments. Sub-contracting to households typically occurs for low-quality products produced for local markets or for export, especially if there are marked seasonal changes or shocks in demand and supply conditions. Outsourcing of parts of the production chain which are part of core activities is now an established aspect of production in global markets, especially in industries like electronics.

Further, it is questionable whether introduction of bans on outsourcing improves the welfare of poorer households. In particular,

---

38. See also Ministry of Manpower, Ministerial Decision No. 100, 2004.

such regulations discriminate against those who are less able to perform jobs on a fixed working schedule or in shift-work, especially older workers and married females. Community policing and solutions rather than straight out bans may be a more equitable outcome.[39]

More generally, the limitations on contract work and the outsourcing of core activities, usually to smaller firms on a seasonal basis, can also affect employment adversely precisely in industries like textiles, where flexibility in output and employment is critical for international competitiveness. The capacity of many large companies to meet the demands of foreign and sometimes domestic buyers at times of peak demand depends crucially on such arrangements in labour-intensive industries like textiles, clothing and footwear.[40] It can be argued that strict limitations on such activities (if they could be enforced) would be a setback for Indonesia, bearing in mind that breaking up, the production process within (and across) countries through intra-industry trade has been a major factor in export growth and employment in East Asia from the latter part of the 20th century (Athukorala, 2004).

5.6. Conclusions

In the short space of some six years since the economic crisis in Indonesia in 1998, there has been a major rewriting of Indonesia's labour code in the fields of industrial relations and labour protection, after little serious reform for almost 30 years. Labour policy has been transformed, both with respect to Basic and Civic (Core) labour rights, as well as Survival and Security Rights. The former were tightly controlled during the New Order period under Soeharto. The latter were regulated quite extensively, but sanctions for non-compliance were low and breaches of the laws were commonplace.

At the same time as labour policy has stressed rights and standards, government statements (and those of all political parties and presidential candidates in 2004) repeatedly emphasised employment creation as one of Indonesia's most important

---

39. Of course, some of the most important solutions often lie well beyond the scope of labour standards, such as incentives and support for the education of poor children unable to attend school.

40. Much hinges on the definition of 'core' activities which is likely to be subjective, especially in components industries like electronics.

challenges.[41] However, few government leaders and political spokespersons have acknowledged the potential for conflict between achieving employment goals—creating better jobs—and tightly regulating Survival and Security Rights in the *reformasi* era in Indonesia. Nor has there been serious discussion of an alternative strategy of setting minimum standards, and allowing firms and workers to bargain over most standards, according to industry and firm circumstances.[42]

In short, in contrast to the pluralism in post-New Order government policy with regard to many other dimensions of public life, Survival and Security Rights have been regulated by government decree in extraordinary detail, ostensibly in favour of workers whose formal protection was seen as neglected during the Soeharto era. We have argued that the regulations are only likely to protect the interests of employed workers in the 'protected' modern sector, in practice, to the exclusion of rights of those in the informal sector and agriculture. The latter are only marginally, if at all, protected by some clauses in the legislation. To the extent that the legislation penalises employment growth, as some research and *a priori* reasoning suggests, it penalises many of these poorer workers, and also younger, new job seekers who seek 'better' modern sector jobs.

Thus, a consistent policy framework is vital to reconcile incentives for job creation by private enterprise with the need to provide basic social protection for workers. In particular, there has been little public discussion on the implications for employment of a raft of clauses which regulate rights in the Manpower Protection Act No. 13, 2003, the most important national policy document for labour standards.

This chapter has examined some of these relationships with special reference to Survival Rights embodied in minimum wage policy, and Security Rights regulated in the clauses in the Act on dismissals and severance pay, contract workers and outsourcing. We have discussed the effects of regulation in both areas in the context of much more difficult labour market conditions in Indonesia since

---

41. For example, the new President cited unemployment as foremost amongst the social challenges faced by the country and employment creation as a major goal of the new government, in his Inauguration Speech of October 20, 2004 ("Our economic growth this year, which is still below 7 per cent, is definitely inadequate in stimulating employment", *Jakarta Post*, October 21, 2004).

42. One important exception is the National Planning Bureau (Bappenas), *White Paper on Employment* published, in 2003.

1998, compared with the Soeharto period. The chapter also notes the importance of the compliance regime in assessing the impact of regulations on Survival and Security Rights. Before the economic crisis, 'compliance costs' were low because employers could 'arrange' settlements in their favour, faced with a weak and tightly controlled labour movement. Employment was determined largely by labour demand associated with the rate of economic growth, and the volume and quality of labour supply. With a significant improvement in Basic and Civil Rights, the compliance regime in relation to labour standards has altered dramatically, with the recognition of freedom of association, together with liberal policies on the formation of trade unions. The comprehensive revision of the labour protection regime and its implications for job creation, need to be viewed in this context.

In short, assuming a downward sloping demand curve for labour and (relatively) competitive product markets in tradable goods industries we have argued that several dimensions of government policy will contribute to slower modern sector employment growth, and less labour market flexibility. The latter is of concern especially in those internationally labour-intensive industries such as TCF, where Indonesia has had a comparative advantage in the past, and in light of the more competitive international environment, in the post-crisis and recovery period in Indonesia.

References

Alatas, V. and L. Cameron (2001). "The Impact of Minimum Wages on Employment in a Low Income Country: An Evaluation Using the Difference-In-Difference Approach", unpublished paper, University of Melbourne, Australia.

Bambang, Widianto (2003). "Kebijakan Upah Minimum dan Perluasan Kesempatan Kerja", *Tinjauan Kebijakan Ekonomi No. 1*, Bappenas, Jakarta.

Berg, E. (1969). "Wages Policy and Employment in Less Developed Countries", in A. Smith (ed.), *Wage Policy Issues in Economic Development*, pp. 294-337, Macmillan, London.

Bhagwati, J. (2004). *In Defence of Globalisation*, Oxford University Press, New York.

Bird, K. and C. Manning (2002). "The Impact of Minimum Wages on Employment and Earnings in the Informal Sector", paper presented at the Eighth *East Asian Economic Association Conference*, November 4-5, Kuala Lumpur.

Cox-Edwards, A. (1997). "Labour Market Regulations in Latin America: An Overview", in S. Edwards and N. Lustig (eds.), *Labour Markets in Latin America: Combining Social Protection with Labour Market Flexibility*, pp. 127-150, Brookings Institute Press, Washington, DC.

Elliot, A.B. and R.B. Freeman (2003). *Can Labour Standards Improve under Globalization*, Institute for International Economics, Washington, DC.

Engerman, S. (2003). "The Evolution of Labour Standards", in K. Basu, H. Horn, L. Roman and J. Shapiro (eds.), *International Labour Standards*, Blackwell, Oxford, pp. 9-83.

Hadiz, V. (1997). *Workers and the State in New Order Indonesia*, Routledge, London.

Hill, H. (2004). "Survey of Recent Economic Developments", *Bulletin of Indonesian Economic Studies*, 40(3).

ILO (International Labour Organization) (2000). *Your Voice at Work*, First Global Report Under the Follow-up to the Declaration of Fundamental Principles at Work, ILO, Geneva.

Islam, I. and Nazara S. (2000). "Minimum Wages and the Welfare of Indonesian Workers", *Occasional Discussion Paper Series No. 3*, ILO, Jakarta.

Lee, J.E. (ed.) (1996). *Labour Standards and Economic Development*, Chung-Hua Institute for Economic Research, pp. 249-73, Taipei.

Manning, C. (1998). "Indonesian Labour in Transition: An East Asian Success Story?", *Trade and Development Series*, Cambridge University Press, Cambridge.

————. (2004). "Labour Regulation and The Business Environment: Time To Take Stock", in P.van der Eng and M.C. Basri (eds.), *Business in Indonesia: New Challenges, Old Problems*, Institute of Southeast Asian Studies, Singapore.

Moene, K-O and M. Wallerstein (2003). "Legislation versus Bargaining Power: The Evolution of Labour Standards", in K. Basu, H. Horn, L. Roman and J. Shapiro (eds.), *International Labour Standards*, pp. 99-104, Blackwell, Oxford.

Nayyar, R. (1995). *Indonesian Labour Legislation in Comparative Perspective: A Study of Six APEC Countries*, Unpublished paper, World Bank, Washington, DC.

Rama, M. (2002). "Globalisation and Workers in Developing Countries", The World Bank, Washington, DC.

Rodrik, D. (1996). *Labour Standards in International Trade: Do They Matter and What Do We Do About Them*, Paper prepared for the Overseas Development Council.

Singh, N. (2003). "The Impact of International Standards: A Survey of Economic Theory", in K. Basu, H. Horn, L. Roman and J. Shapiro (eds.), *International Labour Standards*, pp. 107-181, Blackwell, Oxford.

SMERU (Social Monitoring and Early Response Unit) (2001). *The Impact of Minimum Wages in the Formal Urban Sector*, SMERU, Jakarta.

————. (2002). *Industrial Relations in Jabotabek, Bandung and Surabaya During the Era of Freedom to Organize*, Jakarta.

Srinavasan, T.N. (2003). "Old Wine in New Bottles?", in K. Basu, H. Horn, L. Roman and J. Shapiro (eds.), *International Labour Standards*, pp. 182-187, Blackwell, Oxford.

Van, der Eng, P. and M.C. Basri (eds.) (2004). *Business in Indonesia: New Challenges, Old Problems*, Institute of Southeast Asian Studies, Singapore.

World Bank (1995). "Workers in an Integrating World", *World Development Report*, Oxford, New York.

Part III

Social Impact of
Labour Regulation

6

An Analysis of Severance Pay Policies in India and Sri Lanka

MUKUL G. ASHER
PUNDARIK MUKHOPADHAYA

6.1. Introduction

As India and Sri Lanka address opportunities and challenges arising from globalisation and associated technological and other developments, the functioning of their labour markets has come under increasing scrutiny. Labour laws, regulations, and practices in both countries have traditionally reflected policies which relied on economic planning, public sector expansion, and overall economic growth to provide employment; while the growth strategy implicitly assumed relatively static and inward-looking economic structure. In view of their current strategies which increasingly reflect assumptions of more dynamic and outward-oriented economy, their labour market policies require realignment.

Another reason for the increasing focus on the functioning of the labour markets is that the two countries have achieved only limited success in generating employment, particularly in the so-called organised (or formal) sector which falls within the purview of the labour laws (World Bank, 2004; Sharma, 2005; Sundar, 2005). Importance of analysing microeconomic aspects, particularly, impact of hiring and retrenchment costs, and of incentive structures for individuals and firms arising from current labour regulations and practices for balance between jobs creation and preservation of existing jobs is also being increasingly recognised (Vodopivec, 2004; Sundar, 2005; Nagaraj, 2005; Sabharwal, 2005).

The formal social security systems in the two countries are characterised by dualism and relatively narrow coverage (Karunarathne and Goswami, 2002; Asher and Vasudevan, 2005). In both countries, civil servants, who constitute relatively small proportion (between 2 and 3 per cent) of the labour force, receive non-contributory, defined benefit (DB), inflation indexed pensions, with generous provisions for commutation, and family benefits.

India has, however, fundamentally changed civil service pension system for the Central government employees (except armed forces) who entered after January 2004. The new system is based on defined contribution (DC) principle, with compulsory purchase of annuities at age 60 for part of the accumulations; and appointment of a pensions regulator (Shah, 2005). This system is designed to include voluntary members from both, the organised and unorganised sectors; aims to minimise transaction costs; and ensure scalability.

Sri Lanka has adopted a limited contributory scheme for its civil servants, but it has not changed the DB basis of pensions (Karunarathne and Goswami, 2002). Private sector workers in both countries are covered under a DC scheme, though India has severely under-funded limited DB scheme as part of the national provident fund. These arrangements reflect dualism, and provide disincentives for mobility between public and private sectors.

The coverage of the formal schemes remains limited. In Sri Lanka, about a quarter of the labour force is covered, while in India the corresponding proportion is around 10 per cent (Karunarathne and Goswami, 2002; Asher and Vasudevan, 2005). Social assistance schemes for the elderly in the two countries also have narrow coverage. Most of the work force relies primarily on family support, and own savings for income support in old age.

It is in the above context that this chapter analyses severance pay practices in India and Sri Lanka, two countries with pluralistic institutions and democratic political system. The two countries have a functioning Free Trade Agreement (FTA) since 1998 (the bilateral merchandise trade was US\$ 1.8 billion in 2004), and are negotiating a Comprehensive Economic Partnership Agreement (CEPA) which is expected to link the two economies, including their labour markets, much more closely.

Severance pay refers to payment made by the employers when there is permanent retrenchment of employees.[1] As neither country has implemented unemployment insurance which is the main form

---

1. Temporary retrenchment due to weak demand or maintenance of capital equipment is called in India 'lay-off', during which wages at varying rates continue to be paid.

of severance payment in most middle and high-income countries[2], mandatory (or voluntary) lump-sum severance payments are of critical significance as they are the only short-term income maintenance or safety nets available to covered workers, while permitting restructuring of enterprises.

The analysis of the severance payments in the two countries also includes mandatory gratuity benefits. These are mandated when services of an employee are ended before or at the time of retirement. Thus, gratuity is essentially a part of deferred wage based on the length of service. It thus rewards loyalty to the employer. In both countries, Voluntary Retirement Schemes (VRS) have also been used for restructuring of enterprises. The term severance pay thus denotes all three types of payments in India and Sri Lanka.

As in other areas of public policy, design of severance pay and implementation aspects, with particular emphasis on administration and compliance costs, incentive structures, transparency, affordability, and scalability over time are of crucial relevance. (Vodopivec, 2004; Holzmann *et al.*, 2003). As an example, widely used severance pay formula based on a multiple of years of service and salary, while relatively simple and enabling uniform treatment, may substitute for careful analysis of actual needs and affordability.

The chapter is organised as follows. Section 6.2 provides an overview of the economic, demographic, and labour market characteristics for India and Sri Lanka. The discussion is designed to set the overall context within which severance pay practices in the two countries are examined in Section 6.3. The final section provides concluding observations.

6.2. Economic, Demographic, and Labour Market Characteristics

Table 6.1 summarises selected economic and demographic indicators in the two countries, on the basis of which the following observations may be made.

---

2. Origin of severance pay in the industrial countries was due to creation of labour codes in the beginning of the 20th century, technological changes of the1920s, and the Great Depression of the 1930s. Since then, expansion of welfare state and establishment of ILO (International Labour Organization) in post World War II have provided further impetus to short-term income maintenance measures. ILO conventions and EU (European Union) directives do not provide for severance payments in lump sum, but instead emphasise social risk-pooling unemployment insurance schemes. (Holzmann *et al.*, 2003).

Table 6.1

*India and Sri Lanka: Selected Economics and
Demographic Indicators, 2003*

Category	Unit	India	Sri Lanka
Economic Indicators			
GDP (Current)	Billion US$	600.6	18.2
GDP Growth	Per Cent	8.6	5.9
GDP (PPP)	Billion US$	3078.0	72.7
GDP Per Capita	US$	564	958
GDP Per Capita (PPP)	US$	2880	3740
Aid Per Capita	US$	0.9	34.9
Exports of Goods and Services (% of GDP)	Per Cent	14.5	35.8
Imports of Goods and Services (% of GDP)	Per Cent	16.0	42.4
Inflation Rate (GDP Deflator)	Per Cent	3.2	5.0
External Debt (% of GDP)	Per Cent	16	46
Net Foreign Direct Investment (FDI)	US$ Billion	4.3	0.2
Remittance Receipts	US$ Billion	10.0	1.1
Remittance Receipts (% of GDP)[a]	Per Cent	2.1	7.0
Demographic Indicators			
Population	Million	1064.0	19.2
Population Growth	Per Cent	1.49	1.18
Total Fertility Rate	Births Per Woman	2.86	1.98
Life Expectancy at Birth	Years	63.4	74.0
Urban Population	Per Cent	29	25

Source: Based on *www.devdata.worldbank.org*.

Note: [a]Remittance figures are for 2002.

India's population (second largest in the world) and level of GDP (fourth largest in PPP terms), suggest that it is among the major economies in the world. However, Sri Lanka's per capita income (US$ 958 *versus* India's US$ 568), and outward orientation (as measured by trade to GDP ratio) are both higher than India's. While India's 2003 GDP growth rate at 8.6 per cent was higher than Sri Lanka's 5.9 per cent, sustaining it represents a major challenge for India.

Sri Lanka received 35 times more foreign aid per person than India in 2003. Indeed, India is a significant donor and credit provider to Sri Lanka. Sri Lanka's reliance on remittance receipts in relation to its GDP is more than three times that of India. Job market access for their workers (as well as jobs provided through outsourcing, not captured in remittance receipts) is of crucial importance for economic and social stability in both countries. Sri Lanka's external debt to GDP ratio is three times that of India. The FDI inflows for both countries are relatively low, an area where significant improvement is needed.

A comparison of demographic indicators (Table 6.1) suggests that Sri Lanka's total fertility rate (TFR) at 1.98 is already below the replacement rate level of 2.15. India's TFR, while declining, is not expected to reach the replacement rate till around 2015. Life expectancy at birth is also much higher for Sri Lanka (74 years) than for India (63 years). Thus, Sri Lanka is expected to experience more rapid ageing than India. Urbanisation at about 25 to 30 per cent of the total population is at a moderate level in both countries.

Empirical evidence based analysis of labour force characteristics in both countries is hampered by good quality and timely data; and by insufficient disaggregation of employment categories, particularly for the informal (or unorganised) sector.[3] Both countries need to urgently take steps to improve the quality and timeliness of the labour market data.

Following observations may be made on the basis of available data on selected labour force indicators in the two countries presented in Table 6.2.

First, India's working age population is expected to increase by more than two-thirds (from 620 million to 1048 million) between 2000 and 2050. Policy makers will need to provide opportunities for meaningful activities (including education and jobs) to the growing working age population. This is indeed among the most difficult challenges facing India, requiring reforms in wide range of areas, including labour markets, educational systems, fiscal management, and technology policies.

---

3. Three examples from India may be cited. Deshpande *et. al.* (2004) study uses labour force data for India till only 2000, and in some cases, till only late 1990s. They also report on the difficulties involved on collecting primary data relating to labour market. Sundar (2005) cites data for 1997-98 for distribution of number of workers by size of factories in India. Since then, considerable restructuring of Indian industry has taken place in India. It is indeed undesirable to draw policy implications for nearly decade old data in a period of rapid change experienced by India. Third, Sundaram (2004) shows considerable understatement in the widely used official figures of organised sector unemployment leading to poor quality of public debate on impact of reforms during the 1990s on overall employment. For Sri Lanka, Kelegama (1998), and World Bank (2004) have commented on the need to improve the labour market data.

Table 6.2

Selected Labour Force Indicators of India and Sri Lanka

Category	Unit	Year	India	Sri Lanka
Working Age Population				
	Million	2000	619.7	11.4
	Million	2025	921.5	15.3
	Million	2050	1048.2	14.2
Labour Force				
Total	Million	2002	406.0	8.4
As % of Total Population	Per Cent	2002	63.0	71.0
Employment Share by Industry				
Agriculture	Per Cent	2002	66.8	42.7
Manufacturing	Per Cent	2002	12.9	23.1
Services	Per Cent	2002	20.3	34.3
Employment by Sector				
Organised (Formal) Sector	Per Cent	2002	9.9	48[a]
Unorganised (Informal) Sector	Per Cent	2002	91.1	52[a]
Share of Public Sector Employment in Total Employment	Per Cent	2001	3.3	14.2
Membership of Trade Unions as % of Labour Force	Per Cent	2000	3.0	11.9
Educational Attainment of Labour Force				
Below Primary (Male/Female)	Per Cent	2000	44.0/58.0	4.1/11.0
Degree and Above (Male/Female)	Per Cent	2000	8.3/4.1	1.9/3.6

Source: Adapted from World Bank (2004).
Note: [a] Our estimation.

India's labour force as percentage of working age population is much lower (63 per cent) than Sri Lanka's (71 per cent). If India's ratio approaches Sri Lanka's by 2025, India's labour force will increase from 406 million to 654 million, an increase of nearly 250 million, requiring generation of 10 million additional productive and sustainable jobs every year.

Worryingly, overall employment growth rate in India halved between 1993-2000 to one per cent compared to the preceding six year period; while the growth elasticity of employment declined sharply from 0.52 to 0.15 (World Bank, 2004) per cent. The magnitude of the employment challenge facing India's policy makers and the Indian society is thus enormous, and should create a sense of urgency on the part of all stakeholders. Moreover, the emphasis should be on productive and sustainable jobs as many poor persons in India are economically active, but do not earn enough from these activities (Sharma, 2005; World Bank, 2004).

The working age population in Sri Lanka is expected to grow by one-third between 2000 and 2025, and then decline by about 8 per cent to reach 14.2 million in 2050. This reflects Sri Lanka's demographic trends. Thus, its challenge in providing additional jobs will not be as severe as India's. It will need to rely to even greater extent than India on increased productivity to sustain rising incomes.

Employment share by sector exhibits differing patterns in the two countries. Sri Lanka's employment structure is relatively more balanced. India's share of employment in manufacturing at paltry 13 per cent is about half that of Sri Lanka. However, as share of agriculture in employment declines from current 67 per cent, three times its share in GDP, due to rising productivity, mechanisation, and crop diversification, substantially more jobs will need to be created in manufacturing. This suggests that India's labour market reform will need to be consistent with facilitating growth of manufacturing employment (Nagaraj, 2005; Sharma, 2005; Narayan, 2005). Contrary to widespread perceptions, the share of public sector in total employment at 3.3 per cent is much lower in India than in Sri Lanka (14.2 per cent).[4]

Low rate of unionisation in India (only 3 per cent of the labour force) as compared to Sri Lanka's 12 per cent also reflects low priority given to manufacturing. It also raises an important question concerning the extent to which interests of current labour union membership should govern public policies concerning labour market and social protection in India.

In 2000, Sri Lanka had about 1600 labour unions, while the average size of the labour union was around 600 members. This is a relatively low figure, particularly considering low wage levels, to undertake complex and knowledge-intensive functions of labour unions, such as collective bargaining. In India, it is relatively easy to form labour unions, even when protection of statutory labour laws is absent (World Bank, 2004). Debate on reform of the governance

---

4. The share of public sector employment in India appears understated. Mitra (2005) estimates this share to be 6.0 per cent. This however does not invalidate the point made.

and functioning of the labour unions to better align their management with the interests of the workers is long overdue in both countries

Since the manufacturing sector usually has greater potential for unionisation, enlightened trade union leadership should give priority towards increasing manufacturing employment which is sustainable and productive, consistent with India's current market-oriented strategy. If the labour unions instead opt for prolonging state-led employment creations (outside of productive infrastructure investment), and making it more difficult to restructure unviable enterprises, they and the political parties which sponsor them, will become less and less relevant for meeting needs of India's workers. The challenge is to make political system much more responsive to the needs of all workers, and not just those in the organised sector.

The term organised (or formal) sector in the two countries is used to denote employment covered by various labour laws, including severance pay, and gratuities.[5] Only about 10 per cent of the labour force is in this sector in India as compared with nearly 50 per cent in Sri Lanka. In India, however, the proportion of those having regular incomes is about twice that of the formal sector. Even the broader definition leaves about four-fifths of the labour force in activities where labour protection is weak. Monthly wage differential between organised and unorganised labour at the same skill levels is estimated to be in the range of 3—5 to 1 in India (Mitra, 2005).

The unorganised sector in India is not only large but also quite heterogeneous. This characteristic and the lax enforcement of existing statutory provisions provide methods for bringing about labour market flexibility but without attendant social safety nets, and labour protection, while perpetuating dualism. They also increase uncertainty in business and provide rent-seeking opportunities to those charged with framing the rules and enforcing them, as well as to trade union management intermediating between workers and management.

Increasing the share of organised sector employment is essential even as restructuring of public and private sector organisations is facilitated. Higher employment needs to be pursued by eliminating

---

5. The size of firm to which different labour laws apply varies in India and Sri Lanka. In general, laws in Sri Lanka become applicable at much lower firm size than in India. As a result, size of formal sector estimated on the basis of applicability of labour laws may not be strictly comparable between the two countries.

artificial restrictions on the size of firms (e.g. removing ineffective protection to small-sector activities in India); by making labour laws consistent with current market-oriented economic growth strategy, and by enhancing capacity, accountability, and transparency of organisations entrusted with designing and implementing labour regulations.[6] Formation of new companies and new areas of activities should become the primary avenue for generating additional employment.

Varma (2005) reports that in 2004, entrepreneurs in India were expected to go through 11 steps to launch a business, taking on average 89 days, at a cost equivalent to nearly half of per capita income. This compares unfavourably with 2 days for Australia and 24 days for Pakistan. In 2004, in Sri Lanka, the corresponding figure was 50 days, and only 10.7 per cent of per capita income (World Bank, 2004), Indian policy makers have realised the need to be more competitive in this area,[7] and its structuring of the Special Economic Zones (11 are in operation, with several more awaiting implementation) incorporates the need to drastically reduce the time and cost associated with starting a business. These types of measures also need to be extended to small domestic-oriented businesses as their employment generation potential is high (Varma, 2005; Sabharwal, 2005).

Data concerning educational attainment of the labour force indicate that Sri Lanka has exceptionally good record in providing basic education to mass of workers; while India exhibits moderately better performance in educating its workers at the tertiary level. India is, however, concentrating on improving the basic literacy levels, and its performance is expected to improve significantly.

The above discussion suggests that sustaining high economic growth, managing globalisation, and devising appropriate trade-offs between creating new jobs (and increasing economic efficiency of existing labour and capital resources), and modernisation of labour market organisations should be major priorities for both countries.

---

6. It is instructive that some states in India such as Uttar Pradesh have resorted to suspension of labour inspection of business premises as they are unable to ensure adequate accountability of those charged with such inspection. This is not an equitable and efficient way to bring about labour flexibility as it lowers costs for those employers who do not abide by statutory provisions, giving unfair competitive advantage to them.

7. The Indian Parliament passed the Special Economic Zone Bill in May 2005 but without providing discretion in implementation of the labour laws in these zones.

Therefore, reform of social safety nets, including of severance pay practices, should be consistent with the above priorities.

6.3. Severance Pay Arrangements

This section provides a brief overview of severance pay arrangements in the two countries, and analyses their implications for functioning of the labour markets. As noted, the term severance pay is used broadly to also include gratuity benefits and VRS payments.

6.3.1. India

Under India's Constitution, labour issues are a concurrent subject, i.e. both the Centre and the states share responsibility. In practice, the Centre's role has been predominant with states making relatively minor changes to the laws and regulations of the Centre. India's economic reforms since 1991 have, however, enhanced the responsibilities of the states in economic policy. Some states such as Gujarat, and Andhra Pradesh have, therefore, suggested that the Constitution be amended to make labour issues solely a state subject. It is argued that this will permit those states which give high priority to reforming the current labour laws and regulations with the objective of making them more consistent with the requirements of more market-based and outward-looking economic policies to take a lead and better fulfil their enhanced economic responsibilities. It could also assist in better managing the politics of labour market reform.

India has an impressive list of laws and procedures for protection of workers, primarily in the industrial sector (broadly defined) and in government employment (Samant, 2003). These are the two sectors accounting for bulk of formal sector jobs in India.

The Industrial Disputes Act (IDA), 1947

The IDA, enacted in 1947, is applicable throughout the country and has been amended on several occasions. The last major amendment was in 1984, before India's economic reforms initiated in 1991. It is the main law governing exit, lay-offs, retrenchment, and closures of industrial enterprises. Over the years, the IDA has given rise to an impressive body of case law.

The IDA is applicable to any business, trade, undertaking, manufacture or calling of employer and includes any calling, service, employment, handicraft, or industrial occupation or avocation of workmen. This Act, however, excludes a person employed in air force, army, navy, police service and a person employed in supervisory capacity drawing more than Indian Rupees 1600 (US$ 35) per month.[8] This Act is also applicable to the persons working in the public sector undertakings. In this case, the government is considered as an employer.

The evolution of the Act's provisions may be briefly summarised as follows. Initially it had differing provisions for firms employing between 50 and 100 workers and for firms with 100 or more workers. Firms employing fewer than 50 workers fell outside the scope of the Act.

Initially, this Act did not restrain employers from laying off (i.e. dismissing workers because of slackness in demand and with the intention of re-hiring them when business picks up) or from retrenching (permanent lay-off) workers, or from closing down unprofitable businesses provided they notified the workers or unions well in advance. The 1957 amendment, however, required the employer to compensate the workers affected by closure in the same way as if they were retrenched.

Each of the three amendments of the IDA in 1972, 1976 and 1982 provided greater protection to workers than the preceding ones. It is not a coincidence that more stringent jobs preservation measures coincided with the two energy crisis in 1973 and 1979 respectively; and with general stagnation of the economy. Their legacy is still continuing, primarily in making psychological shift from jobs preservation to jobs creation more difficult to attain.

Chapter V B of the IDA requires employers employing 100 or more workers to give three months notice of a closure to workers (or their representatives) and to the government.[9] After an enquiry

---

8. Courts, including the Supreme Court have interpreted supervisory capacity so strictly that only employees like whole time Directors and Managers at the highest level are included in that category. This implies that most of the employees qualify as workmen under IDA even if they earn a salary above Rs. 1600 per month. In recent years, courts have been taking a more balanced view between needs of the overall economy and society on the one hand and rights demanded by organised workers on the other. This is suggested by the recent decision of the Supreme Court to not permit strikes by government workers (Sharma, 2005).

9. India's Labour Ministry has proposed raising the limit for industrial units seeking to retrench or close without government approval from 100 to 300 workers, while increasing the retrenchment benefits from 15 to 60 days wages for each year of service (*The Financial Express*, April 6, 2005). The proposal is therefore more restrictive than the SNCL's recommendation. Even this modest proposal has been opposed by organised labour. A major industrial state, Maharashtra, has already adopted this proposal in its industrial policy (Sundar, 2005).

(itself a time consuming affair), Labour Department either grants the closure, or refuses. In practice, permission for closure is rarely given, though there have been recent signs of flexibility. This provision of the need for government's permission is quite unusual and goes beyond the recommendations of even the International Labour Organization (ILO). This provision also injects unnecessary political element in business decision making potentially resulting in large opportunity costs to the economy, but permits rent seeking opportunities to those in charge of giving such approvals.

This provision is unsuitable for a market economy where an enterprise management should be able to decide the size of its work force, not just at the start of business but also during its conduct. This view has been endorsed by India's Second National Commission on Labour (SNCL) in a Report issued in 2002, which recommends that the government permission be required only if a firm employing more than 300 workers decides to close (Sundar, 2005).

Employers with 50 or less than 100 workers, however, need only to notify the government, while those with less than 50 workers have no obligation in terms of closure. In practice, workers in such firms can appeal to other laws (for example Indian Contracts Act, 1972) to restrict dismissals.

Greater statutory protection for a section of current organised sector workers need not imply that workers as a group benefit. Based on theoretical reasoning, this has been demonstrated by Basu *et al.,* (2000). Primary channels bringing about this result are reduced job opportunities due to impediments to formation of new companies; resources devoted to finding ways to get around to formal laws leading to inefficiencies and loss of competitiveness; and greater encouragement to adoption of capital intensive technologies.

Fallon and Lucas (1993) found that the 1976 amendments of the IDA, reduced the labour demand by 17.5 per cent in India. An examination of the Indian annual survey of industries corroborates the result. During the 1980s and early 1990s, there was a sharp drop in employment in firms employing more than 100 workers and mild decrease in firms employing between 50 and 99 workers. However, there was a sharp increase in employment for small firms (less than 50 workers). Similar findings have been reported by Deshpande *et al.* (2004).

Retrenchment Payment: The provisions relating to payment of compensation for lay-off and retrenchment was introduced in 1953. An amendment in 1964 (IDA Chapter V A) currently requires an establishment employing 50 or more workers to provide workers with one month's notice and half a month's pay for every year of continuous work by the worker at the firm when retrenchment is undertaken. If notice is not given, then one month's wages are required to be paid. This implies that for a worker with 20 years of service, retrenchment benefit is equivalent to 10 months salary. In comparison with other countries, especially Sri Lanka (see below), this is relatively low. Under the income tax laws, the maximum retrenchment benefit exempted from the income tax is Indian Rupees 0.5 million (US$ 10,900). Any benefit above this amount is subject to individual income tax.

The retrenchment law in India is silent on the treatment of several categories of workers such as those hired from sub-contractors, agency workers, consultants, and home workers (Deshpande *et al.*, 2004). To attain labour market flexibility, firms in India appear to have resorted to greater reliance on types of workers where applicability of formal labour laws is subject to some ambiguity; or where formal labour legislation is regarded as being unduly restrictive in maintaining competitiveness in increasingly open Indian economy (Deshpande *et al.*, 2004).

Currently, for firms employing more than 50 workers, the lay-off compensation is at the rate of 50 per cent of the basic pay plus dearness allowance. This is in addition to the worker's wages during the lay-off period. This applies for those who have been employed for one year or more. For firm employing less than 50 workers, only the wages need to be paid. No changes in this area are contemplated.

India thus combines fairly strong formal labour protection laws for the organised sector workers with relatively modest retrenchment benefit. There are, however, several gaps in the statutory provisions and the enforcement remain uneven and weak. It is these characteristic that perhaps led the SNCL to recommend trade-off involving less rigid formal protection laws and more generous retrenchment benefit varying by size of firms (22.5 to 30 days per year for firms with less than 100 employees, and 45-60 days for firms with more than 300 employees) (Sundar, 2005). In the event of closure, the SNCL recommended somewhat lower retrenchment benefits, though still varying with size of firms, and still higher than the current provisions (Sundar, 2005).

Better enforcement and greater accountability for complying with labour laws are also needed. Both public and private sector firms are among significant numbers who have failed to pay full statutory benefits to their workers, including severance pay and provident fund contributions.

Policy makers recognise that employment potential of various types of non-permanent jobs is high, requiring re-examination of the 1970 Contract Labour Act. Permanent jobs alone will not be sufficient to meet India's daunting employment (and employability) challenge. This is indicated by the SNCL's 2002 Report. The challenge in this area is translating good economics into good politics.

The Payment of Gratuity Act (PGA), 1972

This Act came into force in September, 1972.[10] The main objective of this Act is to provide for a minimum uniform scheme for payment of gratuity to workers (including those retrenched) throughout the country. The Act does not prevent employer-employee contracts providing more generous gratuity benefits. The purpose of the Act is to presumably instil loyalty among workers. This assumes that both employers and employees value long-term continuity of service.

The Act applies to firms employing more than 10 workers. Therefore, it has broader applicability than the retrenchment benefit provision which applies to firms employing 50 workers or more. Moreover, persons employed by government and other public sector organisations also receive gratuity benefits (in addition to pensions and provident fund benefits), but are not covered under the Act (Muthuswamy and Brinda, 2002).

An employee is entitled to gratuity benefits only after five years of continuous employment. But this is waived in case of death or disablement. The rate of gratuity is 15 days salary (basic wage plus dearness allowance) for every year of service, with a maximum

---

10. Though the Act came into force from 16 September, 1972 it is applicable to the employees employed prior to that date. Such retrospective application of the laws creates uncertainty and increases risk premium for businesses and the country, particularly as jobs creation is among the most daunting challenges facing the country.

ceiling of Rs. 0.35 million (US$ 7,600). Since 1994, all employees irrespective of their wages have been eligible for gratuity. Since gratuity is paid to those retrenched, combined severance pay and gratuity payments already amount to one month of benefit per year of service, subject to a ceiling.

Income Tax treats the gratuity received by the government employees and others differently. Any gratuity received by a government (whether state or central) employee is tax free. Gratuity received by employees of private or public sector firms is taxable if it exceeds Rs. 0.35 million over a life time.

The gratuity benefits are wholly borne by the employer. The employer however can obtain gratuity policy from the Life Insurance Corporation of India (LIC), a dominant state-owned provider with nearly 80 per cent market share; or set up Income Tax approved Gratuity Trust to discharge the liability under the Act (Section 4A). This provision potentially permits development of the fund management industry, thereby adding depth to financial and capital markets and enhancing expertise. It is essential, however, that the Gratuity Trust be professionally managed and regulated. Income tax authorities are not the appropriate agency to undertake the regulatory task, though they may still be involved in the granting of income tax exemption.[11]

Funding levels for gratuity liability vary widely among the employers. Many public and private sector employers do not have adequate funding provisions, and this creates additional uncertainty for the workers. Adequate supervision and regulation as well as greater professionalism in managing gratuity liabilities are essential. One option would be to entrust this responsibility to the proposed PFRDA.

Voluntary Retirement Scheme (VRS)

The use of VRS in India has accelerated since the 1991 reforms in both the public and the private sectors (Sharma, 2005). Unlike laws governing retrenchment and closure, there are no statutory rules governing VRS, provided employer and the unions agree among

---

11. The proposed Pension Fund Regulatory and Development Authority (PFRDA) would be an appropriate regulatory authority for the Gratuity Trust. The insurance sector is regulated by the Insurance Regulatory Development Authority (IRDA).

themselves. Consistent with international trends, ability of unions to disrupt operations has weakened due to changing public opinion and requirements of intense domestic and external competition. As a result the benefits provided under the VRS vary considerably from case to case, even for the same firm in their successive rounds of VRS.

There appears to have been insufficient recognition of the need to increase employability of those retrenched under VRS; and little help to the affected workers on financial planning have been forthcoming (Sharma, 2005). This is an area where enlightened employer-union cooperation should be considered.

The first Rs. 0.5 million (US$ 10,900) of VRS payments are exempt from individual income tax. In general, the cost to the employers and the fiscal costs of income tax exemption are generally higher for the VRS than for layoffs, retrenchment benefits and gratuities.

To summarise, the most striking conclusion emerging from the above analysis is that the current labour legislation and employment practices in India neither adequately protect over 400 million in the labour force nor are they conducive to rapid growth creation. The severance pay arrangements, however, are modest by international practices.

Extensive restructuring has nevertheless taken place in both public and private sector firms and organisations, particularly since the early 1990s. This has been made possible by a combination of using gaps in current statutory provisions to increase the share of non-permanent workers; relying on lax enforcement and time consuming procedures; extensive use of the VRS; and adopting more capital-intensive methods of production and distribution. Ironically, the outcome of greater share of non-permanent workers in India is similar to those countries with much more flexible labour markets such as the US and UK.

The key economic concern should be that the economic costs, including opportunity costs of delays in shifting existing physical assets and human resources from low-value to high-value added activities, and in realising requisite scale and scope economies, have been high. As a consequence, in spite of India achieving annual real GDP growth of over 6 per cent for nearly quarter of a century, the challenge of providing productive and sustainable jobs is not being met. Labour market reform will be necessary though not sufficient for meeting the employment challenge as other reforms, including higher and more effective public and private sector investment will also be needed. Both micro and macroeconomic factors need to be considered in the debate on labour market issues.

6.3.2. *Sri Lanka*

As in India, Sri Lanka has an impressive list of laws designed to protect workers. The Sri Lankan Industrial Law is quite complex. It comprises about 40 labour statutes, regulations gazette under the labour statutes, decisions made by the Labour Courts and the Appellate Courts, and collective agreements (Sarveswaran, 2000). Except for the gratuity provisions, major labour legislations pre-date Sri Lanka's economic reforms initiated in 1977.

Legislative Provisions

The main legislation governing the termination of employment in Sri Lanka is the Termination of Employment of Workmen (special provision) Act of 1971 (TEWA), and the Industrial Dispute Act of 1950, as amended (IDA). Both these laws are applied to the workers in the private sector. Sri Lanka established export processing zones in 1977. But to-date, Board of Investment does not have powers to negotiate flexibility in application of labour laws in these zones when negotiating with the investors.

TEWA applies to an extensive range of industries, listed in the Schedule to the Act, including all shops, offices and factories. This reflects the implicit assumption of a relatively static economy. Both the IDA and TEWA define workman broadly as a person who works under a contract of employment in any capacity including apprentices.[12] TEWA however does not apply to the establishment with fewer than 15 workers or to workers with less than six months service.[13]

The legislative provisions governing termination of employment at the initiative of the employer in Sri Lanka do not set any standard for which dismissals can be effected, yet paradoxically provide

---

12. Section 3(2), TEWA, and Section 48, IDA.

13. A worker employed in a firm with less than 15 employees is nevertheless permitted to apply to a Labour tribunal for gratuity benefits. This creates high transaction costs and uncertainty for firms, employees, and the economy as a whole.

stringent procedural controls on dismissal. TEWA specifically provides that the Labour Commissioner (from whom the employer must seek authorisation to dismiss) may decide the application in his absolute discretion.[14] The Commissioner may also order reinstatement of any worker. No distinction is made in the legislation between casual, probationary and fixed term employees. Under the Act, temporary lay-offs may also need the prior authorisation of the Commissioner of Labour. The Labour Tribunals have large and growing backlog of unresolved cases.

Those employees not covered by the TEWA, who are not seasonal employees and work for an establishment of greater than 15 workers, and who have been employed for more than a year are entitled to one month's notice of any retrenchment.[15] In such cases the employer must also give notice to the Government and to any relevant union.[16] The dismissal cannot be effected until two months after the notice has been given, unless an agreement to the contrary has been reached with the employee or his representative (IDA Section 31G).

Since there is no statutory minimum severance pay, the Commissioner of Labour determines the amount of the compensation to be paid to workers who are to be made redundant. In practice, the level of compensation approved by the Commissioner has been up to a maximum of six-monthly wages per year of service, and on average were 1.6 and 3.1 monthly wages per year of service in 2000 and 2001, respectively.[17] The total sums paid out to laid-off workers have been large, amounting to even 36-50 monthly wages, and the average payment in 2002 was Sri Lankan Rupees 57,700, equivalent to more than four-fifths of per capita GDP in 2000. This level of compensation is among the highest in the world.[18]

To reduce the non-transparency of the TEWA payments, employers have requested that the Act is amended so that the

---

14. TEWA, Section 2(b).

15. IDA Section 31E.

16. IDA, Section 31F(a).

17. These figures as well as those in the next sentence are based on communication by the authors with the ILO and World Bank officials based in Sri Lanka.

18. The corresponding figure for Asia as a whole for those with 20 years of service is only 0.8. All other regions including OECD are substantially less generous than Asia, let alone Sri Lanka (Holzmann *et al.*, 2003).

compensation would be determined by a formula. In 2001, the Commissioner General of Labour did suggest a formula involving two to three months salary for each year of actual service or full salary for the remaining period of service up to retirement, whichever is less, subject to a maximum of 50 months salary. ILO prepared a proposal in 2003 for introducing unemployment insurance scheme in Sri Lanka. However neither the formula nor the insurance proposal has received the formal backing of the government.

The unusual and wide discretionary powers given to the Commissioner of Labour creates uncertainty in business planning, and gives rise to rent-seeking opportunities to stakeholders, particular to those entrusted with the discretionary powers, and needlessly politicises economic decision making. This is indicated by the finding that in a significant number of cases unions affiliated to the ruling party have been favoured over the rival unions in adjudicating cases (Kelegama, 1998). These types of powers are unsuitable for a market economy.

The TEWA does not apply to Government-Owned Business Undertakings (GOBUs) or SOEs.[19] This is because under the Sri Lankan laws, a worker in a GOBU is covered only by the government establishment code. Thus, the services of a worker of a SOE can be terminated without the specific permission of the Commission of Labour. A worker of a GOBU or SOE once retrenched is not permitted to seek redresses from the Labour Tribunal. Under the 1987 Act, after conversion of an SOE to a public company, the worker in treated as a private sector worker.

Retrenchment of workers in the SOEs has been particularly contentious in Sri Lanka. The 1992 announcement by the President of the country made voluntary retrenchment the state policy as it guaranteed jobs to existing workers till the retirement age of 55 (Kelegama 1998). The most common compensation applied in restructuring SOEs since 1992 has resulted in an average worker receiving total financial package of around Sri Lankan Rupees 0.25 to 0.3 million. Majority of the voluntarily retrenched workers were below 45 years of age.

---

19. All nationalised private firms under the Business Acquisition Act of 1971 were categorised as GOBU. They are actually SOEs with a different name.

The Gratuity Scheme

Gratuity benefits in Sri Lanka are governed by the Payment of Gratuity Act of 1983. The Act applies to employers with 15 or more employees in private and semi-government sectors. The Act, however, does not cover public sector workers, though they also receive this benefit.

A minimum of 5 years of service is required to be eligible for the benefit. The gratuity amount is 15 days of salary for every completed year of service. Gratuity is paid regardless of the termination of employment. So for workers qualifying under TEWA, this is an additional benefit.

The gratuity funds are not regulated. No data on the extent of funding of gratuity liabilities are available. It would, however, be surprising if the funding levels were high. As in the case of India, there is a strong case to subject gratuity funds to regulatory oversight on governance, funding, and investments.

The above analysis of Sri Lanka's severance pay arrangements suggests the following: First, the labour legislation is strongly procedure rather than outcome oriented. Complexity of laws, which includes a wide ranging right of appeal, makes administration of labour laws unwieldy and time consuming. Nevertheless, considerable restructuring of public and private enterprises has taken place, with extensive use of VRS.

Second, while the statutory gratuity benefits are internationally comparable, retrenchment payments are left to be decided on a case-by-case basis by overburdened labour officials. Resulting needless politicisation of administration of labour laws has led to excessive emphasis on preserving existing jobs rather than creation of new jobs. Not permitting flexibility in application of labour laws in export processing zones after nearly 30 years of operation and when creation of jobs is a major task facing the policy makers, seems to reflect a certain rigidity in political economy and economic thinking.

6.4. Concluding Observations

As India and Sri Lanka continue to link their economies more closely with each other, and further integrate with the world economy, labour market issues, particularly proper balance between preserving existing jobs on the one hand and creating new jobs on the other, have acquired considerable urgency. The influence of their earlier economic, social, and political institutions and thinking however remains strong.

There is a strong resistance among their labour ministries and organised labour (constituting relatively small proportion of the labour force) to applying economic reasoning (e.g. need to minimise transaction costs and opportunity costs) to labour legislation and its implementation. There is also reluctance to shift from excessive procedure-oriented to outcome-oriented approach to labour protection which could enable those not in the organised sector to benefit from jobs creation in many new diverse areas by established as well as newly formed companies. Unwillingness in Sri Lanka to adopt a formula for severance pay which will reduce transaction costs and minimise political influence on business decisions is among the most flagrant examples of the above tendencies. In both countries, there is a need to improve data and understanding of labour markets, with a view to generate policy options on labour issues based on analytical yet evidence-based research.

In both countries, extensive and relatively rigid formal labour laws have coincided with considerable restructuring, by both public and private sector organisations, and fairly low effective labour protection to the vast majority of the workforce. The methods used to bring about this result, such as lax enforcement, time consuming processes, and rent-seeking by privileged few are not conducive to meeting the daunting challenges of jobs creation.

Except for retrenchment benefits in Sri Lanka, severance payments in both countries are modest by international comparisons. So the opportunity for trading-off somewhat higher severance pay on the one hand and greater operational flexibility to public and private sector organisations, greater professionalism in design and implementation of schemes under the Labour Ministries, and emphasis on reducing transaction costs, particularly for formation of new companies on the other, exists.

The overarching challenge in both countries is for the political, business, and labour leadership to help translate sound economics into acceptable electoral politics. Rapid progress in meeting this challenge is not expected, but even small cumulative changes in the right direction have the potential for substantial welfare enhancement. This is a manageable task in both countries, but it should be pursued with a sense of urgency.

References

Asher, M.G. and D. Vasudevan (2005). "Globalisation, Demographic Transition and Reform of Social Safety nets in India", paper presented at the Conference on *Managing Globalisation: Lessons from China and India*, organised by the Lee Kuan Yew School of Public Policy, National University of Singapore, April 4-6.

Basu, K., G.S. Fields and S. Debgupta (2000). *Alternative Labour Retrenchment Laws and their Effect on Wages and Employment: A Theoretical Investigation with Special Reference to Developing Countries*, Cornell University working paper, Ithaca.

Deshpande, L.K., A.K. Sharma, A.K. Karan and S. Sarkar (2004). *Liberalisation and Labour: Labour Flexibility in Indian Manufacturing*, Institute for Human Development, New Delhi.

Fallon, P.R. and R.E.B. Lucas (1993). "Job Security Regulations and the Dynamic Demand for Industrial Labour in India and Zimbabwe", *Journal of Development Economics*, 40: 241-275.

Government of India (2003). *The Workmen's Compensation Act, 1923*, Labour Law Agency, Mumbai, India.

Holzmann, R., K. Iyer and M. Vodopivec (2003). "Severance Pay Programs around the World: Rationale, Status, and Reforms", paper prepared for the Joint World Bank/International Institute for Applied System Analysis/Ludwig Boltzmann Institute for Economic Analysis Workshop on Severance Payments, IIASA/Laxenburg, November 7-8.

IMF (International Monetary Fund) (2001). *India: Recent Economic Developments and Selected Issues, Country Report No. 01/181*, p. 132, Washington, DC.

Karunarathne, W. and R. Goswami (2002). "Reforming Formal Social Security Systems in India and Sri Lanka", *International Social Security Review*, 55(4), pp. 89-106.

Kelegama, S. (1998). "Globalisation and Industrial Relations in Sri Lanka", paper presented at Phase IV of *ILO Regional Programme on Globalisation and Industrial Relations: National Tripartite Seminar on Effects of Globalisation on Industrial Relations*", May 21-24, Trans Asia Hotel, Colombo.

Mitra, B.S. (2005). *Political Success, Economic Challenges: The Untold Story of India*, Liberty Institute, New Delhi.

Muthuswamy and Brinda (2002). *Swamy's Handbook for Central Government Servants*, Swamy Publishers (P) Ltd., Chennai.

Nagaraj, R. (2005). "Fall in the Organised Manufacturing Employment", a paper presented at International *Conference on Employment and Income Security in India*, organised by the Institute for Human Development, New Delhi, April 6-8.

Narayan, J. (2005). "Mere Good Intentions Lead Nowhere", *The Financial Express*, April 8.

Sabharwal, M. (2005). "Give Outsiders a Hand", *Business India*, June 20-July 3, p. 116.

Samant, S.R. (2003). *Employer's Guide to Labour Laws*, Eighth Edition, Labour Law Agency, Mumbai.

Sarveswaran, A. (2000). "Industrial Law: A Critique of the Industrial Law of Sri Lanka in the Context of foreign Investment", *Bar Association Law Journal of Sri Lanka*, VIII(II): 1-6.

Shah, A. (2005). "A Sustainable and Scalable Approach to Indian Pension Reforms", paper presented at the *Conference on Managing Globalisation: Lessons from China and India*, organised by the Lee Kuan Yew School of Public Policy, National University of Singapore, April 4-6.

Sharma, A. N. (2005). "Recent Trends in Indian Labour Market and Emerging Issues of Employment and Income Security", paper presented at *International Conference on Employment and Income Security in India*, organised by the Institute for Human Development, New Delhi, April 6-8.

Singh, J. (2002). "The Law, Labour and Development in India", paper presented at *Annual Bank Conference on Development Economics*, June 24-26, Oslo, Europe.

Sundaram, K. (2004). "Growth of Work Opportunities in India: 1983 to1999-2000", Delhi School of Economics, *Working Paper No. 131*.

Sundar, K.R.S. (2005). "Labour Flexibility Debate in India: A Comprehensive Review and Some Suggestions", a paper presented at *International Conference on Employment and Income security in India*, organised by the Institute for Human Development, April 6-8, New Delhi.

United Nations (2001). "Strengthening Policies and Programmes on Social Safety Nets: Issues, Recommendations and Selected Studies", *Social Policy Paper No.8*.

Varma, A. (2005). "India's Far From Free Markets", *The Wall Street Journal*, June 16.

Vodopivec, Milan (2004). *Income Support to the Unemployed: Issues and Options*, The World Bank, Washington, DC

World Bank (2004). *Labour Markets in South Asia: Issues and Challenges*, World Bank, Washington, DC,

http://www.epfindia.com/epf/legalprovisions.htm.

7

An International Comparison of Health and Safety Regulation and Public Policy from a Gender Perspective

The Case of Australia and Southeast Asia

SUZANNE JAMIESON

7.1. Introduction

This chapter is about women workers and the nature of the work safety laws which are supposed to protect them from the particular hazards they face at work. This work is comparative in nature and looks at the situation in Australia and compares it with the laws in Singapore, Taiwan and Vietnam. Our aim is to gauge whether women workers in these three very different economies work under laws which recognise the specificity of their work lives as women workers or treat them only as mothers (or potential mothers) who also work or laws which ignore questions of gender entirely.

The chapter is about difference and identity and the way in which legal cultures and legal policy makers respond to gender in an increasingly globalised world. We also ponder how to initially scope this question in terms of useful theories and conceptualisation. Ultimately the aim of the wider project will be to examine the gap between the laws as they stand and the way in which they are enforced or not.

Occupational health and safety (OHS) could well prove to be a casualty in a globalising world just as it became during the rapid industrialisation process that overcame Britain in the 18th and 19th centuries the so-called Industrial Revolution (Thompson, 1968; Haines, 2003). That particular revolution prompted intervention by the State in the way of highly prescriptive regulation backed up by State resourced systems of inspection and compliance enforcement.

These arrangements were never adequate, however, largely because inspector numbers were always relatively low and prosecution was always very much a position of last resort (Bohle and Quinlan, 2000: 286; Jamieson, 2001).

Self regulation of OHS in the workplace by the industrial parties has been the official approach in the English/common law legal world (e.g. the United Kingdom, Australia, and New Zealand) since the Robens Report of 1972. In the 1980s, self-regulation was added to the concept of OHS management systems incorporating compliance elements as well as quality management considerations (Parker, 2002: 20). Lamm (2000: 513), in looking in particular at the situation in New Zealand, has noted that "OHS laws are often seen as a barometer of government employment policy and have been used as a precursor for fundamental reforms in employment law." If we characterise the development of OHS laws in Australia since the adoption by the states of Robens-style self-regulation from about 1980 as de-regulatory, Lamm's point is valid because the 1990s saw a widespread deregulation of the employment laws (and labour market) in both state and federal jurisdictions.

Given this time frame, however, the deregulation of the OHS laws was not associated with the onset of globalisation. More will be said below about globalisation. What is obvious from this study (and this is hardly a surprising revelation) is th   story has seen a move from no (or very little) regulation of the physical workplace in pre-industrial times to regulation prompted by industrial and political development (in Britain *circa* 1802 to 1844 and beyond) through to deregulation prompted by changing economic and political attitudes. One of the interesting things which require exploration is the effect of globalisation/deregulation on economies just moving into that second phase i.e. of industrialisation. To adopt an analogy from the physical sciences, it might also be useful to think of history not just as one sinusoidally forward moving wave but rather as the combined effect of multiple waves moving across our field of vision.

What is attempted in this chapter is to look at relevant legal theory in order to explain the position of women in the legal order (especially in the area of OHS) and to suggest ways in which their position might be improved using the traditional instruments of public and legal policy. Before that, however, there are some serious issues of comparative method which need to be dealt with briefly, along with some basic definitional problems. We conclude with some ideas for further research and some general observations that have come out of the project so far.

7.2. Globalisation and Regulation

There is considerable controversy surrounding this term, even extending to whether it is a new phenomenon and not something that has already occurred in the past as markets open up and competition increases in ways not previously experienced. Examples of this might include the Industrial Revolution itself or the chaotic economic events which occurred in Australasia at the end of the 19th century. Recently the International Labour Organization has defined it in this way:

> "Globalisation is a term that is used in many different ways, but the principal underlying idea is the progressive integration of economies and societies. It is driven by new technologies, new economic relationships and the national and international policies of a wide range of actors including governments, international organisations, business, labour and civil society. The social dimension of globalisation refers to the impact of globalisation on the life and work of people, on their families and their societies. Concerns and issues are often raised about the impact of globalisation on employment, working conditions, income and social protection. Beyond the world of work, the social dimension encompasses security, culture and identity, inclusion or exclusion and the cohesiveness of families and communities" (*World Commission on the Social Dimension of Globalisation*, ILO, 2003).

How this impacts on the countries of comparison is mediated by the type of economy they have and their relative levels of development. For the purposes of this Chapter, I characterise Australia and Singapore as developed economies and those of Vietnam and Taiwan as developing, although this is clearly a very clumsy categorisation, revealing huge differences even within the two categories. The other point that needs to be made up front is that this study has not found any evidence of convergence of legal systems or styles at this early stage of globalisation.

Drawing on a model of historical change employed by Todd *et al.* (2004: 265) in relation to Malaysia which they categorise as a developing economy, they suggest that a less developed country moves towards industrialisation by creating a raft of conditions (such as low wages and low levels of unionisation) through public policy that might be seen as attractive in encouraging investment. To this might be added low levels of OHS protection *via* intervention by the

State. In time, however, if this approach is successful, demands for higher wages and generally better conditions will be articulated.

Obvious examples of this might be seen in South Korea and Taiwan over the past decade where labour agitation has increased along with prosperity (Wang, 2002: 198). The developments of these secondary labour conditions (which in fact may operate to reduce the attractiveness of the economy to ongoing investment) pose a strategic choice for the government of the developing economy, according to Todd *et al.*, (2004: 265). The government may choose to continue to exert major control over the labour market, wages, employee rights and the growth of trade unions and their influence which continue to replicate the initial investor-friendly conditions.

On the other hand it may choose to adapt to the conditions created by the early success and allow/encourage trade union activity and the development of collective bargaining underpinned by State-supported investment in human capital by means of educational and skill-enhancing strategies. We argue here that at the critical juncture Australia, Singapore and Taiwan have chosen the adaptive path. It is too early yet to determine what Vietnam will do as it works through its post-socialist economic identity and where the majority of large enterprises remain in State ownership. While the three more developed countries have chosen this route it is not to suggest that they are as union-friendly as some of their critics on the left might wish.

The debate around regulation is likewise intensely political (Hawkins, 2002; Picciotto, 2002: 2) and much written about (Gunningham and Johnstone, 1999; Picciotto, 2002: 1). It would be true to suggest that the regulatory State which grew out of and developed contemporaneously with the rise of modern capital is very much in retreat (Collins, 2003: 95; Gunningham and Johnstone, 1999: 6). The traditional command/control form of regulation is out of favour and calls for reflexive, responsive or smart regulation are in vogue (Gunningham and Johnstone, 1999). That does not mean, however, that the leading writers in this area are calling for the abandonment of criminal prosecutions as one way of regulating hazards in the workplace (Gunningham and Johnstone, 1999: 13) and this is one of the matters we want to pursue in the empirical part of this study.

What we attempt to do below in looking at the OHS legislation in Australia, Singapore, Taiwan and Vietnam is in terms of whether the regulation exercise is likely to produce behaviour or outcomes of an expected standard (Picciotto, 2002: 1) and whether that regulation takes into account the gender of the workers (rather than simply assuming all workers are male). This examination remains centred in the domain of the nation State, a long way from any concept of globalised regulation (Picciotto 2002: 5) or even regionalised regulation (James, 1993). So what might be gendered regulation within that nation State?

7.3. Feminist Legal Theory

Most feminist legal research is situated a long way from the black letter law of the positivist approach used in traditional legal exegesis. Traditional male legal scholarship cannot accommodate or contain women's experience. It could be argued that the positivist legal method couldn't easily explore, explain or elucidate men's legal experience either. The feminist legal approach to the comparative problem below is consistent with a socio-legal approach and in that way the project will eventually encompass not just what the law says but rather why and how it operates as it does. This is particularly useful in a public policy project, remembering that the aim of this project as stated above is to improve the health and safety of women at work. It is also useful to remember that the social relations of men and women are different as we move between societies (Jamieson, 2004: 461).

Naffine (1990) has provided us with a useful way of classifying feminist approaches to legal thought or ways in which the law might be classified according to a feminist vision. Her first category is law as male monopoly (i.e. law is sexist), the second is law as a product of male culture (i.e. law is male) and the third category is law as male dominated but not necessarily representing male interests in a deliberate and cohesive way (i.e. law is gendered). The law as sexist is the approach most law reformers have taken in rewriting laws, especially to take into account concerns for human rights. For example, the anti-discrimination laws across the common law world have been written with this vision of the law as a system in mind. It is the classic liberal formulation of the law whose natural corollary is that once the 'sexism' of the law is removed a mere declaration of equality will make equality a reality.

The second category sees law as always privileging men over women, but this would seem to ignore other important variables operating in social life, such as race, class, religion and physical and intellectual ability. The third category of a gendered law is particularly apposite in the employment/OHS arena where we see laws created on the basis that the 'worker' is an able-bodied male working full-time in the primary labour market and (in Australia at least) represented by a strong trade union. Because the law of employment/OHS is gendered it will affect women's working lives differently to men's and reinforce gender differences. Naffine's 'law is gendered' is the approach used in the comparison below.

In all of these ways of looking at the law woman is always the 'other', never the standard against which all workers are measured. As Curran (1998: 666) points out below it is precisely this concern for the other that makes a feminist legal methodology so appropriate in any comparative legal exercise, because comparative work is always about the 'other' and the different. Furthermore, she suggests (1998: 657) that feminist legal theory has been successful in reconciling concepts of justice and equality with that of difference. Rhode (1989) has also attempted to reconcile these concepts which have had a highly conflicted relationship in both America and Australia. Rhode has brought about this conceptual reconciliation by addressing the idea of disadvantage that might emanate from any law drawn according to ideas of equality or of difference. As we will see below this has been an important debate in the OHS laws in Australia.

7.4. A Role for Trade Unions

The role of unions in the regulation of OHS at the workplace has long been recognised in Britain and Australia (Bohle and Quinlan, 2000: 428-466; Jamieson, 2001: 144-158; James, 1993: 15-19; Woolfson, 1995: 30-33) either by means of their involvement in the formal structures dictated by the Robens-style OHS legislation such as committees or as OHS representatives at the workplace or by means of campaigning around OHS issues or bringing them to the attention of the safety regulators. Trade unions may prove to be a useful form of non-state regulation (Gunningham and Johnstone, 1999; Picciotto, 2002: 4).

We have pointed out elsewhere (Jamieson, 2001) that women's lower rates of union membership and the nature of those trade unions operating as they do in the less strategically placed parts of the economy, has meant that unions are not as critical in the regulation of workplace OHS as they are in respect of some typical male areas of work such as construction and metal manufacturing. In construction in particular, we found that the unions consciously saw their role as keeping the regulator focused on the workplace and its hazards and that this resulted in relatively high levels of prosecutorial activity (Jamieson, 2001). It might be possible to extrapolate from these findings that the absence of a trade union (or at best its very light presence) in a workplace may have two effects. The first effect may be that limited monitoring of hazards may occur at the workplace and a further effect may be that there is no outside pressure by the union to urge greater diligence by the regulator.

The role of unions generally becomes problematic at a time of falling trade union membership, which is apparently a worldwide phenomenon (Gunningham and Johnstone, 1999: 5; Kuruvilla *et al.*, 2002: 439). Kuruvilla *et al.* (2002: 431) point out that, while the picture is different in each of the economies under study (i.e. China, India, Japan, Korea, Singapore, Taiwan, and the Philippines), there was a steady decline in union density across Asia in the 1990s. This is to be weighed up next to their 'union influence' measure which they describe as a proxy for the ability of labour unions to represent their potential membership in addition to exerting influence in the socioeconomic environment (Kuruvilla *et al.*, 2002: 433) based on ILO statistical data.

Not surprisingly, the density figures and the measure of influence are associated, but institutional conditions are very important in determining the strength of that association. For example, China has three times the union density of Singapore (i.e. 63.4 per cent compared to 19.8 per cent) but less than half the level of union influence (i.e. 1.15 compared to 0.38). They note that the Asian wage systems under examination generally show very low collective bargaining coverage and high degrees of decentralisation in their wage fixing structures, and while the Asian nations exhibit lower levels of influence than the European comparators used in the study, low density does not necessarily indicate low influence, and *vice versa* (Kuruvilla, 2002: 439). One wonders as to what extent these findings can be used to suggest that those Asian countries where union influence is reasonably high might also be able to influence government thinking on OHS matters.

7.5. Comparative Law: Theory, Methods and Issues

There are many possible purposes in any comparative legal study. Traditionally the main purposes of the comparative lawyers have been firstly to map or classify the laws of nations into families of laws and secondly to describe in micro-detail the working of those laws (Reimann, 2002: 675), which Twining (2000:174-192) sees as perpetuating the myth that law operates in a vacuum without context. Twining is also very critical of the atheoretical nature of much comparative legal writing, happy as it is merely to describe.

This is not new, of course. Otto Kahn-Freund (1978: 308), in warning of the political misuses of the comparative method, wrote of the importance of understanding and acknowledging underlying power structures within a legal culture. Kahn-Freund was also particularly alert to the ideological uses of the comparative method where it might be used to push legal reform of a deleterious kind by means of comparison with a so-called superior set of laws. Our purpose here is to broaden our legal perspective (Curran, 1998: 65) and to challenge the 'otherness' that women experience in the legal system.

We must make clear that while we have seen the male worker put forward as the benchmark against which women are measured, in no way is Australia put forward as some kind of national ideal to which the Southeast Asian countries under study should aspire. Next is a snapshot of the Australian situation concerning women and OHS laws that will support a comparative investigation of the laws in Singapore, Taiwan and Vietnam.

7.6. Experiences from Australia

In Australia the vast majority of workers (and that includes employees and non-employees) who work under OHS laws created and enforced by the state governments. This constitutional division between the state and federal governments sees only a limited co-ordinating role carried out by the federal government in addition to establishing OHS laws with respect to the employees of the federal government itself and merchant seafarers. The prosecution research carried out by me in the 1990s was entirely concentrated in the state of New South Wales and it is generally to that state to which we refer in the following comparison.

It is very well known that women experience a very different relationship with the workplace compared to male workers. This is partly because of the other unpaid work in the home which they perform and partly because their bodies physically react differently to men's when faced with similar hazards. Of course this does not often happen because across the world, women and men tend to work in very different occupations and in different industries. This gendered division of labour is not consistent between countries, suggesting the importance of local cultural differences, but the division of labour is a fact however differently constituted. The fact that women and men perform such different work tasks and are exposed to such different hazards has dramatic effects in the way in which prosecutions for work injury are carried out in New South Wales.

The history of development of the OHS laws in New South Wales is very much one of copying the British model. In the nineteenth century this was also true in other areas of employment law, e.g. trade union laws and truck laws. Perhaps, surprisingly in the light of that development, is that the creation of the peculiar conciliation and arbitration laws at the end of the 19th century followed not the British model but a thoroughly Australasian model.

This was initially developed in New Zealand and integrally involved the trade unions. The earliest OHS legislation in Britain appears to have been the 1802 Health and Morals of Apprentices Act (Johnstone, 2004: 34) which probably placed greater emphasis on the second rather than the first concern mentioned in the statute's title (Jamieson, 2001: 26). Machine guarding legislation famously followed in the Factory Act of 1844 but we would argue that the rest of the legislative energy of the Westminster Parliament in that century was devoted to the protection of maternal capacity amongst British working class women. Women were not so much regarded as workers with ordinary worker's rights but as future mothers of the Empire. Women were specifically kept out of certain industries, e.g. lead processing and associated manufacturing because evidence was available that foetal damage was likely.

That men might also be damaged was ignored. In the political climate of the time where *laissez-faire* attitudes still predominated amongst the influential classes it was considered that men could take care of themselves and that state intervention to protect them was an unnecessary interference with the rights of capital and a slur on the manhood of male workers. This political concern gained momentum through the century as it was fuelled by race fears that the British race (so-called) would be out-bred by the darker skinned parts of its own Empire and by its enemies in Europe. Interestingly, the enemies in Europe held the same fears as did the American cousins across the Atlantic. The Australian colonists were similarly concerned and banned Chinese labour migration and introduced a number of measures that we would unhesitatingly brand as racist today.

The so-called protective laws included (in New South Wales, at least) bans on working with lead and bans on lifting weights over 16 kilograms, unassisted. This had the result that women working under the NSW Factory Act of 1897 (and its successors until 1992) were not able to work in certain industrial concerns where unskilled work was particularly well paid, e.g. the Port Kembla steelworks. This clearly resulted in the kind of disadvantage referred to above in the author's discussion of Deborah Rhode's work. The legislation categorised women as different rather than equal, and this led to disadvantage. Interestingly, in the very many areas of typical women's work which remained effectively unregulated until the advent of the Robens-style Occupational Health and Safety Act of 1983, women were free to lift weights far greater than 16 kilograms, unassisted. Obvious examples include the work of nurses, child-care workers and teachers whose work was all beyond the purview of the factory legislation.

The 1983 Occupational Health and Safety Act (only recently superseded by the 2000 Act of the same name) followed the British Robens model of introducing a system of self-regulation by the workplace parties backed up by a regime of inspection by the state. The 1983 and 2000 versions of the Act differed in respect of representation of worker interests but were identical in terms of gender neutral language. The Acts contain no references to gender at all and no special provisions exist for the protection of women workers. The difference/equality debate appears to have been resolved in favour of the equality approach. In terms of protection from the effect of lead in various lead manufacturing processes steps have finally been taken to reduce the levels of exposure, which male workers may experience. In the same way a single standard for manual handling of heavy weights has been adopted nationally.

The narrative presented above would seem to suggest that women are now treated in New South Wales as workers with full rights, equal to those of male workers. The OHS legislation quite specifically does not treat them merely as mothers or potential mothers. Equality has been achieved (at least in terms of the legislation) but that is really only part of the story. To apply Naffine's categorisation of law which we used above, formal equality has been achieved by taking the obviously discriminatory effects out of the legislation. The language of the 1983/2000 Acts implies that female workers' needs are considered to be equal of those of men by the state. Unfortunately this is not borne out when we examine the prosecution history of the NSW Workcover Authority. We have argued elsewhere (Jamieson, 2001) that the practices of the Authority are in fact highly gendered and that many of the OHS needs of women are not met by the prosecution practices of that organisation.

Over many years the major resources of the Authority in respect of prosecutions have been devoted to two areas of work, namely construction and manufacturing. There is evidence that this is partly the result of historical practice going back to the days of the Factories, Shops and Industries Act, 1962 (the most recent iteration of the 19th century legislation, now repealed) and partly in response to the activism of the trade unions in those industries (Jamieson, 2001: 144-157). This has meant that up at least until 2000 when the inspectorial service was reorganised, few inspections and almost no prosecutions were taken by Workcover outside the construction and manufacturing industries. Not only were women's interests ignored in the perpetuation of these practices but clearly the interests of many male workers working outside these industries were also neglected. The symbolism thus is stark (Hawkins, 2002: 333). Some prosecutions are now being carried out beyond these industries but overcoming the practices and organisational culture of long standing does not happen quickly.

To sum up, we argue that while the obviously gendered and discriminatory language of the past has been eliminated by the reforms in the past 25 years, one must look beyond the words of the statute. Gendered implementation and administration of gender-neutral legislation and public policy can be just as disadvantageous to women workers (to use Rhode's language) as obviously sexist acts of Parliament. But what is the situation in our selected Southeast Asian countries?

7.7. Experiences in Taiwan and Vietnam

Of the three countries under examination, Singapore is most obviously closest to Australia in terms of economic, social, legal and political development. Singapore also shares some British background with Australia that includes legal history and form (Thio, 2004: 186-190) and English language and both are very much multicultural in composition. Taiwan's history is of course quite different as is its colonial history. This might also be said of Vietnam. In terms of legal system/family Taiwan also has many links with the civil law tradition of Europe, having largely adopted the German approach to law before the time of its foundation after the Chinese revolution of 1949 (Wang, 2002: 186 and 193-196). There are, however, remaining areas of non-adherence to legal regulation deriving from its history (Cooney, 2004). Vietnam, while having had a very different colonial history, is now developing a legal system which must deal not just with globalisation and the emancipation of women that we have described in relation to Australia, but also with the creation of a locally appropriate response to capital while remaining a socialist state (Gillespie, 2004: 146-157; Nicholson, 2002: 127-133).

Singapore's revised Factories Act of 1998 (original Act 1973) is very much a mixture of the old-style prescriptive factory legislation welded onto some aspects of the Robens regime that we have described above in relation to Britain and Australia. The legislation provides for inspection and the creation of workplace committees which are intended by the legislation to be part of the regime of self regulation by the workplace parties. Workers are always referred to as 'persons' (*vide* S.28 on the training and supervision of inexperienced workers). No specific provisions relating to women workers appear in the Act and as is the case in Australia, one wonders (prior to the fieldwork which must follow these observations) the extent to which women participate in the operation of the committees and other structures (especially where men and women work together). Maternity protection, however, is found in the Employment Act of 1968 in Clause 76. This is very much analogous to the situation in Australia where provisions for maternity leave and the like are to be found outside the OHS statutes.

Prima facie then, it would seem that the legislative situation of women workers in Singapore is very much like that described above in relation to Australia in that the legislation is written in gender neutral language (although this is not the case with all Singaporean legislation) and women are situated in the workplace as workers and not as mothers or potential mothers, which as we have seen above will almost inevitably lead to disadvantage. Fieldwork will suggest whether the implementation of that legislation is gendered or not and whether or not women workers in Singapore are disadvantaged in the terms we have established in this study.

The situation in our remaining two countries is quite different. In Taiwan the Labour Standards Law (revised in 2002) states clearly in Article 25 that employees must not be treated differently by their employer on the basis of sex. Article 49 of the same statute, however, lays down a complex and detailed scheme for the differential treatment of all women workers with respect to night work. This must be read in conjunction with the highly prescriptive Labour Safety and Health Law of 1974.

Less controversial would seem to be the maternity protection provisions which follow on immediately in Articles 50-52. More recently (i.e. in January 2002) we have seen the passage of a Gender Equality in Employment Law which mirrors the positive approach taken in these matters in Europe. (It is useful here to remember that there is no such law in Australia as the anti-discrimination statutes at state and federal levels merely provide a complaint mechanism rather than any positive legislative guarantees of equality). Inspection arrangements in Taiwan are light (Hwang, 1993: 279) and remain so (Wang, 2002: 196-207) in keeping with its developing status as is trade union membership and recognition (Wang, 2002: 190-191).

Presumably, projected field work will reveal the ways in which the inspectorate carries out its work. One might predict whether this is an under-resourced area of public policy (as discovered by this author on previous field work in Taiwan in 1993 and 1996). Priority in inspection activity will be given, as is appropriate to industries where fatalities occur. As we know from the Australian research, this will most likely be found in traditional areas of male work (Jamieson, 2001).

The Labour Code of the Socialist Republic of Vietnam of 1994 (amended on 2 April, 2002, becoming effective from January 1, 2003) contains specific provisions relating to women's work which seems not only designed to protect the maternal status of working women but also to encourage them into the paid workforce (see Articles 109 and 110). Foetal protection is specifically mentioned in Article 112 and this is detailed further in Article 113. Article 113 also specifically bans women from permanent work in mines (and here we are reminded of the British and Australian legislation of the mid-19th century which is now repealed due to the ongoing resentment of some male miners!). Further maternal protection is afforded in Article 115 which appears designed to protect women from heavy work in the later stages of their pregnancies.

Interestingly, menstruating women are entitled to 30 minutes of rest during the workday under Article 115/3. (One wonders whether this provision is actually used by the women workers.) Article 118/2 sees the legislative requirement that there should be an appropriate number of women inspectors among the labour inspectorate. *Prima facie*, these highly prescriptive differences based provisions are not dissimilar from those promulgated in Britain and Australia during the 19th century when rapid industrialisation took a particular toll on the health of working mothers (Luong, 2003). In a poor, still developing country the position of women will require much attention. Again, how this is managed in practice will only be revealed through empirical work.

7.8. Conclusions and Further Questions

Two principal hypotheses will be tested. In respect of Singapore it will be whether, while gender neutral laws sit on the statute books, the laws are actually administered in a way that does not ignore the OHS concerns of women workers. The results, one might hypothesise in Taiwan and Vietnam, may be more problematic. Put simply, we seek to measure the extent to which appropriately framed laws may produce unintended consequences where women workers become invisible to the regulatory agencies of the state. It may be possible to begin to develop an analysis of these laws that incorporates some sense of historical progress in the framing of the laws that may be dependent on economic development. Over time, the effect of globalisation may be apparent where it is not apparent in the framing of the laws now. That effect may well only surface in the way in which law is implemented.

The next step in this project is to be able to measure the way in which the laws in the three Southeast Asian countries actually operate in workplaces. This will involve an analysis of the way in which the inspectorates go about their work in circumstances that may be either under-resourced because the problem is simply too big in a developing nation or because conscious decisions have been made within the nation State that serious regulation is inappropriate where a low-wage development strategy operates. From such a study, proposals for reforms that benefit women workers should develop. That reform should recognise the specificity of the hazards women face at the workplace without reducing them to the status of mothers who work, and denying them their full status as industrial citizens.

References

Bell, G. (1999). "The Singapore Legal System in Context-Whither the Concept of the National Legal System", in K. Tan (ed.), *The Singapore Legal System*, Singapore University Press, Singapore.

Bohle, P. and M. Quinlan (2000). *Managing Occupational Health and Safety-A Multidisciplinary Approach*, second edition, Macmillan, Melbourne.

Collins, H. (2003). *Employment Law*, Oxford University Press, Oxford.

Cooney, S. (2004). "The Effects of Rule of Law Principles in Taiwan", in R. Peerenboom (ed), *Asian Discourses of Law-Theories and Implementation of Rule of Law in Twelve Asian Countries* , France and the U.S., Routledge, London.

Cooney, S., T. Lindsey, R. Mitchell and Y. Zhu (eds.) (2002). *Law and Labour Market Regulation in East Asia*, Routledge, London.

Cooney, S. and R. Mitchell (2002). "What is Labour Law Doing in East Asia?" in S., Cooney, T. Lindsey, R. Mitchell, and Y. Zhu (eds.), *Law and Labour Market Regulation in East Asia*, Routledge, London.

Curran, V. (1998). "Dealing in Difference: Comparative Law's Potential for Broadening Legal Perspectives", *American Journal of Comparative Law*, 46 : 657-668.

Deery, S. and R. Mitchell (eds.) (1993). *Labour Law and Industrial Relations in Asia*, Longman Cheshire, Melbourne.

Gillespie, J. (1995). "Current Directions in the Vietnamese Commercial Legal System", in A. Tay and C. Leung (eds.), *Vietnam: An Emerging Giant in the Asia-Pacific Region*, Continuing Legal Education, The University of Sydney.

————. (1999). "Vietnam: Legal Framework for Foreign Investment and Trade", in A. Tay (ed.), *East Asia—Human Rights, Nation-Building, Trade*, Nomos Verlagsgesellschaft, Baden-Baden.

————. (2004). "Concept of Law in Vietnam: Transforming Statist Socialism", in R. Peerenboom (ed.), *Asian Discourses of Law-Theories and Implementation of Rule of Law in Twelve Asian Countries, France and the U.S.*, Routledge, London.

Gunningham, N. and R. Johnstone (1999). *Regulating Workplace Safety: System and Sanctions*, Oxford University Press, Oxford.

Haines, F. (2003). "Regulatory Reform in Light of Regulatory Character: Assessing Industrial Safety Change in the Aftermath of the Kader Factory Fire in Bangkok, Thailand", *Social and Legal Studies*, 12: 461-487.

Hawkins, K. (2002). *Law as Last Resort: Prosecution Decision–Making in a Regulatory Agency*, Oxford University Press, Oxford.

Hwang, Y. (1993). "Taiwan" in S. Deery, and R. Mitchell (eds.), *Labour Law and Industrial Relations in Asia*, Longman Cheshire, Melbourne.

ILO (International Labour Organization) (2002). *Seventh Synthesis Report on the Working Conditions Situation in Cambodia's Garment Sector*, ILO, Geneva.

————. (2003). *Time for Equality at Work-Global Report under the Follow-up to the ILO Declaration on Fundamental Principles and Rights at Work*, ILO, Geneva.

James, P. (1993). *The European Community: A Positive Force for UK Health and Safety Law?*, Institute of Employment Rights, London.

Jamieson, S. (2001). *Invisible Women Workers: Women and Prosecution for Work Injury in New South Wales*, unpublished SJD thesis, Faculty of Law, University of Sydney.

————. (2004). "Feminist Theory, Globalisation and Comparative Law: Women Workers in Australia and Ireland", *International Journal of Human Resource Management, 15:* 459-465.

Johnstone, R. (2004). *Occupational Health and Safety Law and Policy-Text and Materials*, Thomson, Sydney.

Kahn-Freund, O. (1978). *Selected Writings*, Stevens, London.

Kerkvliet, B. (2003). "Authorities and the People: An Analysis of State-Society Relations in Vietnam", in H. Luong (ed.), *Post-war Vietnam–Dynamics of a Transforming Society*, Institute of Southeast Asian Studies, Singapore.

Kuruvilla, S., S. Das, H. Kwon and S. Kwon (2002). "Trade Union Growth and Decline in Asia", *British Journal of Industrial Relations*, 40: 431-461.

Lamm, F. (2000). "Occupational Health and Safety Regulation: A New Zealand Perspective", in P. Bohle, and M. Quinlan (eds.), *Managing Occupational Health and Safety-A Multidisciplinary Approach*, second edition, Macmillan, Melbourne.

Luong, H. (2003). "Gender Relations: Ideologies, Kinship Practices, and Political Economy", in H. Luong (ed.), *Post-War Vietnam—Dynamics of a Transforming Society*, Institute of Southeast Asian Studies, Singapore.

————. (ed.) (2003). *Post-War Vietnam–Dynamics of a Transforming Society*, Institute of Southeast Asian Studies, Singapore.

Naffine, N. (ed.) (1990). *Law and the Sexes: Explorations in Feminist Jurisprudence*, Allen and Unwin, Sydney.

Nicholson, P. (2002). "Vietnam's Labour Market: Transition and the Role of Law", in S. Cooney, T. Lindsey, R. Mitchell and Y. Zhu (eds.), *Law and Labour Market Regulation in East Asia*, Routledge, London.

Parker, C. (2002). *The Open Corporation–Effective Self-regulation and Democracy*, Cambridge University Press, Cambridge.

Peerenboom, R. (ed). (2004). *Asian Discourses of Law-Theories and Implementation of Rule of Law in Twelve Asian Countries, France and the US*, Routledge, London.

Picciotto, S. (2002). "Introduction: Re-conceptualising Regulation in the Era of Globalisation", *Journal of Law and Society*, 29: 1-11.

Reimann, M. (2002). "The Progress and Failure of Comparative Law in the Second Half of the Twentieth Century", *American Journal of Comparative Law*, 50: 671-700.

Rhode, D. (1989). *Justice and Gender*, Harvard University Press, Cambridge, MA.

Robens, Lord (1972). *Report of the Committee on Safety and Health at Work*, HMSO, London.

Scully, C. and R. Johnstone (2004). "The Nature of Regulatory Compliance: An Analysis of the Responses of Business Organisations to Constitutive Regulation of Working Relationships", in *New Economies: New Industrial Relations-Proceedings of the 18th AIRAANZ Conference*, Volume 2 Un-refereed Papers, AIRAANZ, Noosa.

Tan, K. (1999). *The Singapore Legal System*, Singapore University Press, Singapore.

Tay, A. (ed). (1999). *East Asia–Human Rights, Nation-Building, Trade*, Nomos Verlagsgesellschaft, Baden-Baden.

Tay, A. and C. Leung (eds.) (1995). *Vietnam: An Emerging Giant in the Asia-Pacific Region*, Continuing Legal Education, The University of Sydney.

Thio, L. (2004). "Rule of Law within a Non-liberal 'Communitarian' Democracy: The Singapore Experience", in R. Peerenboom (ed.), *Asian Discourses of Law-Theories and Implementation of Rule of Law in Twelve Asian Countries, France and the U.S.*, Routledge, London.

Thompson, E. (1968). *The Making of the English Working Class*, Penguin, London.

Todd, P., R. Lansbury and E. Davis (2004). "Industrial Relations in Malaysia: Some Proposals for Reform", in *New Economies: New Industrial Relations—Proceedings of the 18th AIRAANZ Conference*, Volume 2 Un-refereed Papers, AIRAANZ, Noosa.

Twining, W. (2000). *Globalisation and Legal Theory*, Butterworths, London.

Wang, H., S. Cooney (2002). "Taiwan's Labour Law: The End of State Corporatism?", in S. Cooney, T. Lindsey, R. Mitchell and Y. Zhu (eds.), *Law and Labour Market Regulation in East Asia* , Routledge, London.

Woolfson, C. (1995). *Deregulation: The Politics of Health and Safety*, University of Glasgow, Glasgow.

Workcover Authority of NSW (2003). "Annual Report", Workcover, Sydney.

————. (2004). *Compliance-Policy and Prosecution Guidelines*, Workcover, Sydney.

8

Promotion and Regulation of the Informal Economy in Southeast Asia

LUCITA LAZO

8.1. Introduction

The debate on the informal economy has spanned three decades since the coinage of the term by the International Labour Office in the 1970s in Kenya. Scholarly works on informal employment have been done in Latin America, Africa and Asia.

Why the attention on the informal sector? Contrary to orthodox economic thinking, informal employment did not disappear even when economies were supposed to have modernised and industrialised. Globally, the informal sector appears to be growing for varied reasons. For example, poverty and the need for survival, and the lack of employment opportunities may have pushed the growth of street vendors in Nairobi or Manila rather than the avoidance of regulations imposed on merchants in the formal sector.

A World Bank study showed that in the mid-1990s, about 57 per cent of non-agricultural employment in Latin America and the Caribbean was in the informal sector. The comparable figure for Africa was high as 78 per cent while the informal sector accounted for 83 per cent of newly created jobs in Latin America and 93 per cent in Africa. In Asia, 45-85 per cent of non-agricultural employment is in the informal sector (Charmes, 1998, cited in WIEGO, 2000: 8) Employment outside the formal sector accounts for 15 per cent in high-income countries and 80 per cent in the low-income countries.

The potential for generating surplus and wealth accumulation exists in the ranks of the informal enterprises and workers and could be a 'crucial factor in determining the long-run evolution of the informal sector in both developed and developing countries' (Swaminathan, 1991: 4). However, this aspect needs more empirical study. How many informal workers emerge with enterprises of their own over the long term?

A large number of women workers are employed in the informal sector and they constitute a significant proportion of all women workers. Estimates of women in the informal sector, however, are not very reliable as many women workers are engaged in home-based activities that tend to be omitted from official records and statistics. The majority of women in the informal sector are either self-employed traders/producers or casual/sub-contract workers; relatively few are employer-owners who hire others to work for them.

At the lowest end of the ladder of informal workers are home-workers who are sometimes viewed as disguised wage workers. Home-workers perform piece rated jobs under sub-contracting arrangements from formal enterprises and in some instance, informal enterprises.

Average incomes of both men and women are lower in the informal sector than in the formal sector and the gap exists even when women are self-employed. The gender gap in incomes appears higher in the informal sector, largely due to two relatively interrelated factors:

- Informal incomes worldwide tend to decline as one moves across the following types of employment: employer, self-employed, casual wage worker, sub-contract worker or outworker.

- Within the informal sector, women are under-represented in high-income activities and over-represented in low income activities (notably, sub-contract or industrial outwork).

Globalisation and trade liberalisation are fuelling the growth of the informal economy. The new economic order has led to stiffer competition among producers all over the world and has pushed firms to streamline for greater productivity and efficiency and to practice labour flexibilisation and casualisation. One consequence of this is downsizing leading to job cuts which in turn push retrenched workers into the formal economy. The Asian financial crisis dramatised this phenomenon so well.

In Southeast Asia, there have been concerted efforts in policy-making *vis-à-vis* informal employment and there is an emerging grassroots movement on informal employment in Thailand, Indonesia and the Philippines. The issue became particularly acute and visible during the Asian financial crisis of 1997 which drove the laid-off workers into informal enterprises and/or informal employment. For example, in Thailand the impetus to count home workers and informal workers came out of the government's desire to come to the rescue of those who were badly hit by the crisis, many of whom went into informal employment.

In this chapter, we shall focus on the experience in Southeast Asia in policymaking for the informal economy. Pragmatic responses that emerged from the financial crisis of 1997 have helped crystallise and consolidate official policy in respect of informal workers. The process continues to evolve up to this day.

8.2. Understanding the Informal Sector

After many years of work, the debate on defining the informal sector continues. Even with the passage of the ILO Convention 177 on Homework, the notion of the informal sector has eluded a firm definition, usually settled at country level by adopting an operational definition.

Banerjee (2002), a scholar in economics, states "there is no agreement on the set of economic characteristics or conditions that are essential to identify an informal sector activity ... reviewing these numerous studies one can only conclude that the defining characteristic of the informal sector is its capacity to accommodate a mixture of widely differing productive activities." She argues that the term informal sector has no meaningful definition that can be used for cross-country comparison or, in some cases, even within country comparisons. However, in practice, the informal sector does include several distinct kinds of work and that worker in each can be identified through standardised definitions and procedures.

She further suggests that the core of the informal sector includes:

- The self-employed form an enterprise, accept all risks of production involved and also perform at least a part of the necessary labour in the production; employ some productive resources owned, borrowed or acquired by usufruct rights,   take their own production decisions.

- Casual wage workers working outside the household for a wage, either in cash or in kind, who have no time contract and no security of employment. The wage may be paid by a piece rate or time rate.

- Regular wage workers working outside the household who have a time-bound contract but no long-term security of employment.

- Home-based workers working on work put out to them by distant employers on piece-rated payment. They bear the costs of providing some inputs, such as space and power, may use their own tools and bear some risk of their finished work being rejected without payment. Employment is strictly at the discretion of the employer.

- Unpaid workers who work in any productive industry but have no decision-making rights, get no wage for the work they do even though they may bear a share of the risks.

- Productive workers in the care economy working on those tasks that produce for the use of household members, goods and services for which substitutes are readily available on request.

When an enterprise is in the informal sector then the workers in that enterprise belong to what can be termed as informal sector employment. The reverse is not always true.

Of the many characteristics used to identify the informal sector, the following three features of an activity recur frequently in the literature—regulation by the state forms of ownership and nature of employment.

There is a need to distinguish between informal enterprises and informal employment. Informal enterprises are those whose existence or status is not regulated i.e. licensing, such as obtaining a permit from authority or registration. Informal employment is where labour process and conditions of work are outside the sphere of public scrutiny. Employment in the informal sector has been defined as comprising of self-employed workers, family workers and causal labourers; where there is no regulation of employment contracts.

There is a link between the formal and informal sectors of the economy. The two sectors could be seen as part of a continuum of economic activities. The informal sector is heterogeneous. It is made of sub-sectors including—home workers; street vendors and traders: small construction operators; small transport operators such as pedicab drivers and others, i.e. service workers like laundry women, etc.

The informal sector remains an integral part of most economies of the developing world and is unlikely to disappear. Initially, the informal sector was regarded as a 'residual set of production relations carried over from more primitive stages of development'. It was considered as a transitory phenomenon that would disappear with political and economic modernisation.

As economies reach higher stages of development, it was earlier expected that the informal sector would wither away. In the meanwhile, the sector was not seen as a major contributor to the national product but as a means of livelihood for many who had failed to find a living in the modern economy (Banerjee, 2002).

8.3. Policy Implications of the Informal Sector: Experience in Southeast Asia

Informal employment involves micro and small enterprises and has been used as a deliberate strategy for promoting job creation and employment. But, there are those who disagree with such an approach for varied reasons, namely: 1) that informal sector is the breeding ground for vulnerability and exploitation which come in the form of women and child labour, low wages and poor working conditions, long hours of work, income and social insecurity; 2) low growth potential of many subsistence and survival firms and to support them would mean economic inefficiency; 3) marginal contribution to government revenues.

> "It is commonly believed that the Urban Informal Sector (UIS) and governments are antagonistic to each other because being outside the domain of laws and government regulations, the UIS does not contribute to government revenues, and more importantly calls into question the legitimacy of government by demonstrating the limits to its powers. Yet the evidence from developing countries indicates that governments have lately devised various policies to facilitate income and employment generation within the UIS" (Sanyal, 1991: 54).

An array of questions has been posed in respect of policies on the informal sector. For example, to what extent should the state be involved in the informal economy? Should the informal sector be encouraged? Should the state support small firms or large firms or should it withdraw from intervening in the market (deregulation, debureaucratisation and privatisation)? How should the appropriate and efficient institutional environment needed for democracy and a market economy be achieved? Should the informal sector be regulated? What are the implications of promotion of the informal sector for changing the balance of power, for long range planning, for implementation of programmes and plans, for the legitimacy of the state?

Bringing informal into the policy arena and supporting micro-enterprises may lead to empowerment and democratisation but will it lead to a more rational and competitive economy? Should the most dynamic firms be promoted, should the playing field be levelled, or should competition be allowed to weed out the most inefficient? Would expansion of the informal sector be a better means of creating jobs and increasing production? Should policy focus on 'modern' activities for export markets or on small enterprises that cater to local markets?

Should and can the informal sector be incorporated into formal sectors (e.g. legalised, taxed) or provided special privileges and subsidies even if it is unlikely that they can graduate to formal status? How should the self-employed and small enterprises be included in decision-making and policy formulation? What kind of social protection should be extended to them?

Regulation refers to the specific rules and regulations imposed by the state on economic activities. In the formal sector, labour legislation serves as the framework for work relations and thus workers are protected. In contrast, informal enterprises or informal workers are excluded from labour legislation; therefore, the informal sectors are unregulated by the institutions of society in a legal and social environment in which similar activities are regulated" (Swaminathan, 1991: 21).

The De Soto study of the informal sector in Peru concludes that state intervention and regulation hinder the development of enterprises and so calls for a new kind of legal system, one that promotes "economic efficiency...to allow informal activities to develop their full potential." De Soto calls for greater private property rights and less state intervention (Swaminathan, 1991: 23).

There are those who advocate 'virtual neglect' of small enterprises, concentrating resources on building up large capitalist or state-owned firms. In this view, strategies to help small enterprises are simply regressive, slowing the overall development process and the redistribution of capital and labour associated with that process" (Bromley, 1978: 1037).

The debates on the formal-informal dichotomy have raged from the 1970s to date and have not been categorically resolved. While the theoretical debate raged on, globalisation and liberalisation spawned more informal employment with flexibilisation and casualisation in the world of work.

Meantime, grassroots practitioners and civil societies in developing countries have proceeded to organise workers in informal employment and to advocate for and promote their social protection. Global movements such as the WIEGO (Women in Informal Employment: Globalising and Organising) and the HOMENET (Network of Home workers) and Clean Clothes Campaigns in the UK and North America have emerged to address the social issues surrounding those in informal employment and casual work in the nineties.

One result of the global, regional and national campaigns is the adoption of a global policy in 1996–ILO 177, the Convention on Home Work which stipulates provisions for home workers, which includes the self-employed and those working under subcontracting arrangements.

8.4. The Policy Experience in Southeast Asia

The campaign for social protection of informal workers began as early as the 1970s when the Self-employed Women's Association of India was established under the leadership of a former trade union leader, Ela Bhatt. Similar movements emerged in Southeast Asia, particularly Thailand, Indonesia and the Philippines under an ILO technical cooperation programme launched in June 1988. Worldwide, parallel movements such as the organisation of street traders in South Africa had also begun. The main advocacy was for social protection of informal workers. The campaign found greater visibility in the late nineties.

In Southeast Asia, the debate on the informal sector was virtually mooted by the 1997 Asian financial crisis, which dramatised the informal workers' need for social protection. The crisis meant joblessness for many; and informal work became the coping response. One common example is the conversion of erstwhile millionaires to sandwich vendors in Bangkok during the crisis, to graphically illustrate the turn to informal employment.

Because many of the own account workers and casual workers were vulnerable to the pauperising impact of the crisis, the entry of government to provide for social safety nets became the order of the day. Because many informal workers belonged to the poor or near poor and vulnerable groups who were affected by the crisis they were the object of government intervention to extend social protection.

The crisis was a blessing in disguise for the informal sector because it brought forth policies to assist them. In Thailand and Indonesia which were hit hard by the crisis, social protection measures were expanded to cover those impacted by the crisis.

In the Philippines, the informal sector saw major impetus for government support which fostered organising the sector, representing them in government bodies such as the National Anti-Poverty Commission under the Arroyo administration. With UNDP technical support, a country programme on the informal sector had been drawn up and adopted at the level of the national development planning body with the consensus of Cabinet undersecretaries.

The strategic issues of the informal sector were identified to be: invisibility, lack of access and control over productive resources and lack of access to social protection. Policy measures were, therefore, designed to address these strategic issues and in effect, recognised and acknowledged the existence of the sector in the economy.

Invisibility is a compound of statistical and legal invisibility which leads to invisibility in policy, programmes and budgets. Informal workers are among the statistical category of unpaid family workers, self-employed or own account workers. An exact count of them is hard to obtain because definitions are unclear and there are no specific categories to enumerate them. This implies reforming statistical systems in order to accommodate the proper enumeration of informal workers as well as the quantification of their economic contribution in the gross national product. Not all countries were open to statistical reforms of this nature, however.

The consequence of the statistical invisibility of the informal sector is the absence of institutional support, assistance and services to facilitate their access to economic and social empowerment. This also implies lack of access to social protection because their income poverty makes it difficult for them to be part of established social insurance systems which require monthly premiums or contributions.

8.5. Reducing Invisibility: Counting the Informal Workers and their Contribution to the Economy

The matter of visibility and counting the informal workers drew official attention during the financial crisis of 1997. For instance, in

Thailand, the reluctance to count informal workers in national statistics softened considerably as the Thai government strongly felt the need to know and track how many needed to be assisted by government as a result of the crisis.

Added to this is the greater willingness to factor-in the gender dimensions in national statistics on the recognition that many women were bearing the brunt of the crisis as well as the fact that women form the bulk of those in informal employment. For example, over 85 per cent of home-based workers in most countries are women (HOMENET). Home-based workers comprise a significant share of the work force in key industries and increasingly, in service industries. In Asia and Latin America, home-based workers account for 40-50 per cent of the work force in key export industries, notably textiles, garments, and footwear.

Efforts to quantify the economic contribution of informal workers have been initiated in both the Philippines and Thailand and other Asian countries, partly as an initiative to concretise the value of women's unpaid work and show women's unrecognised value in the national economy. Such initiatives were stimulated and supported by the UN agencies including the UNIFEM, UNESCAP and UNDP. This is still work in progress.

8.6. Voice and Political Representation: Organising the Informal Workers

A vital change in official policy was the inclusion of women in national consultations and decision making. For example, home-workers in Thailand, through their organisation, the HOMENET, were consulted in the implementation of the health insurance scheme. Likewise, in the Philippines, an Informal Sector Council was formed as part of the National Anti-Poverty Commission (NAPC) and was constructively engaged in high-level policy discussions that reached the level of the President. This constructive engagement was put to good use in the crackdown on street vendors of the Metropolitan. Manila authorities which reclaimed footpaths and pavements from the peddlers and vendors that plied the public spaces and city streets.

An important prerequisite to this was the proper organisation of the informal workers so that the process of consultation and dialogue with them could be systematically approached by the national and local government authorities. The crackdown on street vendors in

Metro Manila gave further impetus for the street vendors of Metro Manila to organise and dialogue with their respective local and city governments who had the ultimate say in the fate of their livelihood—street vending.

A consequent policy challenge to the local and city governments was how to balance the provision of livelihood, employment and income to the urban informal workers and the recovery of public goods—the city streets, walkways, and footpaths. A genuine clash of interest between the informal sector and general public led to acrimonious battles between the city authorities and informal workers in Metro Manila. Dialogues upon dialogues were held to harmonise interests and find appropriate solutions and alternative vending sites for the street vendors.

8.7. Facilitating Access to Productive Resources

Essential to releasing whatever dormant dynamism that existed in the informal sector was their access to productive resources, namely skills training, credit, market linkages and technology to increase productivity. Economic empowerment of the informal workers was an important ingredient in enabling their micro-enterprises and products to become competitive and ensure stable and regular income over the long term.

Policies of this nature were relevant to the own account and self-employed workers among the informal sectors but of less impact to those in home-based subcontract work or casual wage work. The need for special policies geared for the informal workers became necessary because small enterprise policies often cover those that are well above the micro-enterprises of the informal sector (i.e. firms with capitalisation of one million baht/pesos and/or with employees of 10 and above). Hence, small enterprise promotion policies tend to skip informal enterprises and workers.

For the more dependent groups such as the subcontracted home-workers, the pertinent policy reform was their inclusion in the social insurance systems which were generally designed for wage workers. In both the Philippines and Thailand, social reforms have led to schemes that brought the homeworkers into the fold by treating them as self-employed workers making their monthly contributions. These policy changes occurred as a result of nearly a decade of advocacy among the homeworkers of Thailand and the Philippines.

8.8. Regulatory Measures for the Informal Sector

The regulation of workers in informal employment continues to exist alongside the promotional policies. In fact, there are current efforts to formulate and enforce regulatory measures in respect of the informal sector. Examples can be cited from Thailand and the Philippines, especially in the regulation of street vendors.

In Thailand, a number of regulations for street vendors were issued from the year 2000 onwards. The Governor of Bangkok issued a notification on street vendor trading to bar vendors from the street every Wednesday and to declare guidelines for selling products in public spaces:

- Vendors can sell at spots arranged by the Bangkok Metropolitan Authority (BMA) everyday without having to pay any fees, but for cleaning service of the footpath on which they put their stalls, as provided by the BMA Municipality Statute on Fees B.E. 2543.

- Should any vendors be required to pay fees besides the cleaning service, they should notify the Governor, or the Office of Municipality, or the BMA's Complaint Centre.

- All vendors must strictly observe regulations issued by the BMA, cleaning and putting away stalls after selling.

The BMA procedures to regulate vendors include: 1) survey and regulate the vendors, only those who have been practising this trade are allowed to continue their occupation; 2) colour spray is used to draw the lines for specified areas, each of which is well numbered; 3) create identity cards for vendors, or ask from other vendors to establish if a particular vendor always comes to use the vendor space; 4) put up signs that specify durations of street vending.

The BMA started to enforce the BMA regulation regarding the collection of fee for cleaning footpath used by street vendors. Officers from the Department of Sanitation and Environment of each district were assigned to collect the cleaning fee. Every 15 days, the fee is collected for 150 baht per one square metre per month with a receipt given to vendor (Daily News Online, 2001).

In addition, there are efforts to formulate labour regulations to protect home workers in Thailand. Discussions are now ongoing for a Home workers' Act.

In the Philippines, regulation is explicitly provided for in the Labour Code. The basic policy of the Labour Code is that: "The state shall afford protection to labour, promote full employment, ensure equal work opportunities regardless of sex, race or creed, and regulate the relations between workers and employees. The state shall assure the rights of workers to self-organisation, collective bargaining, security of tenure, and just and humane conditions of work."

Under the Labour Code, there are laws and issuances intended to provide protection to the informal sector. These are Articles 154 and 155, Rule XIX, Book III of Implementing Rules. Specifically, Article 155 of the Labour Code directs the Secretary of Labour to regulate employment of industrial home workers.

In the 1990s Department Order No.5 of the Implementing Rules of Book III of the Labour Code on employment of home workers was promulgated, which provided for:

- the right to self-organisation of home workers and the registration of home-workers' organisations which "shall be entitled to the rights and privileges granted by law to legitimate labour organisations" ;

- registration of employer, contractor, and sub-contractor;

- immediate payment for homework after delivery of goods, and remittance by the contractor/sub-contractor or employer of contribution to the SSS, Medicare, and ECC;

- standard output rates determined by time and motion studies to equalise piece rates received by workers in the factory or main undertaking of the employer and home workers performing the same job or activity, individual/collective agreement between employers and home workers or tripartite consultations among representatives of government, employers and workers;

- prohibition of any deduction from home workers' earnings for materials lost, destroyed, soiled or damaged save for certain conditions;

- requirement for home worker to redo the work improperly executed or returned only once without payment;

- liability of the employer, jointly and severally with the contractor or subcontractor if the latter fails to pay wages or earnings of his/her workers;

- regulation of employment of minors as home workers;
- prohibition of homework in dangerous occupations;

In South Korea, as an aftermath of the 1997 economic crisis, "irregular workers totalled 50 per cent of the overall workforce. Women were the first to be fired from their jobs and delegated to irregular work. It was difficult for women to fight against the patriarchal, male-oriented society.... protests by regular workers who had been transferred to irregular employment have been continuing since 2000..... wages of these workers are 40-80 per cent of that of the regular workers. This difference is continuously increasing and the wages of women irregular workers are only 40 per cent of the wages of male regular workers. In the banking sector, sex differentials in wages could range from 23-83 per cent of men's wages. In addition, irregular workers are excluded from insurance" (Park and Choi, 2004: 3, 5, 19).

Under the current Korean labour laws, all workers have the right to get legal protection regardless of type of employment. Discrimination against irregular workers obviously belies this provision of law. However, initiatives have begun to bring the phenomenon of irregular work into the fold of the law and regulate it. Thus, in 2003, the South Korean government announced the abolition of discrimination as one of its major targets and the Ministry of Labour announced its intention to call for legislation to prevent discrimination against irregular workers. The Presidential Commission of Labour has called for legislation of a special law to guarantee formation of unions, collective bargaining, maternity protection and other working conditions and protective measures for the application of industrial accident insurance (Park and Choi 2004: 18). The case of South Korea clearly illustrates a trend toward reregulation.

8.9. Conclusions

Globallydriven events such as the Asian financial crisis in 1997 have effectively overtaken the theoretical and policy debate on the informal sector in Southeast Asia. Pragmatic policies to redress the situation of the poor, a category that overlapped to a large extent with the workers in informal employment became the moral imperative. As a result, countries like the Philippines and Thailand evolved a policy mix that addressed the strategic issues of the informal sector—invisibility, lack of access to productive resources and lack of social protection.

The informal sector is not homogeneous and would therefore require a mix of policy interventions in accordance with the critical issues and concerns of the sub-sectors. Clearly, there is a role for the state, particularly in ensuring that the informal workers do not fall through the bottom of the income and social ladder. Regulation as in the case of hawkers and vendors remains with the state.

Releasing economic dynamism from the ranks of the informal enterprises is a function that would require promotion and encouragement on a selective or purposive basis. An assessment of economic growth potential would be necessary in the process of provisioning social services such as credit, technology and market links.

The phenomenon of the informal sector is now gaining better recognition and acknowledgement by the official authorities. Initial fuzziness of the notion is gaining some degree of clarity. Further work in research and policy is needed at country level to address the needs of the informal economy.

References

Banerjee, Nirmala (2002) *Gender-Sensitive Statistical Measures for the Informal Sector*, UNIFEM.

Bromley, Ray (1978). "The Urban Informal Sector–Why is it Worth Discussing?", *World Development*, Pergammon Press, 6, (9/10): 1033-1039.

Case Study Report: Problems and Possible Solutions for Stall Sellers and Street Vendors, unpublished paper read at the CAW Workshop in Bangkok, 16-18 March 2004, Bangkok, Thailand.

Parilla, Josephine and Cabanilla Phoebe (2004). *Legal Policies and the Situation of Women in the Informal Sector in the Philippines*, unpublished draft, March, Bangkok.

Rakowski, Cathy (1994). "Convergence and Divergence in the Informal Sector Debate: A Focus on Latin America, 1984-92", *World Development*, 22, (4): 501-516.

Sanyal, Bishwapriya (1991). "Organising the Self-Employed: The Politics of the Urban Informal Sector, *ILO Review*, 130, (1): 39–54.

Standing, Guy (1999). "Global Feminisation Through Flexible Labour: A Theme Revisited", *World Development*, 27, (3): 583-602.

Swaminathan, Madhura (1991). *Understanding the Informal Sector: A Survey*, Centre for International Studies, pp. 1- 39, Cambridge, Massachusetts, July.

Women in Informal Employment: Globalising and Organising (WIEGO), Carr Centre for Human Rights, Kennedy School of Government, Harvard University, Cambridge.

9

Pension Regulation in Japan: Issues and Reforms

HARUKA URATA
NORIYUKI TAKAYAMA

9.1. Structure of Japanese Retirement System

The current Japanese retirement system consists of the three-tiered system. The first and the second tiers are the social security system. Participation in the social security system is mandatory. The third tier is employer-sponsored private retirement system.

The first tier, National Pension (NP), provides flat amount benefits based on years of participation. All Japanese citizens who are between age 20 and 60 must participate in NP. About 70.2 million people participated in NP as of the end of March 2002. Self-employed, farmers, their spouses, and students pay a fixed contribution of 13,300 yen per month, regardless of their income level. On the other hand, employees and their dependent spouses do not need to pay contributions to NP. Instead, employees pay contributions to Employee's Pension Insurance (EPI) or Mutual Aid Pension (MAP). Their contributions include NP ones. Minimum 25 years of participation is required to receive old age benefits. Benefits start at the age of 65 and benefit levels depend on contribution periods. If you continue to pay contributions for 40 years, you can receive the maximum benefit, which is 66,000 yen per month from age 65. Benefits are fully indexed to inflation. If contribution period is less than 40 years (480 months), benefits are reduced accordingly. Two-thirds of funds for paying benefits come from contributions and subsidies from EPI and MAP. The remaining one-third and operational expenses are budgeted by the government. Although the Japanese social security is operated as pay-as-you-go system, there are some accumulated assets. NP had the assets of 9.9 trillion yen as of the end of March 2001.

The second tier, Employee's Pension Insurance (EPI), provides earning-related benefits to private sector full-time employees. Part-time employees who work for three quarters or more of working hours of regular full-time employees also participate in EPI. Employees under the age of 70 who work for corporations or for sole proprietorships that are always hiring 5 or more employees must join EPI. 32.1 million people participated in EPI as of March 31, 2003. Employers and their employees each pay one-half of the contributions. The current contribution rate is 13.58 per cent of monthly standard remuneration and of standard bonus. Participants receive fixed benefits (NP portion) and earnings-related benefits as old age benefits. Benefit levels are indexed to reflect wage increase and price increase. EPI had assets of 137.4 trillion yen as of the end of March 2001.

The second tier for public employees, Mutual Aid Pension (MAP), is operated separately from Employee's Pension Insurance. There are three kinds of MAP plans: National Public Service Personnel Mutual Aid Pension Plan, Local Government Officials Mutual Aid Pension Plan, and Private School Teacher and Employee Mutual Aid Pension Plan. About 5.2 million people participated in MAP as of March 31, 2002. EPI and the three MAPs adopt different contribution rates. Nonetheless, the basic structure of MAPs is the same as EPI except that each MAP has additional benefits that correspond to employer-sponsored pension plans for private sector employees. MAP had assets worth 48.7 trillion yen as at end of March 2002.

The third tier is employer-sponsored retirement plans. Historically Japanese companies have paid lump-sum retirement benefits when employees leave companies. These lump-sum retirement plans are book-reserved systems. When two kinds of Defined Benefit (DB) plans, Qualified Pension Plan (QPP) and Employee Pension Fund (EPF) were introduced during the mid-1960s in Japan, many companies transferred all or part of the lump-sum retirement benefits into DB plans to take advantage of the tax benefits as well as to smooth out cash outflows. In October 2001, Defined Contribution (DC) Plan was introduced in Japan. Soon after that, another kind of DB plan, called New Defined Benefit Plan (New DB) was introduced in April 2002. They are different in terms of applicable laws, regulatory body, plan management rules, taxation, and so on. EPFs had assets worth 51.6 trillion yen and QPPs had assets worth 22.7 trillion yen at the end of March 2001. EPFs have

10.9 million participants and QPPs have 9.2 million participants as of the end of March 2002. Some employers adopt both EPF and QPP. As a result, the number of participants in these two plans has duplication. The number of DC plan participants was 645,000 as of November 2003. There are no public data available at present as to the new DB plan.

People voluntarily purchase individual annuity products from financial institutions to prepare for retirement by themselves. Self-employed can voluntarily participate in National Pension Fund to supplement their retirement provision.

This chapter focuses on regulations and deregulations of the Japanese third tier pensions. Discussions on Japanese social security pensions are beyond the scope of this chapter (see Takayama, 2004, for current reforms on social security pensions of Japan).

9.2. Environment Surrounding Japanese Retirement System

9.2.1. *Ageing and Future Reduction in Old-age Benefits of Social Security System*

Because of the rapid ageing and the decline in the number of births in the Japanese society, old-age benefits of the social security system are expected to be reduced. To compensate for the shrinkage of social security benefits, the role of private pension plans must be larger and larger.

9.2.2. *Adverse Investment Environments*

Since the bubble economy ended in the early 1990s, Japan has experienced sluggish stock market performance and super-low interest rates. Due to these adverse investment environments, employers were required to make additional contributions to the existing DB plans. However, most employers could not afford to do so in the depressed economy. Some employers have dissolved retirement benefit plans, leaving employees without employer-sponsored retirement provision. Many employers wanted to shift investment risks associated with DB plans to employees. As a result, employers and trade groups have requested the introduction of DC plans.

9.2.3. *New Accounting Rule on Benefit Obligation*

A new accounting rule similar to Financial Accounting Standard No. 87 in the US took effect in March 2001. Projected benefit obligations (PBO) under a defined benefit retirement scheme must be recognised and any unfunded portion must be disclosed on the company's balance sheet.

Japanese traditional book reserve retirement plans and funded defined benefit plans inflate companies' liabilities on the balance sheets under the new accounting rule, which is expected to impact companies' credit ratings and stock prices negatively. Many companies wanted to replace existing DB schemes with DC plans which have no PBO exposure or with cash balance plans which are somewhat immune to interest rate fluctuations. Employers and trade groups have demanded these new types of pension plans as these plans create a more predictable and manageable cost pattern.

9.2.4. New HR Policy (Performance-based Benefits)

Recently many companies are replacing seniority-based pay systems by performance-based pay systems. Traditional retirement benefit plans that favour long-time workers are not in line with them. More and more companies are trying to reflect individual work performance in retirement benefits. Companies are also trying to improve employee understanding and appreciation of retirement benefits. More visible retirement plans such as DC plans and cash balance plans with individual (hypothetical) accounts are preferred.

9.2.5. Breakdown of Lifetime Employment Model

The Japanese labour market is becoming increasingly mobile these days. To attract talented people in a labour market and to reward them properly, traditional retirement plan designs are not suitable.

9.2.6. Business Reorganisation

Mergers and acquisitions have become prevalent in Japan, after several deregulations on business reorganisation rules. Harmonisation of retirement benefits is required in M&A situations. Employer-sponsored pension plans need to be flexible to accommodate these organisational changes.

9.3. Company-sponsored Plans

Retirement benefits in Japan have traditionally been provided as cash lump sum benefits at the time of retirement/separation of employment, but pension/annuity provisions are becoming more prevalent. The amount of the benefit is usually lower in the case of voluntary termination (resignation) than in the case of involuntary termination (retirement, pre-retirement death, disability, discharge). Normal retirement age in Japan is often referred to as the mandatory retirement age. Market practice is age 60. This is now the legally mandated minimum age.

9.3.1. Defined Benefit (DB) Plans

Pay-related Plans

Pay-related plans are based on either final pay or career average pay. Benefits are defined as pensionable pay times a multiple, where the multiple is according to years of service and reason for termination. Pensionable salary is usually set as equal to monthly base salary. In some cases, pensionable salary is set equal to monthly standard remuneration (MSR), which is the social security pay base and is equal to total monthly salary-subject to a maximum of 620,000 yen per month.

Points Plans

Benefits are defined as equal to career accumulated points times a unit value. Points accrue annually based on the employee's salary grade or job position, age or service, or any combination of the above. Unit value is increased at employer's discretion or through union negotiation.

Cash Balance Plans

After Defined Benefit Corporate Pension Act became effective on April 1, 2002, Cash Balance plans are allowed to be established in Japan. Cash Balance plans are technically DB plans that look like DC plans.

9.3.2 DB Funding Alternatives

DB plans can be funded through various methods in Japan. The selection of the funding approach can be independent of the plan design. There are currently five different fund types for DB retirement plans:

- Retirement Allowance Plans (RAP);
- Employee Pension Funds (EPF);

- Qualified Pension Plans (QPP);
- Fund-Type New DB plans; and
- Agreement-Type New DB plans.

9.4. Retirement Allowance Plans (RAP)

A RAP is an unfunded plan, with liability recognised *via* a book reserve (accounting reserve). There used to be tax deductibility of RAP book reserves, but it effectively ended as of March 31, 2002.

The fund reserve is usually not segregated and security of accrued benefits depends upon the financial soundness of the employer. Because benefits are not funded, companies usually administer such plans themselves. For ease of administration, usually benefit payments are made in lump sum form only. Employers retain more flexibility to change RAPs than they do for other plan types.

9.5. Employee Pension Funds (EPF)

An EPF was introduced in October 1966 by amendment of Employee Pension Insurance Act, and now is one of the main private pension schemes in Japan. An EPF is a separate independent legal entity established by a single employer or jointly by several employers with the approval by the Minister of Health, Labour, and Welfare. An EPF is an externally funded plan and its principal purpose is the payment of old age pension benefits to participants. An EPF contracts out a part of the earnings-related old age pension under EPI (the social security system) and provides additional pension by employers on top of the contracted-out portion. In return for paying the earnings-related old age pension on behalf of the government, an EPF receives a part of social security premiums, called exempt premiums. This entire system under an EPF is called 'Daiko System'.

9.5.1. *Types of EPF*

There are three types of EPFs; single-employer-type EPF, affiliated-employer-type EPF, and multi-employer-type EPF. Single-employer-type EPF can be established by a single employer with 500 or more participants. Affiliated-employer-type EPF can be established by affiliated employers with 800 or more participants. If the number of participants of the main/parent company of affiliated companies is 500 or more, the threshold number is reduced down to 500. On the other hand, if the main/parent company does not join the affiliated-employer-type EPF, the threshold number is increased to 2,000. Multi-employer-type EPF is usually established within the same industry and/or within the same region with 3,000 or more participants. As of February 25, 2004, 406 out of the total 1,450 EPFs are single-employer-type EPFs, 459 are affiliated-employer-type EPFs, and 585 are multi-employer-type EPFs.

9.5.2. Benefit Components of an EPF

An EPF must offer a plus alpha benefit and an additional benefit on top of the contracted-out benefit. Formula for the plus alpha benefit is the same as that for the contracted-out benefit, which is average MSR, times multiple times months of credited service. MSR is a measure to classify employee earnings into 30 categories with the minimum of 98,000 yen and the maximum of 620,000 yen based on which EPI premiums and benefits are calculated. Formula for the additional benefit varies from employer to employer. Benefits must be non-discriminatory and the total level of plus alpha benefits and additional benefits must be at least 10 per cent higher than that of the contracted-out portion. The contracted-out benefits and the plus alpha benefits are called 'basic part' while additional benefits are called 'additional part'.

Basic Part Benefits

Eligibility for receiving benefits for the basic part is one-month participation in an EPF. Benefits must be life annuity. If a participant terminates within 15 years of service, the assets equal to the present value of his/her accrued benefits are transferred to Pension Fund Association (PFA), which takes over the responsibility of paying benefits.

Additional Part Benefits

Maximum benefit eligibility requirements are 20 years of service for an annuity and three years of service for a withdrawal lump sum. Annuity payments must begin as late as age 65 years. Over one-half of accrued benefits for the additional portion and the plus alpha portion must be paid in life annuity with the maximum guarantee period of 20 years or/and up to a maximum age of 85 years. Beneficiaries can opt to receive a lump sum instead of life annuity, but the amount of the lump sum must be less than the present value of life annuity calculated using the statutory minimum assumed interest rate. As to a withdrawal lump sum, beneficiaries can defer the receipt of all or part of it. EPF may provide disability benefits and survivor benefits. Employers usually pay premiums for the plus alpha benefits and the additional benefits although employee contributions are allowed.

9.5.3. Taxation on EPFs

Employer contributions to an EPF are a tax-deductible company expense. Employer contributions are not treated as taxable income to employees. Employee contributions can be fully deducted in calculating an income tax as well as a residence tax. This is the difference in EPF taxation from QPPs and New DB Plans, explained later. Investment earnings are tax-deferred. Plan assets are generally not subject to an annual special corporation tax unlike other type of pension plans (explained later). However, plan assets over the level corresponding to 2.84 times the contracted-out benefits are subject to a special corporation tax. Lump sum benefits paid to beneficiaries are favourably taxed as retirement benefits (with a service-related deduction[1]). Annuity benefits are subject to a special income deduction.[2] Survivor benefits are tax-free. This is another difference in EPF taxation from QPPs and New DB Plans.

---

1. **Deductions for Lump-sum Payment**

Years of Service	Deductions
Up to 20 years	Years times 0.4 mil. yen
Beyond 20 years	Years over 20 times 0.7 mil. yen + 8 mil. yen

All lump-sum money from retirement benefits, DB plans, and DC plans are combined before applying the deductions. The amount remaining after the deductions is divided by 2 to reach the taxable income, and then separately taxed.

2. **Deductions for Annuity Payments**

For those who are age 65 or over

Amount of Annuities	Deductions
Less than 2.6 mil. yen	1.4 mil. yen
2.6 mil–4.6 mil. yen	Amount times 25%+0.75 mil. yen
4.6 mil–8.2 mil. yen	Amount times 15%+1.21 mil. yen
More than 8.2 mil. yen	Amount times 5%+ 203 mil. yen

For those who are less than age 65

Amount of Annuities	Deductions
Less than 1.3 mil. yen	0.7 mil. yen
1.3 mil–4.1 mil. yen	Amount times 25%+0.375 mil. yen
4.1 mil–7.7 mil. yen	Amount times 15%+0.785 mil. yen
More than 7.7 mil. yen	Amount times 5%+ 1.555 mil. yen

All annuities from social securities, DB plans, and DC plans are combined before applying the deductions.

9.5.4. Dissolution of EPFs

Mainly due to deteriorated investment environment, more and more EPFs have been dissolved these days. In 1994 and 1995 only one EPF was dissolved. Since then, the number of EPF dissolution has increased from 29 in fiscal 2000 to 50 in fiscal 2001 to 92 in fiscal 2003.

The Minister of Health, Labour, and Welfare must approve EPF dissolutions before EPFs settle their assets. There are stringent prerequisites to apply for approval of dissolution. If EPF assets are less than those corresponding to contracted-out benefits, one time contribution to cover the shortage is required. Once EPF is dissolved, the assets value corresponding to contracted-out benefits will be transferred to Pension Fund Association (PFA), which takes over the responsibility of payments of contracted-out benefits. Any residual assets are allocated to participants and beneficiaries according to the rule of distribution stipulated by EPF plan documents. Participants can choose to receive it as a lump sum or to transfer to PFA for future annuity payments. Participants can also mix lump sum payment and transfer to PFA.

9.5.5. Return of Contracted-out Benefits
to the Government (Daiko-henjo)

As of April 2004, 777 EPFs have already received approval to give back the social security contracted-out benefits of the plan. Although the contracted-out benefits are in essence social security benefits, employers must compensate for the investment loss derived from the contracted-out portion and recognise PBO for contracted-out portion in their books. The contracted-out portion used to bring in extra profits to EPFs in the era of good investment environment. But once investment environment turned adverse, the contracted-out portion began to affect EPF operation negatively. Many employers and trade unions lobbied for a legislation that allows EPFs to return the contracted-out portion back to the original social security regime. With the passage of Defined Benefit Corporate Pension Act, it has become possible for EPFs to surrender the contracted-out benefits to the government (Daiko-henjo), effective from April 1, 2002.

Once EPFs have returned the contracted-out portion, additional benefits and plus alpha benefits are transformed into New DB plans explained later. EPFs are supposed to return plan assets to the government in cash, but as an exceptional rule, they can return in the form of securities if certain requirements are met.

9.6. Qualified Pension Plans (QPP)

A Qualified Pension Plan (QPP) was introduced in 1962 by amendment of Corporation Tax Act and Income Tax Act, and now is one of the main private pension schemes in Japan. A QPP is externally funded, tax favoured retirement benefit plan. Because there is no minimum participation requirement unlike an Employee Pension Fund, QPPs are popular among small-to-medium employers although the number of QPPs is constantly decreasing in the last years.

A QPP is established as a contract between the employer and a trust bank, a life insurance company, or the National Mutual Insurance Federation of Agricultural Cooperatives (lead manager). The Chief of National Tax Agency must approve QPP contracts as satisfying 14 requirements stipulated in the Corporation Tax Ordinance. As a practice, lead managers handle this approval procedure on behalf of employers. Plan documents must be filed with the Labour Standards Inspection Office.

A QPP is established by a single employer or jointly by affiliated employers. The coverage and benefit formula must be non-discriminatory. Only full-time regular employees can be covered. QPPs are regulated in terms of benefit structure, benefit reduction constraints, rate of funding, amortisation of past service liabilities, and non-reversion of assets to the employer. Actuarial revaluation must be done at least every five years. Assumed interest rate can be changed only at actuarial revaluation, but the rate must not be less than the standard interest rate stipulated in the Corporation Tax Ordinance. The lead manager generally enforces these regulations.

It has been pointed out that QPP regulations are less restrictive than those for EPFs and not enough to protect employee rights of receiving benefits. As a result, with the passage of Defined Benefit Corporate Pension Act, employers cannot establish new QPPs on or after April 1, 2002. Employers must convert existing QPPs to other types of pension plans such as New DB plans, EPFs, or DC plans by March 31, 2012.

9.6.1. Benefits of QPPs

QPP benefits are paid upon termination of employment. This is different from EPFs and new DB plans that pay benefits when participants attain a prescribed advanced age. There are no benefit eligibility requirements unlike EPFs and new DB plans. The form of payment must be fixed annuity of 5 years or longer, or life annuity. Most of QPPs provide fixed annuity only. Beneficiaries can opt to receive a lump sum instead of annuities, but the amount of the lump sum must be less than the present value of annuities calculated with the interest rate stipulated in the plan document. QPPs may provide survivor benefits, but not disability benefits. The benefit formula can be a flat scheme, pay-related scheme, and point scheme. Cash balance scheme is not allowed in QPPs.

9.6.2. Taxation on QPPs

Employer contributions to a QPP are a tax-deductible company expense. But employer contributions are not treated as taxable income to employees. Employees can contribute to a QPP up to one half of the total contributions at their discretion if a QPP is a contributory plan. Employee contributions are subject to tax deduction, but are coordinated with the deduction for life insurance premiums (maximum: 50,000 yen per annum). Investment earnings are tax-deferred, but plan assets are subject to an annual special corporation tax of 1.173 per cent of the book value of plan assets excluding employee contribution portion. There is currently a moratorium on this tax until March 31, 2005, reflecting adverse investment environments during the last several years in Japan. Lump sum benefits paid to beneficiaries are favourably taxed as retirement benefits (with a service-related deduction). Annuity benefits are subject to a special income deduction. Benefits corresponding to employee contribution portion are excluded from taxable income. Survivor benefits are subject to an inheritance tax.

9.7. New DB Plans

Two kinds of New DB plans, Fund-Type and Agreement-Type, were introduced on April 1, 2002, by Defined Benefit Corporate Pension Act. The purpose of Defined Benefit Corporate Pension Act is to unify regulations among DB plans and to enhance protection of vested benefits for participants.

As is explained previously, employers maintaining EPFs want to surrender the contracted-out portion to the government. As a result of lobbying activities, Defined Benefit Corporate Pension Act has created a new DB scheme, Fund-Type New DB Plan. Fund-Type is similar to EPF structure with a separate governing board, but without contracted-out benefits. The legal minimum number of participants for this Fund-Type is 300. Existing EPFs can switch to the new DB plans by surrendering contracted-out benefits to the government.

QPPs have problems in protecting vested benefits because plan operation is not strictly regulated. There are no rules to check the funding status annually for QPPs. As a result, funding status of most QPPs has deteriorated in the adverse investment environment and many of them have been terminated without enough assets to pay benefits. In order to enhance protection of participants and beneficiaries rights, Defined Benefit Corporate Pension Act has created another new DB scheme, an Agreement-Type New DB Plan to replace QPPs. Agreement-Type is similar to QPP structure with contract with a lead manager, but is subject to minimum funding rules, fiduciary duties, and disclosures. There is no legal minimum number of participants for Agreement-Type.

9.7.1. Benefits of DB Plans

Form of payment must be fixed annuity of 5 years or longer, or life annuity. Old age annuity benefit commencement must be between ages 60 and 65 for normal retirement and as early as age 50 for early retirees. Beneficiaries can opt for a lump sum payment instead of annuity payments. The lump sum value must be equal to or less than the present value of annuities for a guaranteed period. Maximum benefit eligibility requirements are 20 years of service for an annuity and 3 years of service for a lump sum. Survivor and disability benefits are permitted.

9.7.2. Contributions to New DB Plans

Employers make contributions to fund plan assets. Employees are permitted to contribute up to 50 per cent of total contributions if plan documents allow them to do so. Actuarial revaluation must be performed at least every five years. Each employer determines an assumed interest rate based on a long-term expected investment return. However, it must be equal to or above the minimum assumed interest rate set by the Minister of Health, Labour and Welfare.

9.7.3. Minimum Funding Requirements

To protect vested benefits for participants, strict funding rules apply to new DB plans. There are two tests related to minimum funding requirements, minimum ongoing basis contribution requirements and minimum termination basis contribution requirements. Both tests are carried out every year. Minimum ongoing basis contribution test compares plan assets with actuarial reserve (the amount that plan should possess for future benefit payments). The purpose of the test is examining whether pension plan assets are properly accumulating or not. If assets minus actuarial reserve are less than the allowable shortfall amount that is stipulated in plan documents, no action is required. Otherwise, actuarial revaluation must be carried out and a new contribution determined. Minimum termination basis contribution test examines whether plan assets are enough for benefit payments for past services of participants and beneficiaries, assuming that the plan were to dissolve. The test compares plan assets with the present value of minimum benefits. Minimum benefits are accrued benefits as of the test date. Additional contributions must be made if plans are regarded as under-funded.

9.7.4. Maximum Funding (Contribution Holiday)

Contributions are reduced or suspended if assets exceed 1.5 times liabilities that are defined as the larger of actuarial reserve or minimum funding requirement.

9.7.5. Cash Balance Plans

In New DB plans cash balance-type plans are allowed to be introduced. Pay credit is given to 'notional accounts', along with an interest credit based on:

- Fixed rate;
- Government bond rate or other objectively measurable stable index (national wage index or cost of living are acceptable; equity index is not permissible);
- Combination of fixed rate and government bond rate;
- Fixed or government bond rate with applicable minimums or maximums. Conversion rate between annuity and lump sum can be indexed regardless of the plan design structure.

9.7.6. *Switching among Different Pension Schemes*

Because QPP must be terminated within eight years from now, The Defined Benefit Corporate Pension Act allows plan sponsors to switch among several different schemes, Thus so far, some QPP sponsors have switched to other types of pension plans but a majority of the sponsors have just terminated QPPs and left employees without any retirement plans.

9.8. Deregulations of DB Plan Investment

Investment for private pension plan assets was subject to strict regulations in Japan. But during the 1990s a series of deregulations have been implemented.

9.8.1. *EPF*

Only trust banks and life insurance companies could be investment managers of EPF assets until March 1990. In April 1990, EPFs were allowed to invest new money in those products offered by investment advisory contracts with investment advisory companies, separately-invested products provided by trust banks, and dedicated separate account products by life insurance companies, but up to the limit of one-third of EPF assets. In November 1994, old money too was allowed to be invested in those products (one-third limit still applied). The limit was raised from one-third to one-half of EPF assets in April 1996, and eventually abolished in April 1999. In-house investments were allowed to EPFs with assets of over 50 billion yen in 1990. Assets-size test was eliminated for in-house investment in June 2000. As a result of these deregulations, the market share among investment managers has changed substantially. Especially, investment advisory companies have increased their market share.

There used to be so-called '5-3-3-2' rule regarding asset allocation of EPFs until 1997. The rule requires that 50 per cent or more EPF assets are invested in bonds/loans, 30 per cent or fewer assets are in stocks, 30 per cent or fewer assets are in foreign currency investments, and 20 per cent or fewer are in real estate. The purpose of this rule was to ensure security of pension investments. However, it was gradually deregulated and finally abolished in December 1997. Since then, stock investment and foreign investment have increased while the general accounts of life insurance companies have decreased. In exchange for investment deregulation, EPFs must develop a formal investment policy where a strategic asset mix and principles for manager selection and evaluation are defined. Based on the formal investment policy, EPFs develop investment guidelines for each investment managers.

9.8.2. QPP

Deregulation for QPP asset investments was slower than those for EPFs. Investment advisory companies were allowed to manage QPP assets in October 1997, which was seven years after the deregulation in EPFs. Trust banks seized 41 per cent of total QPP assets and life insurance companies had 59 per cent shares just before the deregulation. As of March 2000 the market share was as follows: trust banks, 43 per cent; life insurance companies, 48 per cent; investment advisory companies, nine per cent.

There were rules regarding asset allocation with QPPs, too. But this rule applied to each investment manager as opposed to EPFs where asset allocation rule applied to the entire EPF assets. Trust banks were subject to '5-3-3-2' rule similar to EPFs. Co-mingled separate accounts of life insurance companies were subject to '3-3-2' rule where 30 per cent or fewer assets are invested in stocks, 30 per cent or fewer assets be in foreign currency investments, and 20 per cent or less, be in real estate. These asset allocation rules were eliminated in April 1997.

QPP assets used to be invested in co-mingled funds by trust banks and life insurance companies. With these deregulations QPPs became able to manage their assets according to their demographic and funding status. QPP sponsors vary widely by size. Some large employers sponsoring QPPs form pension committees under management supervision and develop a formal investment policy. However, small-to-medium companies with QPPs are slow in adapting themselves to deregulated environments.

9.8.3. Outcomes of Investment Deregulations

With these deregulations, the pension market has generated new players, services and products. Since investment advisory companies were allowed to enter the market in 1990s, independent advisory companies, subsidiaries of banks, securities companies, property and casualty insurance companies, and foreign financial institutions have been established, and fierce competition for pension money has begun. Investment managers are required to demonstrate high-level speciality and capability in asset management with a clear investment philosophy and style. Investment managers, specialising in specific types of investment, have become popular. New services such as master trust service and new products such as alternatives have been introduced. Plan sponsors are required to construct the best portfolio, to select competent investment managers, and to evaluate their investment performance properly. Consulting firms have expanded their services to provide plan sponsors with asset consulting services. These deregulations have shifted a substantial amount of pension money to stock and foreign investments, thus making the pension plan a major player in capital markets.

9.9. Defined Contribution Plans

Defined Contribution (DC) Plans was first introduced in Japan on October 1, 2001. DC plan rules are prescribed by Defined Contribution Act and associated ordinances of the government and the Ministry of Health, Labour and Welfare. There are two types of DC plans in Japan, Corporate-Type DC plans and Individual-Type DC plans. One person can participate in either of them according to his/her status. Only employers can contribute to Corporate-Type DC plans, and the amounts of contributions are fixed regardless of employers' profits. Employee contributions are not allowed in Corporate-Type DC plans. On the other hand, in Individual-Type DC plans employees or the self-employed can contribute to the plan at their discretion. But employers cannot make matching contributions to Individual-Type DC plans.

9.9.1. Eligibility and Contribution Limits

Private employees who are covered by Employee's Pension Insurance (social security system) are eligible for Corporate-Type DC plans once their employers establish a DC plan. There are two separate contribution limits for Corporate-Type DC plans. If employers maintain a QPP, EPF, or new DB at the same time, contribution limit to individual accounts is 18,000 yen per month. Otherwise the limit is 36,000 yen per month.

If employers do not sponsor a DB plan or a Corporate-Type DC plan, an applicant is eligible to participate in Individual-Type DC plans. The limit then is 15,000 yen per month. The self-employed as well can participate in Individual Type DC plans, and their limit is 68,000 yen per month, although this is an aggregated limit with the premiums to National Pension Fund. In any case those who are less than age 60 years can become DC participants. Public employees and housewives (or house husbands) are not eligible for either of Corporate-Type or Individual-Type DC plans.

9.9.2. Corporate-Type DC Plans

Consent of a union representing over one-half of the insured covered under Employee' Pension Insurance for those under the age of 60 years is necessary to establish a Corporate-Type DC plan. If there are no such unions, consent from an employee representative that represents over one-half of the insured covered under Employees' Pension Insurance for those under the age of 60 years, is necessary.

The plan administrator plays a key role in DC plans operations. A plan administrator's functions include:

- recordkeeping participants' individual account data and inform participants of their account balances periodically;
- handling each participant's investment direction;
- confirming benefit claims;
- selecting investment options for the plan;
- providing participants with information on investment options.

9.9.3. Eligibility

Those who are up to 60 years and covered by Employee's Pension Insurance (social security system) can be participants if employers implement Corporate-Type DC plans. Being a participant means receiving contributions. Those insured of Employee's Pension Insurance who are of age over 60 years are not eligible to participate in Corporate-Type DC plans. Employees who are not insured of Employee's Pension Insurance are also ineligible to participate in Corporate-Type DC plans even though they are under 60 years old. The latter includes part-time workers. Employers can cover a limited group of employees with Corporate-Type DC plans on a non-discriminatory basis.

9.9.4. Contribution Formula

The contribution formula must be a fixed percentage of participants' pay or fixed amount for every participant. In any case the amount of contributions must be within the contribution limits (18,000 or 36,000 yen per month).

9.9.5. Investment Options

Participants select investment options from those presented by the plan for their individual account balance in DC plans. At least three options must be provided for participants to make diversified investment. Bank deposits, mutual funds (investment trusts), and insurance products are commonly presented as investment options. One of the investment options must be a capital guaranteed product such as time deposit and Guaranteed Investment Contract (GIC). Securities of the employer can be presented although it is rare. No real estate investment option is permitted. Participants can change their investment options at least once every three months. Plan administrators must provide information on account balances to participants at least once a year.

9.9.6. Participant Education

Since participants make investment decisions in DC plans, it is important to give enough information to participants. Defined Contribution Act classifies such information into three types, 'Explanation about DC Plans', 'Basic Investment Theory' and 'Information on Investment Options'. Providing 'Explanation about DC Plans' is plan sponsors' legal obligation. They must explain how DC plans work and what the contents of the plan documents are. Plan sponsors should provide 'Basic Investment Theory' on the best efforts basis. Such knowledge as trade-offs between risks and returns, diversification, and dollar-cost-averaging should be given to the participants. Providing 'Information on Investment Options' is the plan administrators' legal obligation. Information on each option's structure, historical performances, risk/return profiles, and so on must be given to participants.

9.9.7. Benefit Payments

Benefits are payable when attaining age 60 with over 10 years of participation. When participants leave the company before the age of

60 years, they cannot receive benefit payments and must rollover the account balances to a new employer's DC plan or to Individual-Type DC plan. They have no choice on whether to receive cash payment or rollover to another plan at termination of employment. There is an exception to 'age 60 years requirement'. If an employee leaves with no more than three years of participation and becomes ineligible for any type of DC plan (e.g. housewives or public employees), the vested account balance, if any, can be paid out in cash. This exception was made to eliminate burdens of keeping records and holding small assets for short-time participants. Participants can start receiving benefits any time between the age of 60 and 70 years. Benefits are paid in lump sum or instalments extending over 5 to 20 years. Life annuities can be offered.

9.9.8. Vesting Rules

With three years of service, participants are 100 per cent vested in Corporate-Type DC plans. Participants can be partially vested within three years if the plan documents provide so, like 50 per cent vested after one year of service, 75 per cent vested after two years of service, and 100 per cent vested after three years of service. Employers are not allowed to forfeit once employees attain at least three years of service. In other words employers are allowed to forfeit the accumulated assets of employees who leave the company within three years of service on voluntary basis.

9.9.9. Portability

Rollover is mandatory unless participants are over 60 years of age. The fully vested account balance of a participant must be rolled over into the new employer's Corporate-Type DC plan or Individual-Type DC plan. When participants in Corporate-Type DC plans change jobs, their account balances must be rolled over to the new employers' Corporate-Type DC plan. If a new employer does not sponsor Corporate-Type DC plan or if participants become self-employed, their account balances are rolled over to Individual-Type DC plans. When participants in Individual-Type DC plans change jobs to become employes, their account balances must be rolled over to the new employers' Corporate-Type DC plan. If a new employer does not sponsor Corporate-Type DC plan, their account balances remain with Individual-Type DC plans.

9.9.10. Taxation on DC Plans

In Corporate-Type DC plans employer contributions are a tax-deductible business expense. Employer contributions are not treated as taxable income to employees. In Individual-Type DC plans participants can deduct contributions from their taxable income. Investment earnings are tax-deferred. However, Plan assets are subject to an annual special corporation tax of 1.173 per cent of the book value of plan assets, regardless of whether they gain or lose on investment (as for QPPs). There is currently a two-year moratorium (until March 31, 2005) on this tax. Rollover is tax-free. Lump sum benefits paid to beneficiaries are favourably taxed as retirement benefits (with a service-related deduction). The contribution period is considered as the service period. Annuity benefits are subject to a special income deduction (same treatment as for annuities paid from QPPs, EPFs, and social security).

9.9.11. DC Market Outlook

The number of Corporate-Type DC plan documents approved by the government has constantly increased since the introduction in October 2001, as of the end of March 2004, 845 plan documents have been approved covering 2379 employers. (Note that several employers can maintain DC plans under a single plan document.) The number of participants is 620,000 for Corporate-Type DC plans (as of November, 2003) and 25 thousand for Individual-Type DC plan (as of December, 2003).

9.9.12. DC Deregulations

In order to compensate for social security benefit reduction, the tax committee of the ruling Liberal Democratic Party and Komei Party approved a future increase in the monthly contribution limits applicable to DC plans in December 2003.

Corporate-Type DC plans: The monthly contribution limit for employers that do not sponsor another funded DB plan will increase to 46,000 yen from the current limit of 36,000 yen. For employers that do sponsor another funded DB plan, the new limit will increase to 23,000 yen from the current limit of 18,000 yen. Individual-Type DC plans: The monthly contribution limit for employees who work for employers that do not sponsor a funded DB plan or Corporate-Type DC plan will increase to 18,000 yen from the current limit of 15,000 yen. For the self-employed, the limit remains the same at 68,000 yen.

In addition to the increase in contribution limits, it is scheduled that the limits applicable on transferable amounts when an existing DB plan is converted into a Corporate-Type DC plan will be eliminated. The new rule applies retroactively to those employers that have converted to DC plans before the rule takes effect.

The rule for withdrawal payments is expected to be relaxed. Currently, only those who become ineligible for DC plans after three years or less participation can receive lump sum withdrawal of money before attaining the age of 60 years. A new rule will introduce a small amount provision for the lump sum withdrawal money. If an account balance is 500,000 yen or less, a withdrawal payment can be received, regardless of participating period.

The scheduled increases and abolishment of the cap on transferable money helps make DC plans more viable for the future, which provides employers further additional plan design options to help better meet their employee retirement needs and objectives. These deregulations have come as a result of strong lobbying activities by employers, trade groups, and financial institutions. However, the following requests were not realised at this time: allowing taking cash payments at the termination of employment, before the age of 60 years; allowing employees to contribute to Corporate-Type DC plans to supplement their retirement provision.

9.10. Scheduled Private Pension Scheme Reform

The comprehensive Pension Reform Bill in 2004 includes the following items for private pension scheme.

9.10.1. Special Rules for EPF Dissolutions

As a condition to EPF dissolution, EPF assets must be not less than the value corresponding to contracted-out benefits. Otherwise, EPF cannot be dissolved under the current rule. The new rule will allow dissolution of under-funded EPF on condition that the shortage below assets value corresponding to contracted-out benefits is amortised within five years. The new rule is effective for three years after enforcement (April 2005).

9.10.2. Portability involving DB Schemes

Portability is currently allowed within DC schemes and from EPF to Pension Fund Association (PFA) in Japan. The scheduled pension reform will expand portability involving DB schemes. When EPF or PFA participants change jobs, they can choose to transfer their portion of assets into an EPF or a New DB plan of a new employer as far as plan documents permit such transfers. Alternatively, they can choose to transfer the assets into a Corporate-Type DC plan of a new employer or an Individual-type DC plan. The same rule applies to New DB participants. When they change jobs, they can choose to transfer their portion of New DB assets into PFA, an EPF, a New DB plan, or a Corporate-Type DC plan of a new employer, or an Individual-Type DC plan. Note that QPP is not included in the new portability scheme.

When New DB participants resign before normal retirement age or when New DB plans are terminated, participants can choose to transfer their portion of New DB assets into PFA, and then to receive benefits in annuities from PFA.

9.11. Conclusion

Pension deregulations in Japan have given employers wider plan options, including DC plans and CB plans. These plans enable employers to respond to change in financial and labour markets. Investment deregulation has made pension plan an important player in the capital market. On the other hand, reregulation to enhance protection of participants' vested rights has been implemented with the scheduled abolishment of QPPs and the introduction of New DB plans. However, it does not seem that this reregulation is welcomed. It remains the issue how to motivate employers to provide retirement benefit plans while pursuing participants' vested rights.

Reference

Takayama, N. (2004). "A Balance Sheet Approach to Reforming Social Security Pensions in Japan," paper presented at Joint PBC-IMF Seminar on *China's Monetary Policy Transmission Mechanism*, Beijing, April 12-13, *http://www.ier.hit-u.ac.jp/~takayama/index-e.html*.

Index

A

Acharya, Sarthi 29, 61
adjustment process 27
administered prices 62
Africa 183
ageing 145
agrarian economy 57
agriculture 57
        share of employment 82
agricultural workers, seasonal 72
Ahmedabad 64
Andhra Pradesh 150
Annuity benefits 204, 216
anti-discrimination laws 169
Arnold, L. 45
Asher, Mukul 30, 141, 142
Asia 183, 191
Asia-Pacific 21, 39, 43, 46
        countries 38, 45
        region 21, 34, 50, 115
Asian countries 17
Asian financial/economic crisis 27,
        63, 74, 184, 185, 189, 195
Australia 22, 34, 38, 39, 165, 168,
        172, 176
Australian colonists 174
autarkic economic development model
        57
Ayres, I. 47

B

Bacungan, F. 40, 42, 43
Bakshi, R. 64

Bales, S. 89
Banerjee, Nirmala 185
Bangkok 189
Bangladesh 48
Bardach, E. 35, 47
basic rights 113
Basri, M.C. 112
Batley, R. 75
Bhatt, Ela 189
Bhatt, P.R. 65
Bhattacharya, D. 61
Blackett, A. 49
blue-collar workers 65, 66
Bohle, P. 170
Braithwaite, J. 47
Brassard, Caroline 29
Breman, J. 64, 65, 75
Britain 176
British rule 34
bureaucracy 61
bureaucratic decision-making 62
Business India 72
business process outsourcing (BPO)
        65, 66

C

capital, financialisation of 24
capital, free mobility of 22
capital goods industries 58
capital intensive fashion 73
capital-intensive industries 66
capital markets, deregulation of 24
capitalists 24

captive markets 63

Caribbean 183

Castells, M. 38

casual wage workers 184, 185

casual workers 48

Chan, A. 36, 45

Chatterjee, R. 60

child labour 117

    abolition of 114

    issues 104

China 23, 35, 36, 38, 39, 41, 43, 44, 45, 49

Chinese labour migration 174

civic rights 113

civil servants 141

civil societies 72, 105, 189

closures 150, 151

    permission for 152

codes of conduct 49

collective bargaining 26, 34, 123

    power 105

Collins, H. 36, 168

command legislation 47

common law 169

community policing 134

Compaq 24

compensation for lay-off 153

competitive market, perfectly 24

compliance costs 136, 143

compliance regime 136

computer software sector 66

concurrent subject 150

contract 73

    labour 67

    work, fixed-term 133

Contract Labour Abolition and Regulation Act of 19 67

Contract Labour Act 154

contract workers 68

control legislation 47

Cooney, S. 28, 35, 38, 40, 42, 46, 50, 176

corporatisation 38

corruption 31, 39, 40

cross-country comparison 185

currencies, free movement of 24

D

Das, G. 63

Datta, R.C. 61

Davala, S. 67

DB Plans, benefits of 208

DB Plans, new 207

DB Plans, new, contributions to 208

DC Plans, corporate-type 213, 215, 216

DC Plans, defined contribution 212

DC Plans, explanation about 214

de-bureaucratisation 187

de-industrialisation in West Bengal 69

Deery and Mitchell, 1993 34

defined benefit 198

Defined Benefit Corporate Pension Act 205, 207

Dell 24

demand curve, downward sloping 136

democratisation 188

    of capital 24

demographic indicators 145

depression of the 1930s 23

deregulation 17, 22, 58, 74, 187

    argument 23

deregulation for QPP 211

deregulation, logic of 24

deregulation process 29

Deshpande, L.K. 153

Deshpande, S. 65,

Dev, M. 72

developed economies 167

developing economies 167

developing nation 178

development 17

Deyo, F. 35, 40

Dharmadhikari, A. 65

Dick, H. 39

direct foreign investment 71

dispute settlement 115

distortions 25, 73

    in the labour market 42

Dorf, M. 47

downsizing 184

dual wage system 87

dualism 141

Dutta, S. 75

E

East Asia 44, 46

East Asian countries 40

economic composition 58

economic crisis 128

    in Indonesia 134

Economic factors 42

economic growth 21, 58, 63

    high 64

    overall 141

    pattern of 29

economic partnership agreement, comprehensive 142

economic planning 141

economic reforms since 1991 150

economic restructuring 34

educational systems 145

effect of globalisation 178

electoral politics 161

electronics 133

Employee Pension Funds 198, 201, 202, 204-206

Employee Pension Insurance Act 202

Employee's Pension Insurance 197, 198

employment growth 117

    in the modern sector 117

    low 27

employment growth *(contd. ...)*

    nature and extent of 58

    pattern of 82

    termination of 157

employment regulation 38

empowerment 188

end-use norms 59

enforcement pyramid 47

enforcement strategies 51

ethical trading initiative 50

European Parliament 50

exit 150

export markets, modern activities for 188

export-led industrialisation 29

export-promoting zone 70

external environment 28

F

factor markets 24

factor price fixation 22

Factories, Shops and Industries Act 175

Fallon, P.R. 74, 152

family-controlled managements 63

FDI 23

    inflows 145

feminist legal research 169

financial crisis in Southeast Asia 83

financial markets, deregulation in the 64

fiscal management 145

forced coercion 114

forced labour 46, 114

forced savings 58

Fordian mode 23

formal schemes 142

formal sector 150, 188

free economies 22

Free Trade Agreement 142

Freeman, R.B. 61, 73, 74

Frenkel, S. 48

Frost, S. 38
Fund-Type 207
    New DB plans 202
fundamental rights 113

G

Gallagher, M. 41, 44
gender equity 21
gender gap 184
gender neutral language 176
gender neutral laws 178
gender-neutral legislation 175
gender-related problems 104
gendered division of labour 173
gendered law 170
General Agreements on Trade and
    Tariffs 22
geographical mobility of labour 23
Gillespie, J. 176
Ginsburg, T. 36
global markets 133
globalisation 72, 111, 141, 167, 184,
    188
globalisation, challenges of 64
globalisation, impact of 167
globalisation, managing 149
globalised world 165
good governance 69
Goswami, R. 141, 142
governmental agencies 35
Grabosky, P. 47
gratuities 148
gratuity benefits 154, 155
    in Sri Lanka 160
gratuity benefits, mandatory 143
gratuity, rate of 154
growth 17
    of employment 62
    rates 57
    strategy 141
    pattern of 58

guaranteed investment contract 214
Gujarat 150
Gunningham, N. 35, 47, 168, 170, 171

H

Hawkins, K. 168, 175
Hirway, I. 75
home computers 24
human capital 27
human resource development 76
human welfare 25

I

IBM 24
ILO 34, 50, 74, 75, 115
    Convention 182 46
IMF 90
incentive packages 59
incentive structures 143
income distribution 58
India 22, 27, 28, 30, 34, 37, 38, 48,
    117, 141, 142, 145, 150
    economic reforms since 1991
    150
India's
    GDP growth rate, 2003 144
    Constitution 150
    population 144
    share of employment 147
    TFR 145
    working age population 145
indivisible assets 24
Indonesia 28, 40, 42, 43, 44, 48, 112,
    136, 184, 189
    economic crisis in 134
Indonesian labour market 29, 118
Industrial Act 61
industrial conglomerates 63
    in South Korea 63
Industrial Disputes Act of 1947 61,
    150
    amendments of the 151, 152

industrial growth 62
industrial relations 44, 165
industrialisation 58, 167
informal economy 34, 183, 184, 185
informal employment 183, 184, 187
    in Thailand 184
informal enterprises 183
informal sector 30, 145, 183, 184,
    185, 187, 188, 190, 195, 196
informal systems 44
institutional economists 25, 26
institutional support 190
insurance companies 69
Intel 24
intellectual property 22
internal compliance processes 49
international agencies 50
international capital mobility 58
International Development
    Association 90
international environment,
    competitive 136
International Labour Office 183
International Labour Organization 25,
    48, 167
intervention 25
    in labour markets 26
interventionist 22
Investment deregulation 218
investment in human capital 77, 168
investment theory, basic 214
investment options, information on
    214
inward-looking economic structure
    141

J

James, P. 170
Jamieson, S. 30, 170, 173, 175
Japan 22, 34, 38
Japanese labour market 200
Japanese retirement system 197

Java-Bali 29
Jayasuriya, K. 40
Jiminez, R. 40
joblessness 72
jobs creation 141
    in the modern sector 121
jobs, preservation of existing 141
Johnstone, R. 35, 47, 168, 170, 171,
    173
Joshi, V. 61

K

Kagan, R. 35, 47
Kahn-Freund, Otto 172
Kelegama, S. 159
Karunarathne, W. 141, 142
Kent, A. 35
Kolkata 64
Korean labour laws 195
Korean War 43
Kulshreshtha, A.C. 70
Kuruvilla, S. 35, 171

L

labour abuses, egregious forms of 46,
    47
labour code 83, 85, 88, 194
    of the Socialist Republic of
    Vietnam 177
labour, composition of 65
labour flexibility 29, 67, 72
labour force characteristics 145
labour force participation rate 82
labour force, non-agricultural 48
labour intensity 66
labour issues 150
labour laws 28, 29, 41, 42, 46
labour law framework 37
labour law regime, relaxed 70, 114
labour laws, complying with 154
labour laws, rigid 27, 66, 71

labour leadership 161
labour legislation 43, 188
    in India 77
    in Indonesia 118
labour markets 22, 24, 28, 31, 34, 44, 91, 141, 145
    current state of 21
    deregulated 28
    deregulation in 74
    flexibility 153
    functioning of the 141
    imperfections 89, 91
    intervention 27
    regulation 17, 28, 33, 45, 46, 121
        formal 40, 44
    rigidity 73
labour organisations 43
labour protection regime 136
labour regulation 21, 29
    economic impact of 29
    formal 35
    Indian experience of 29
    responsive forms of 38
labour relations process 43
labour rights 134
labour standards 26, 49, 112
    in poor countries 111
labour surplus 29
    country 59
labour-intensive projects 89
laissez-faire attitudes 173
Latin America 23, 183, 191
lay-off compensation 153
lay-offs 150
laying-off 64
Lazo, Lucita 30
Lee, C.S. 42
Lee, J.E. 115
less developed country 167
liberalisation 64, 117, 188
    process 57

liberalisation (*contd. ...*)
    reforms 29
liberalised system 58
licence regime 59
licence-quota system 63
life annuity 203
life expectancy at birth 145
life insurance companies 210
Lindsey, T. 36, 39, 40, 42, 43, 44
Little, IMD 61
Liu, Amy Y.C. 43
Liu, K.M. 47
Liubicic, R. 49
low-income countries 27, 74
Lucas, R. 74, 152

M

MacIntyre, A. 40
Madheswaran, S. 65
Mahadevia, D. 75
Malaysia 27, 34, 74, 167
Mamic, I. 49
Manila 183
Manning, Chris 29
Manpower Protection Act 125, 126, 129, 133
manufacturing activities, newer 65
manufacturing employment 128
market economy 89
market economies, regulated 57
market support 59
market-oriented economic growth strategy 149
market-oriented economy 92
markets 64
Masduki, T. 36, 40, 42, 43, 44
Medoff, J. 61
Mehmet, O. 34
mergers and acquisitions 200
microeconomics 25
millennium development goals 21
minimum funding requirements 209

minimum wages 26, 28, 42, 60, 71, 75, 81
  policy 135
  regulation 102, 126
misallocation of resources 25
Mitchell, R. 38
Mitra, S. 66
modern enterprises 70
modern industries 57
modern labour codes 133
modern small-scale industries 62
monopolies, inefficient 63
Mukhopadhaya, Pundarik 30
multi-stakeholder initiatives 51
multilateral organisations 25
multinational sectors 62
Mumbai 64
Murray, J. 49
mutual aid pension 197, 198

N

Naffine, N. 169
Nairobi 183
National Anti-Poverty Commission 190, 191
National Commission on Labour, Second 152
national labour code 116
national labour legislation 118
national pension 197
National University of Singapore 21
Nayyar, R. 115
neoclassical theory 24
neoclassical viewpoint 73
new economic order 184
Nicholson, P. 39, 83, 176
non-agricultural sectors 58
non-governmental organisations (NGOs) 49, 50, 117
non-standard employment 35
Nossar, I. 38

O

obsolete industries 64
occupational health and safety 165
Occupational Health and Safety Act 174
OECD countries/economies 23
Ofreneo, R. 40, 42, 43
OHS concerns of women workers 178
OHS laws 172, 173
  deregulation of the 166
OHS legislation 169, 174
  in Britain 173
OHS, role of unions in the regulation of 170
OHS, self regulation of 166
oil-crisis 22
old economy 64
old-age benefits 199
older industries 64
optimal allocation of labour 73
organised labour 64
organised sectors 59, 72
  activities 73
  employment 148
  workers 69, 72
organised trade unions 64
O'Rourke, D. 49
outsourcing 73, 132
  of activities 132
  of core activities 134
outsourcing, bans on 133
outward orientation 144
outward-oriented economy 141
Owens, A. 49

P

Pakistan 117
Park, S.I. 40
Parker, C. 49

patronage 64
Payment of Gratuity Act 154, 160
Pearson, R. 49
Peerenboom, R. 39, 40, 41
Peiyan, Zeng 44
pension system 142
pension plan, qualified 198, 202, 206
Peru 188
petroleum prices 23
Philippines 38, 40, 41, 42, 184, 189,
     190, 191, 194, 195
Phung, Duc Tung 91
Picciotto, S. 168, 170
Piramal, G. 63
pluralistic institutions 142
political patronage 60
political tug-of-war 72
population growth rate 82
Porges, J. 43
poverty 29
     alleviation in Vietnam 88
     levels in Vietnam 81
poverty line, those below the 72
political system, democratic 142
President Soeharto, downfall of 123
primary sectors 27, 57, 73
primitive stages of development 187
private sector 64
private sector, formal 83
privatisation 34, 38, 187
product markets, competitive 136
product reservation 59
production relations 187
profits, repatriation of 22
protection 72
     informal workers 189
public policy 30, 143
public regulatory frameworks 49
public sector 27, 62, 83
     banks 69
     expansion 141

public sector (*contd. ...*)
     organisations 69
     ownership 58
pure theorist 26

Q

QPP assets 211
QPPs, benefits of 207
Quinlan, M. 170
quotas 59

R

Rani, U. 65
RAP 202
Red River Delta 92
Reebok 49
regulated regime 59
regulation 17, 21, 33
     of outsourcing 133
     of the Vietnamese labour market
     88
regulation, formal 34
regulatory regime 29
regulatory state 168
regulatory frameworks, formal 50
Reimann, M. 172
rent seeking 61, 62
     opportunities 159
replacement rate level 145
reservation policies 66
restructuring of enterprises 143
retirement allowance plans 201
retirement benefits in Japan 200
retirement benefits, harmonisation of
     200
retirement plans, employer-sponsored
     198
retrenchment 72, 150
     benefits in Sri Lanka 161
     law in India 153
Rhode, D. 170

rights 113
> of collective bargaining 114
Robens regime 176
Rodgers, R. 35
rural communes 29

S

Sabel, C. 47, 49
Sabharwal, M. 149
Samant, S.R. 150
scams 64
Scandinavia 27
Second World War 23
secondary sector 57, 73
securities 214
security rights 113, 114, 126, 135
self-regulatory practices 51
semi-skilled 66
Sen, Amartya 66
services 57
> industry 65
> sector 66
severance pay 143, 148
> arrangements 156
> practices 150
> payments 161
sexism of the law 169
sexist acts of Parliament 175
Seyfang, G. 49
Sharma, A.N. 141, 147, 155
Singapore 22, 34, 165, 168, 176
Singapore's revised Factories Act of 1998 176
Singh, A.K. 65, 113
Singh, G. 70
skill-enhancing strategies 168
skilled labour, supply of 27
small and medium sized enterprises (SMEs) 37
small-scale industries, promotion of 59

social assistance schemes 142
> for the elderly 142
social dialogue 76
social impact of labour regulation 30
social insurance systems 192
social protection of informal workers 189
social safety nets 189
> reform of 150
social security 21, 29, 34
> package 76
> systems 30, 199
socialist revolution 35
socialist states 41
Soeharto 112
> New Order 122, 134
> post period 112
South Africa 189
South Korea 34, 40, 41, 43, 168
Southeast Asia 23, 27, 28, 30, 74, 184, 185
Southeast Asian countries 22, 175, 178
Southeast Asian financial crisis 82
Soviet-style industrialisation model 58
Sri Lanka 28, 30, 37, 141, 142, 145, 157
Sri Lankan
> Industrial Law 157
> demographic trends 147
> employment structure 147
> external debt to GDP ratio 145
> per capita income 144
> severance pay arrangements 160
> total fertility rate 145
Sri Lanka, working age population in 147
stagflation 22
stakeholders 147
state agencies 50
state owned enterprises reform 89

state, role of the 29
state subject 150
state, shadow 45
stock markets 64
Stone, K.W. 38
structural change process 82
sub-contract worker 184
sub-contracting to households 133
subsidiary rules 35
subsidised inputs 59
Sundar, K.R.S. 141, 153, 154
supply-side incentives 58
survival and security rights 134
survival rights 113, 114, 135
sustainability 17
    of Vietnam's development 89
Swaminathan, Madhura 183
systemic inefficiency 62

T

Taiwan 22, 40, 41, 42, 165, 168
    history 176
Tan, S. 43, 47
tariff barriers 22
Tata, Ratan 72
taxation on QPPs 207
technology policies 145
technology transfer 58
tertiary sector 57, 73
Teubner, G. 47
TEWA 157, 159
Thailand 28, 48, 74, 185, 189, 191,
    193, 195
Thio, L. 176
Third World countries 111, 115
Thompson, E. 165
Todd, P. 168
Toshiba 24
tradable goods industries 136
trade liberalisation 184
trade reform 117

trade regimes 64
Trade Union Act 124
trade unions 50, 76
trade unions, registered 69
trade-offs 149
tripartite negotiation 26
trust banks 210
Tulpule, B. 61
Twining, W. 172

U

underemployment 83
    rate of 72, 83
UNDP 190, 191
unemployment insurance 142
UNESCAP 191
UNIFEM 191
unionisation 70, 83, 148
United Nations 21
Unni, J. 65
unorganised sector 59, 62, 65, 70
    in India 148
unprotected workers 72
unregulated 36
unskilled workers 66
urban Informal Sector 187
urbanisation 145
    level of 82
US 27

V

Van, der Eng 112
Varma, A 149
Vasudevan, D. 141, 142
vertical integration processes 24
Vietnam 28, 35, 38, 39, 41, 45, 81,
    165
Vietnam Living Standard Survey 29,
    82, 91
Vietnamese Labour Code of 2002 83
Vietnamese labour market 82, 83, 88

Vietnamese unions 45
Voluntary Retirement Scheme (VRS)
    143, 155
vulnerable workers 45

W

wage differentials by skill 128
wage differentiation 82
wage income, gender differentiation
    of 104
wage-inflation indexing 60
wages, rigidities in 23
wages, sex differentials in 195
Walters, D. 48
Wang, Z. 42, 45, 168, 176
Washington consensus 22
wealth accumulation 183
welfare goals of workers 74
welfare of poorer households 133
welfare-distribution of gains 17

western economies 22
white-collar 65
WIEGO 183
Wiens, Thomas B. 91
Winn, J.K. 36
women workers 165
Woolfson, C. 170
work force 57, 72
workers 24
workers' well-being 21
workplace committees 176
World Bank 48, 73, 74, 83, 86, 90,
    114, 141, 147
      poverty line 90
WTO 22, 63, 81, 102, 115

Z

Zhu, Y. 35, 36
Zimbabwe 27